A TOLKIEN
BESTIARY

A TOLKIEN BESTIARY

DAVID DAY

ILLUSTRATED BY
IAN MILLER
MICHAEL FOREMAN
ALLAN CURLESS
LIDIA POSTMA
JOHN BLANCHE
PAULINE MARTIN
SUE PORTER
LINDA GARLAND
JAROSLAV BRADAC
VICTOR AMBRUS
JOHN DAVIS

CHANCELLOR
PRESS

TO ROSALIE VICARS-HARRIS

A Tolkien Bestiary was edited and designed by Mitchell Beazley,
a division of Octopus Publishing Group Ltd

A Tolkien Bestiary
First published in 1979 by Mitchell Beazley
Reprinted in paperback 1982, 1983, 1984, 1985, 1986, 1987, 1988, 1989
This edition published in 2001 by Chancellor Press
an imprint of Bounty Books, a division of
Octopus Publishing Group Ltd,
2-4 Heron Quays, London, E14 4JP

© Octopus Publishing Group Ltd 1979

ISBN 0 7537 0459 5

Typsetting by Conway Group Graphics Limited, London
Origination by Culver Graphics Limited, High Wycombe, Buckinghamshire
Produced by Toppan (HK) Ltd
Printed in China

ILLUSTRATION CREDITS
The work of artists who contributed to this book appears on these pages:

IAN MILLER pages 26-7, 28-9, 38-9, 51, 58-9, 60-1, 62-3, 68, 69, 70, 71, 73, 74, 75, 92-3, 94-5, 100-1, 129, 130-1, 142-3, 144, 145, 172-3, 180-1, 198-9, 200-1, 202-3, 205, 220-1, 226-7, 228-9, 236-7, 248-9, 250, 252 and 276

MICHAEL FOREMAN pages 36-7, 40-1, 46-7, 48, 97, 161, 230-1 and 240

ALLAN CURLESS pages 12-13, 22, 23, 24, 25, 30, 31, 49, 52-3, 54, 76-7, 78-9, 80, 81, 82, 83, 116, 117, 146-7, 150, 158-9, 166-7, 170-1, 178-9, 184-5, 186-7, 195, 196, 206, 208-9, 232-3, 238-9, 244, 245, 246-7, 266-7, 268-9 and 274-5

LIDIA POSTMA pages 102-3, 132-3, 134-5, 136, 137, 138, 139, 162-3 and 234-5

JOHN BLANCHE pages 104-5, 106-7, 110-11, 112 and 168-9

PAULINE MARTIN pages 33, 164-5 and 225

VICTOR AMBRUS pages 56-7, 84-5, 86-7, 90-1, 114-15, 118-19, 120, 126-7, 148-9, 182-3, 188, 190-1, 192-3, 214, 215, 216-17 and 242-3

SUE PORTER pages 44-5, 108-9 and 174-5

JAROSLAV BRADAC pages 20-1, 140-1, 152, 153, 154-5, 156-7, 222-3, 254, 255, 256, 257, 258, 260-1, 264, 265, 270-1 and 272-3

LINDA GARLAND pages 34-5, 42-3, 98-9 and 176

JOHN DAVIS pages 64-5, 66, 67, 122-3, 124-5, 210-11 and 212

ALSO BY DAVID DAY
A - Z of Tolkien

CONTENTS

PREFACE

A bestiary is a book about beasts. In the Middle Ages, when the bestiary was most popular, it was the equivalent of an encyclopedia of natural history, revealing fabulous beasts and monsters to the curious.

Bestiaries have a particular fascination for me. For most of my life I have been a student of the world's mythologies, which I have found reveal a truer and fuller vision of the human mind and soul than all the historical, psychological and anthropological studies ever devised. Bestiaries provide a means by which the wild and unruly creatures peculiar to mythology can be contained and brought under observation. Teratology – the study of monstrous and miraculous beings – is a much neglected science. As the Argentinian writer Jorge Luis Borges once stated in his marvellous "Book of Imaginary Beings": "We are as ignorant of the meaning of the dragon as we are of the meaning of the universe, but there is something in the dragon's image that appeals to the human imagination, and so we find the dragon in quite distant places and times. It is, so to speak, a necessary monster."

On reading J. R. R. Tolkien's "The Lord of the Rings", "The Hobbit", "The Adventures of Tom Bombadil" and "The Silmarill-ion", I was immediately struck not only by their value as wonderful tales beautifully told but also by the immense cosmology behind these works. Indeed, it is the largest, most complex and detailed invented mythological system in our literature. I soon found the vast inhabited landscapes of Middle-earth and the Undying Lands a fruitful area to study and chart. To this end, this book was begun, and it seemed to me that the bestiary structure would be ideal. What better way to study Tolkien's world than to cage all of its inhabitants and one by one bring them under close scrutiny – physically examining them, noting their habitation, their habits and foibles, charting their evolution and histories.

The traditional bestiary was an illustrated reference work compiled by scholarly monks about beasts and beings both exotic and mundane. It was rooted in the Greek and Roman classics and was based on the Greek-Egyptian "Physiologus" of the second century AD. It codified the ancients' knowledge of magical and monstrous animals and races and what the medieval mind observed and understood of the natural world.

What emerged was a work of imagination and beauty: an art form rather than a simple compilation. The medieval scholars who painstakingly lettered and illustrated the bestiaries channelled all their creative energies into these exquisite books. Bestiaries of many kinds were translated into more than a dozen languages and were, after the Bible, the most widely read and disseminated written works in the West. They were highly regarded as source books on the natural world, as allegorical documents of religious instruction and as books of popular entertainment.

"A Tolkien Bestiary" is a bestiary in the broadest sense of the word; it includes not only fantastical beasts and monsters but also races, nations, deities and flora: in Tolkien's terms, all the "kelvar" and "olvar". It is a comprehensive encyclopedia that describes, illustrates and historically delineates all his creations.

Like its medieval predecessors, this Bestiary lays strong emphasis on illustrations. One of the most important and original contributions to this book has been made by its eleven excellent illustrators and its gifted designer, Debra Zuckerman.

All drawings in the Bestiary are imaginary fantasies complementing the information in Tolkien's own writings. The black and white illustrations are of races, creatures and plants, whereas the colour illustrations, which are placed chronologically from the creation of the World to the end of the War of the Ring, are of broad landscapes, great kingdoms and major battles and events in Arda.

In "A Tolkien Bestiary" I have worked within the ornate conventions of the bestiary form; consequently, the language has a certain archaic flavour. References to Tolkien's real books are not made in my text; I do not refer, for example, to "The Hobbit" and "The Lord of the Rings" but to the "Red Book of Westmarch", from which both were allegedly translated. Certain races are referred to in the present tense because in Tolkien's books there is no record of their ever dying; for example, Elves and Valar remain alive and active in the Undying Lands.

In entries under an alternate name for a race or beast, their most usual name appears in capital letters to refer the reader to the main entry. For example, in the Periannath entry the word Hobbit will appear in capital letters, as Periannath is the Grey-elven word for Hobbit. To indicate that certain phrases or words are translations from other languages the appropriate words have been put in quotation marks, as have Tolkien's book titles (real or imaginary) and the song and tale cycles.

At the beginning of "A Tolkien Bestiary" there is a composite map of Middle-earth and the Undying Lands. It is an original interpretation from Tolkien's writings and should be used only for general orientation. It shows all the lands of Arda, even though many of them, as well as many of the great realms, did not exist at the same time; in fact, much of Arda seems to have vanished completely by the time of the War of the Ring. An accurate re-creation of the geography of Beleriand of the First Age of Sun and west Middle-earth of the Third Age will be found in the detailed maps of J. R. R. and C. J. R. Tolkien themselves (© George Allen & Unwin Ltd, 1937, 1954 and 1977) in "The Hobbit", "The Lord of the Rings" and "The Silmarillion".

Two time charts are provided for chronological orientation. The first is a sweeping visualization of the entire time span that Tolkien's writings embrace; the second is a closer view of the Ages of Sun and is designed primarily to show the interrelation of various major kingdoms on a chronological scale. For a detailed listing of events and incidents of the Second and Third Ages of the Sun, the reader must consult Tolkien's own exhaustive indexes.

At the back of the book are genealogy tables of the races and kingdoms of Men and Elves and two indexes. All Bestiary entries are listed in the first index, where reference is given to their principal sources in Tolkien's books. It is followed by a general index to all the races, places, characters and events mentioned in my text.

Primarily, I meant "A Tolkien Bestiary" to be a useful reference work to Tolkien's world of Arda, but it is also a celebration of the imagination of a great story-teller and the creator of a world. This book was written and designed in the belief that, had the scribes of Middle-earth compiled a work on the natural history of Arda, the result would have been something very similar to this.

David Day

LIST OF ILLUSTRATIONS

COLOUR ILLUSTRATIONS
The colour illustrations are arranged in four groups, each reflecting a major phase in the history of the Undying Lands and Middle-earth. The first two groups illustrate events described by J.R.R. Tolkien in "The Silmarillion", the third illustrates episodes from "The Hobbit" and "The Lord of the Rings" and the fourth the latter part of "The Lord of the Rings."

BLACK AND WHITE ILLUSTRATIONS

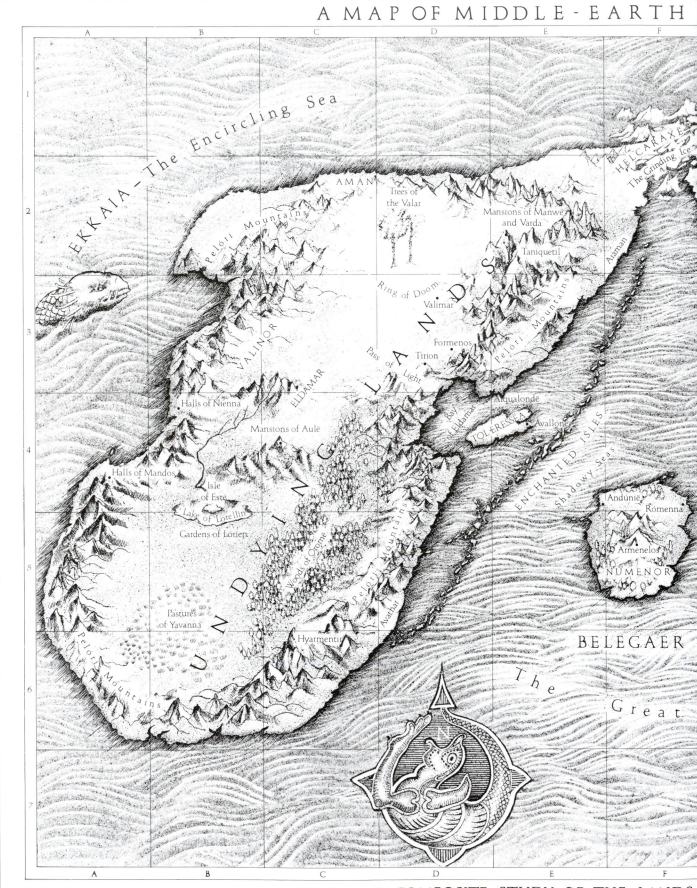

EKKAIA – The Encircling Sea

HELCARAXE

The Grinding Ice

AMAN

Trees of the Valar

Mansions of Manwe and Varda

Pelóri Mountains

Taniquetil

Araman

Ring of Doom

Valimar

Pelóri Mountains

VALINOR

Formenos

Tirion

Pass of Light

ELDAMAR

Halls of Nienna

Aqualondë

Mansions of Aulë

Bay of Eldamar

TOL-ERESSËA

Avallon

Halls of Mandos

ENCHANTED ISLES

Shadowy Seas

Isle of Estë

Andunië

Rómenna

Lake of Torellin

Gardens of Lórien

Armenelos

NÚMENOR

Woods of Oromë

U N D Y I N G   L A N D S

Pelóri Mountains

Pastures of Yavanna

Avathar

BELEGAER

Hyarmentir

Pelóri Mountains

The

Great

ANGBAND

Iron Mountains

Gondolin

Tol Sirion · Mountains of Terror

Menegroth

DORIATH

Belegost

Nogrod

Nargothrond
Brithombar
Eglarest

BELERIAND

OSSIRIAND

Blue Mountains

FORODWAITH

Foroche

ARNOR

Angmar

Grey Mountains · Iron Hills

Lonely Mountain

Esgaroth

RHOVANION

Hobbiton

Barrow Downs

LINDON

Grey Havens

Old Forest

Rivendell

Mirkwood

THE SHIRE

Eregion

Dol
Guldur

Moria

Lothlórien

Gulf of Lune

DUNLAND

Isengard

ROHAN

Dead
Marshes

Black
Gate

Barad-dûr

Mt Doom

Minas
Morgul

MORDOR

KHAND

Minas Tirith

GONDOR

Dol Amroth

Bay of Belfalas

NORTHERN WASTE

MIDDLE-EARTH

Lamp
of the
Valar

Illuin

UTUMNO

Inland
Sea of
Helcar

Mountains of the East

Cuiviénen

RHÛN

HILDÓRIEN

Almaren

HARAD

City of Corsairs

Umbar

FAR HARAD

Forests of Harad

The Great Sea

Gulf

GREAT DESERT

Lamp
of the
Valar

Ormal

CREATION	Eru ("He that is Alone")	Timeless Halls fashioned Ainur created Music of the Ainur	Vision of Eä Creation of the World (Arda)	SHAPING OF ARDA	Valar and Maiar entered Arda Arda shaped
AGES OF TREES ERA ONE UNDYING LANDS	Valinor founded Trees of the Valar created	Eagles created	Ents conceived	AGES OF TREES ERA TWO UNDYING LANDS	FIRST AGE Light for the Stars gathered by Varda
AGES OF DARKNESS MIDDLE-EARTH	Sleep of Yavanna began Angband built	Balrogs, Vampires, Winged Beasts, Serpents, Great Spiders, Werewolves appeared	Dwarves conceived	AGES OF STARS MIDDLE-EARTH	FIRST AGE Stars rekindled Elves awakened
THIRD AGE Teleri arrived on Tol Eressëa	Teleri built first ships	Alqualondë founded	FOURTH AGE Tengwar alphabet devised by Noldor	Melkor released	FIFTH AGE Silmarils made
THIRD AGE Falathrim allied with Sindar	Dwarves entered Beleriand	Menegroth founded	FOURTH AGE Orcs driven out of Beleriand	Laiquendi entered Ossiriand	FIFTH AGE Cirth alphabet devised by Sindar
SECOND AGE Avallónë founded	Ban of the Valar	Elves of Avallónë traded with Númenor	Elves of Avallónë brought the Palantíri to Númenor	Númenórean Invasion Change of the World	THIRD AGE The Long Peace of Valinor began
SECOND AGE Lindon founded Númenor founded	Mordor built by Sauron	The One Ring made War of Sauron and the Elves	Nazgûl appeared	Downfall of Númenor First fall of Mordor and Sauron	THIRD AGE The One Ring lost

Arda marred Melkor expelled	 AGES OF LAMPS	Lamps of the Valar forged	Almaren founded Great Forest of Arda grew	Utumno built Rebel Maiar and demons entered Arda	Lamps and Almaren destroyed
	Oromë discovered Elves	Valar departed for War of Powers	SECOND AGE Chaining of Melkor Peace of Arda began Summons of the Valar	Vanyar and Noldor arrived in Eldamar	Tirion founded
Ents awakened Dwarves awakened	Orcs bred Trolls bred Khazad-dûm founded	War of Powers Utumno destroyed	SECOND AGE Great Journey began	Melian the Maia appeared Great Journey ended	Nogrod and Belegost founded Doriath founded by Sindar
Peace of Arda ended Formenos built	Trees of the Valar destroyed First Kinslaying Flight of the Noldor	 AGES OF SUN UNDYING LANDS	FIRST AGE Moon and Sun fashioned by Valar	Melian the Maia returned to Valinor	Valar departed for War of Wrath Melkor expelled
	Melkor and Ungoliant returned Sleep of Yavanna ended	 AGES OF SUN MIDDLE-EARTH	FIRST AGE Men awakened War of the Jewels began	Dragons bred Noldor and Sindar kingdoms destroyed	War of Wrath Angband destroyed War of the Jewels ended
	Istari departed for Middle-earth	Eldar ships from Lothlórien and Dol Amroth arrived	Valar rejected Sauron's spirit	FOURTH AGE Ringbearers' ship arrived	Last Eldar ship arrived
Barbarian Invasions began	Sauron re-appeared Hobbits appeared Balrog re-appeared	The One Ring found Uruk-hai bred Battle of Five Armies	Olog-hai bred War of the Ring Final fall of Mordor and Sauron	FOURTH AGE Ringbearers' ship departed Dominion of Men began	Last Eldar ship departed

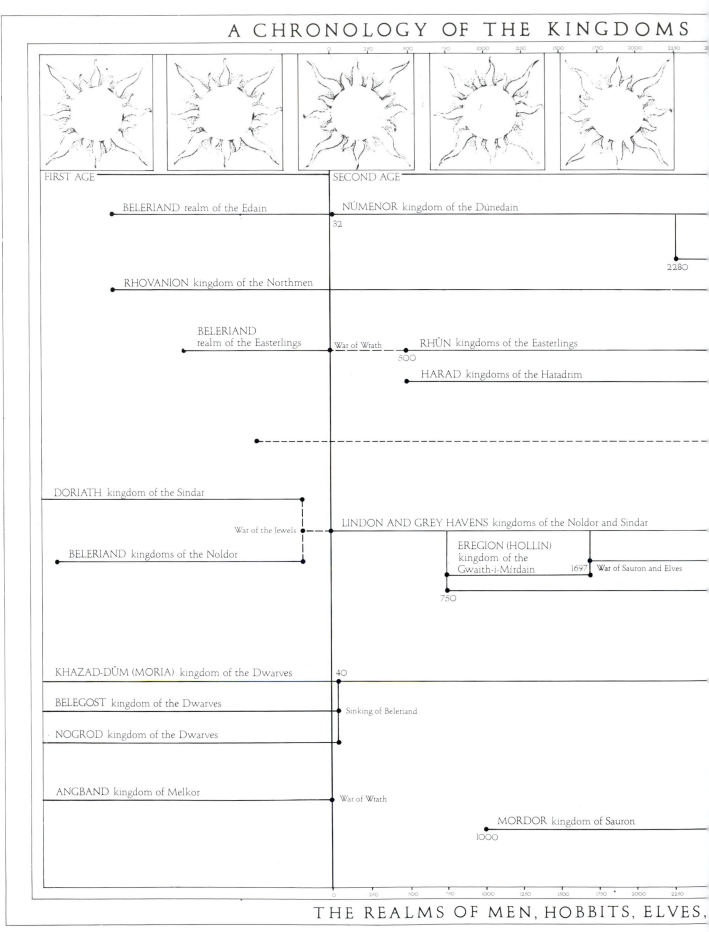

FIRST AGE

SECOND AGE

BELERIAND realm of the Edain

NÚMENOR kingdom of the Dúnedain

32

2280

RHOVANION kingdom of the Northmen

BELERIAND
realm of the Easterlings

War of Wrath

RHÛN kingdoms of the Easterlings

500

HARAD kingdoms of the Haradrim

DORIATH kingdom of the Sindar

War of the Jewels

LINDON AND GREY HAVENS kingdoms of the Noldor and Sindar

BELERIAND kingdoms of the Noldor

EREGION (HOLLIN)
kingdom of the
Gwaith-i-Mírdain

1697   War of Sauron and Elves

750

KHAZAD-DÛM (MORIA) kingdom of the Dwarves

40

BELEGOST kingdom of the Dwarves

Sinking of Beleriand

NOGROD kingdom of the Dwarves

ANGBAND kingdom of Melkor

War of Wrath

MORDOR kingdom of Sauron

1000

THE REALMS OF MEN, HOBBITS, ELVES,

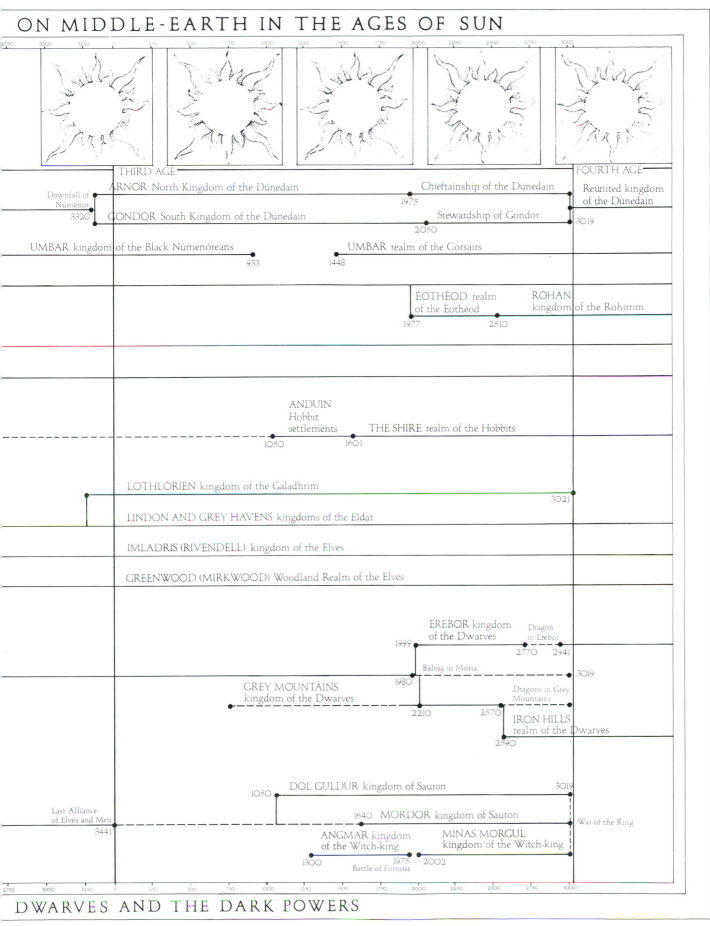

THIRD AGE   FOURTH AGE

ARNOR North Kingdom of the Dúnedain   Chieftainship of the Dúnedain   Reunited kingdom
                                                                                    of the Dúnedain
Downfall of   1975
Númenor
                GONDOR South Kingdom of the Dúnedain   Stewardship of Gondor
3320   2050   3019

UMBAR kingdom of the Black Númenóreans   UMBAR realm of the Corsairs

                                    933   1448

                                ÉOTHÉOD realm   ROHAN
                                of the Éothéod   kingdom of the Rohirrim

                                1977   2510

                        ANDUIN
                        Hobbit
                        settlements   THE SHIRE realm of the Hobbits

                        1050   1601

        LOTHLÓRIEN kingdom of the Galadhrim

                                                                    3021

        LINDON AND GREY HAVENS kingdoms of the Eldar

        IMLADRIS (RIVENDELL) kingdom of the Elves

        GREENWOOD (MIRKWOOD) Woodland Realm of the Elves

                                EREBOR kingdom   Dragon
                                of the Dwarves   in Erebor
                        1999   2770   2941
                                Balrog in Moria   3019
                        1980
        GREY MOUNTAINS   Dragons in Grey
        kingdom of the Dwarves   Mountains
                                2210   2570
                                                IRON HILLS
                                                realm of the Dwarves
                                        2590

                DOL GULDUR kingdom of Sauron   3019
        1050
Last Alliance   1640   MORDOR kingdom of Sauron
of Elves and Men   War of the Ring
3441   ANGMAR kingdom   MINAS MORGUL
                        of the Witch-king   kingdom of the Witch-king
                1300   1975   2002
                        Battle of Fornost

A BESTIARY OF THE BEASTS, MONSTERS, RACES, DEITIES AND FLORA

AINUR In the very beginning there was Eru, the One, who dwelt in the Void, and whose name in Elvish was Ilúvatar. As is told in the "Ainulindalë", Thoughts came forth from Ilúvatar to which He gave eternal life through the power of the Flame Imperishable. Ilúvatar named these creations Ainur, the "holy ones". They were the first race and they inhabited the Timeless Halls that Ilúvatar had fashioned for them.

The Ainur were great spirits and each was given a mighty voice so that he could sing before Ilúvatar for His pleasure. When He had heard each sing, Ilúvatar called them to Him and proposed that they should sing in concert. This was what the tales call the Music of the Ainur, in which great themes were made as individual spirits sought supremacy or harmony according to their nature. Some proved greater than others; some were powerful in goodness, some in evil; yet in the end, though the battle of sound was terrible, the Music was great and beautiful. From this harmony and strife Ilúvatar created a Vision that was a globed light in the Void. With a word and the Flame Imperishable He then made Eä, the "World that Is"; Elves and Men later named it Arda, the Earth. The Music became the Doom of Arda and the fate of every race was bound to it, save that of the late-coming race of Men, whose end nobody but Ilúvatar knew.

So it was that after Arda was made, some of the Ainur went down into this newly created World, where they were known as the Powers of Arda. Later they were thought by Men to be gods. Those who were good among them were guided by their knowledge of the Will of Ilúvatar, while others strove to fulfil their own ends. Whereas in the Timeless Halls they had been beings of pure spirit, within Arda they were limited in power by choosing to inhabit the bounds of Time and the small space of the World. Further, within Arda they took on separate shapes, each according to his nature and the elements he loved, and, though not bound to a visible form, they most often wore these shapes as garments, and in later Ages they were known to Elves and Men in these forms.

In the "Valaquenta" a part of the long history of the Ainur who inhabited Arda and shaped the World is written. It tells how the kingdoms of Almaren, Utumno and Angband were built in Middle-earth; and how the kingdom of Valinor was made in the Undying Lands of Aman. It speaks also of how the Ainur brought forth Light and the Count of Time, and how there were terrible wars among them that shook Arda; and it gives the names and forms of many of the mightiest of the race.

In Arda the Elves divided this race into the Valar and the Maiar. Those of the Ainur counted among the Valar are: Manwë, the Wind King; Varda, Queen of the Stars; Ulmo, Lord of the Waters; Nienna, the Weeper; Aulë, the Smith; Yavanna, Giver of Fruits; Oromë, Lord of the Forest; Vána, the Youthful; Mandos, Keeper of the Dead; Vairë, the Weaver; Lórien, Master of Dreams; Estë, the Healer; Tulkas, the Wrestler; Nessa, the Dancer; and Melkor, later named Morgoth the Dark Enemy.

Many of the Ainur were counted among the Maiar, but only a few are named in the histories that have come down to Men: Eönwë, Herald of Manwë; Ilmarë, Maid of Varda; Ossë, of the Waves; Uinen, of the Calm Seas; Melian, Queen of the Sindar; Arien, the Sun; Tilion, the Moon; Sauron, the Sorcerer; Gothmog, Lord of the Balrogs; and Olórin (Gandalf), Radagast and Curunír (Saruman) – the Wizards. In the histories of Middle-earth there also appear others who may have been Maiar: Thuringwethil, the Vampire; Ungoliant, the Spider; Draugluin, the Werewolf; Goldberry, the River-daughter; and Iarwain Ben-adar (Tom Bombadil).

As has been said, only some of the Ainur went down to Arda. A greater part has always lived in the Timeless Halls, but it has been foretold that at the World's End the Valar and Maiar shall rejoin their kindred, and among those who return will also be the Eruhíni, the Children of Ilúvatar, who came forth upon Arda. Once again there shall be Great Music: this shall be mightier than the first. It shall be unflawed, filled with wisdom and sadness, and beautiful beyond compare.

ALFIRIN One of the many sad songs sung by the Grey-elves of Middle-earth tells of a flower called Alfirin. Its flowers were like golden bells and it grew on the green plain of Lebennin near the delta lands of the Anduin, the Great River. The sight of them in the fields, with the sea-wind blowing, would tug at the hearts of the Eldar and awaken the sea-longing that always drew these Children of Starlight westwards, over Belegaer, the Great Sea, to where their immortal brethren lived.

In the minds of Elves, the Alfirin were in miniature like the great gold bells of Valinor, which always toll upon the ears of the Blessed in the Undying Lands.

AMANYAR In the time of the Trees of the Valar, many of the Elven peoples made the Great Journey from Middle-earth to the continent of the Undying Lands, which is also known as Aman. Thereafter, in the Ages of Stars and Sun, Elves also came to Aman and all those who reached the Undying Lands, soon or late, were named the Amanyar, "those of Aman".

APANÓNAR When the Sun first rose on Arda and its light shone in the land of Hildórien in eastern Middle-earth, there arose a race of mortal beings. This was the race of MEN, who were also named the Apanónar, which means "afterborn", because they were not the first speaking people to come to Arda. Elves, Dwarves, Ents and the evil races of Orcs and Trolls had been in the World for many Ages before Men arrived.

ARATAR Among the Powers of Arda there are the Valar, eight of whom are named the Aratar, the "exalted". Their might far exceeds that of all others in the Undying Lands. Two Aratar are Manwë, the Wind King, and Varda, Queen of the Stars, who both live on Taniquetil in Ilmarin, the "mansion of the high airs". Two others, called Aulë the Smith and Mandos the Doomsman, live in halls beneath the Earth, while Yavanna, who is Queen of the Earth, and Oromë, the Forest Lord, live on the open land. Another is Ulmo, the Lord of the Waters, who inhabits the seas. The last Aratar is Nienna the Weeper, whose home is a great house in the West from which she looks upon the Door of Night.

ASËA ARANION From the land of the Númenóreans, a herb of magical healing powers came to Middle-earth. In the High Elven tongue this herb was named Asëa Aranion, the "leaf of kings", because of the special powers that it possessed in the hands of the kings of Númenórë. More commonly, Elven-lore used the Sindarin name, ATHELAS; in the common Westron tongue of Men it was Kingsfoil.

ATANATÁRI Of the race of Men, there were those who, in the First Age of Sun, came from the East of Middle-earth, went West and North, and came to the realm of Beleriand where the Noldor and Sindar Elves lived. The Noldor named these Men the Atanatári, the "fathers of Men", though more often this name took the Sindarin form, which is EDAIN.

These Men learned great skills from the wise Elves who had recently come from Aman, the Land of Light, and had themselves been taught by the Powers of Arda, whom Men greatly feared and worshipped as gods.

So the Atanatári were truly the fathers of their race, for though, later, other Men came from the East, where they had learned much from the Dark Elves of those lands, their lore was as nothing when compared with that learned by the Atanatári from the Calaquendi. For this reason the Atanatári were destined to become the teachers of all their people in the Ages of Sun that were to follow. Much that has been counted great and noble in all Men has its source in these ancestors.

ATANI Of all Men in the First Age of Sun the mightiest were the Atani of the Three Houses of Elf-friends, who lived in Beleriand. Even by the measure of the Eldar the deeds of these mortals during the War of the Jewels were great. Much is told in the "Quenta Silmarillion": how Húrin killed seventy Trolls and endured the tortures of Morgoth; how Túrin slew Glaurung, Father of Dragons; how Beren cut a Silmaril from Morgoth's crown; and how Eärendil the Mariner sailed the skies in his jewelled ship. And through the Atani, Men were first ennobled by the mixture of Elven-blood, for three times in the First Age an Atani lord wed an Elf-princess: Beren wed Lúthien, Tuor wed Idril and Eärendil wed Elwing. Thus the Atani were the noblest and strongest of Men, and taught much that they learned from Elves to their descendants and to the lesser Men that came after.

However, the name Atani was given to the Men of the Three Houses only for a brief time by the Noldor. Its true meaning is "Secondborn", which is what all the race of mortals who arose in the East of Middle-earth were called. For as Elves, who came into the World at the time of the Rekindling of the Stars, were named the Firstborn, so Men, who came at the time of the Rising of the Sun, were named the Secondborn – the Atani.

In time, however, the name Atani faded altogether, for the Quenya tongue of the Noldorin Elves was not widely used in Mortal Lands. The Men of the Three Houses became the EDAIN in the more common Sindarin language of the Grey-elves, and it is under that name that the greater part of the tales of these Men in the lost lands of Beleriand are told.

ATHELAS Among the many tales in the "Red Book of Westmarch" is recorded a part of the Grey-elven rhyme concerning the healing herb Athelas. The meaning of the rhyme had in the passing of Ages been lost to the understanding of all but the wisest of Men, though by the time of the War of the Ring it remained a folk cure for mild ailments of the body.

In the terrible days of that war Aragorn, son of Arathorn, who was a true descendant of the kings of Númenórë from where the magical woodland herb had come, came to the kingdom of Gondor. It is told in tales that Aragorn, who had the healing hands of these kings, broke the long-leafed herb into cauldrons of steaming water and released its true power. The fragrance of orchards, the coolness of mountain snow, and the light of a shattered Star poured into the dark rooms where the victims of poisoned wounds and black sorcery lay, until they stirred again with life and youth, and the long trance that had held them in sway broke before it had taken them to an evil death.

So Athelas was named Kingsfoil, the "leaf of kings", by Men and its use by a true king of Númenórë was a sign of the end that would soon come to that greatest evil of Mordor, east of Gondor, which threatened all who inhabited Middle-earth.

AVARI At the Time of Awakening, all Elves lived in the East of Middle-earth near Orocarni, the Mountains of the East, on the shore of Helcar, the Inland Sea. But in time the summons of the Valar came and all the Elves had to make a choice between starlight and the promise of a land of eternal light. Those who chose eternal light and set out on the Great Journey were named the Eldar, while those who remained were called the Avari, the "unwilling".

The Avari became a less powerful people, for their land became barbarous with Dark Powers and evil races, and so the Elves dwindled and hid themselves. They became as shadows and sprites that mortal eyes could not perceive. They lived always close to the wooded land, built no cities and had no kings. Later, in the years of Sun, the Avari were named Silvan or Wood-elves, and some of them wandered westwards and became involved in the great affairs of their Eldar kindred under whom they grew prosperous and strong for a while, before dwindling once again.

BALCHOTH During the time of Cirion, the twelfth Ruling Steward of Gondor, some fierce barbarian people lived in Rhovanion on the eastern borders of the realm. They were the Balchoth and they were part of the Easterling race. The Balchoth caused great terror in the southern Vales of Anduin, for their ways were evil and their deeds were directed by the Dark Lord Sauron, who resided in Dol Guldur in Mirkwood.

The savagery of the Balchoth was legendary and their numbers were great. In the year 2,510 of the Third Age of Sun, the Balchoth launched a huge fleet of boats upon the Great River and at last crossed into the realm of Gondor. They despoiled the province of Calenardhon and slaughtered its people, until they were set upon by the Men of Gondor in a mighty army led by Cirion. Yet, a black army of Orcs came from the mountains and attacked the Men of Gondor from behind. In that darkest moment aid came to the Men of Gondor: the Rohirrim sent into battle a great force of cavalry that routed both Balchoth and Orc. This was the Battle of the Field of Celebrant, at which the power of the Balchoth was broken for ever. The barbarian army was annihilated and no history tells of the fierce Balchoth after that day. They were a vanquished people and they soon disappeared completely from the lands of Middle-earth.

B

BALROGS The most terrible of the Maiar spirits who became the servants of Melkor, the Dark Enemy, were those who were transformed into demons. In the High Elven tongue they were named the Valaraukar, but in Middle-earth were called Balrogs, the "demons of might".

Of all Melkor's creatures, only Dragons were greater in power. Huge and hulking, the Balrogs were Man-like demons with streaming manes of fire and nostrils that breathed flame. They seemed to move within clouds of black shadows and their limbs had the coiling power of serpents. The chief weapon of the Balrog was the many-thonged whip of fire, and, though as well they carried the mace, the axe and the flaming sword, it was the whip of fire that their enemies feared most. This weapon was so terrible that the vast evil of Ungoliant, the Great Spider that even the Valar could not destroy, was driven from Melkor's realm by the fiery lashes of the Balrog demons.

Most infamous of the Balrog race was Gothmog, Lord of the Balrogs and High Captain of Angband. In the Wars of Beleriand three High Elven-lords fell beneath the whip and black axe of Gothmog. After the Battle under Stars, Fëanor, the most renowned of Elven-kings, was cut down by Gothmog at the very doors of Angband. In the Battle of the Sudden Flame, he slew Fingon, High King of the Noldor. Finally, again in the service of Melkor, Gothmog led the Balrog host and its Troll-guard and marshalled the Orc legions and the Dragon brood, before storming and sacking the kingdom of Gondolin and killing Ecthelion, the Elf-lord. But it was here at the Fall of Gondolin, in the Square of the King, that Gothmog met his end, by the hand of Ecthelion, whom he himself had just slain.

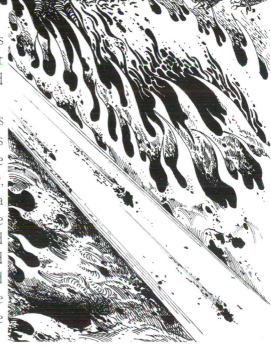

In each of Melkor's risings and in each of his battles, the Balrogs were among his foremost champions, and so, when the holocaust of the War of Wrath ended Melkor's reign for ever, it largely ended the Balrogs as a race.

It was said that some fled that last battle and buried themselves deep in the roots of mountains, but after many thousands of years nothing more was heard of these evil beings and most people believed the demons had gone from the Earth for ever. However, during the Third Age of Sun the deep-delving Dwarves of Moria by accident released an entombed demon. Once unleashed, the Balrog struck down two Dwarf-kings, and, gathering Orcs and Trolls to aid him, drove the Dwarves from Moria for ever. As is told in the "Red Book of Westmarch", the Balrog's dominion remained uncontested for over two centuries, until he was cast down from the peak of Zirakzigil by the Wizard Gandalf after the Battle on the Bridge of Khazad-dûm.

BANAKIL It was not until the first thousand years of the Third Age of Sun had passed in the Vales of Anduin, east of the Mountains of Mist, that Men first became aware of the Banakil, the "Halfling" race. Smaller than Dwarves and shy of other races, they lived quietly and no history tells of their beginning before this time. Though they were of little importance to Elves and Men, the "Red Book of Westmarch" tells how their deeds determined the wars of the mightiest that inhabited Middle-earth in the Third Age. Under the name HOBBIT they became far-famed in the songs and tales that tell of the great War of the Ring, which ended the evil dominion of Sauron, the Dark Lord of Mordor.

BARDINGS Among the strong Northmen who lived between Mirkwood and the Iron Hills, there were those who, in the last century of the Third Age of Sun, were called the Bardings. Previously these people had been known as the Men of Dale and had inhabited the wealthy city of Dale below the Lonely Mountain. But, when the Dragon Smaug came to the Lonely Mountain, Dale was sacked and the people fled. The Lake Men of Esgaroth gave them sanctuary for almost two centuries. In that time among these exiles of Dale rose the heir of the king who was called Bard the Bowman. He was a great warrior and a grim and strong man. When the Dragon of the Lonely Mountain attacked again, it was Bard who shot the beast through the breast with a black arrow and freed the land of the fiery terror.

So Bard became the ruler of his people and, with a portion of the wealth of the Dragon's hoard, he rebuilt Dale and once again made a rich kingdom around it. Thus, in honour of this hero, all the people of Dale from that time proudly bore his name.

BARROW-WIGHTS West of the Brandywine River beyond the Old Forest were the Barrow-downs, the most ancient burial ground of Men in Middle-earth. There were no trees or water there, but only grass and turf covering dome-shaped hills that were crowned with monoliths and great rings of bone-white stone. These hills were the burial mounds that were made in the First Age of Sun for the Kings of Men. For many Ages the Barrow-downs were sacred and revered, until out of the Witch-kingdom of Angmar many terrible and tortured spirits fled across Middle-earth, desperately searching to hide from the ravening light of the Sun. Demons whose bodies had been destroyed looked for other bodies in which their evil spirits could dwell. And so it was that the Barrow-downs became a haunted and dread place. The demons became the Barrow-wights, the Undead, who animated the bones and jewelled armour of the ancient Kings of Men who had lived in this land in the First Age of Sun.

28

The Barrow-wights were of a substance of darkness that could enter the eye, heart and mind, or crush the will. They were form-shifters and could move from shape to shape and animate whatever life-form they wished. Most often a Barrow-wight came on the unwary traveller in the guise of a dark phantom whose eyes were luminous and cold. The voice of the figure was at once horrible and hypnotic; its skeletal hand had a touch like ice and a grip like the iron jaws of a trap. Once under the spell of the Undead the victim had no will of his own. In this way the Barrow-wight drew the living into the treasure tombs on the downs. A dismal choir of tortured souls could be heard inside the Barrow as, in the green half-light, the Barrow-wight laid his victim on a stone altar and bound him with chains of gold. He draped him in the pale cloth and precious jewellery of the ancient dead, and then ended his life with a sacrificial sword.

In the darkness these were powerful spirits and they could be held at bay only with the spell of strong incantations. They could be destroyed only by exposure to light, and it was light that they hated and feared most. The Barrow-wights were lost and tortured spirits and their last chance to remain on Earth depended on the dark security of the burial vaults. Once a stone chamber was broken open, light would pour in on the Barrow-wights and they would fade like mist before the sun and be gone for ever.

BATS Of the many creatures that Melkor the Dark Enemy bred in darkness from the birds and beasts of Middle-earth, the blood-sucking Bat was one. No story tells whether they were made from bird or beast but they were always known to be servants of evil. The lusts and habits of the Bat were well suited to evil purposes, and tales tell how even the mightiest of Melkor's servants used the Bat shape in times of need. Such was the form of Thuringwethil the Vampire, "woman of secret shadow", and Sauron himself changed into a great wide-winged Bat when he fled after the Fall of Tol-in-Gaurhoth. The "Red Book of Westmarch" also tells how, at the Battle of Five Armies in the Third Age of Sun, black storm clouds of Bats advanced in open war with legions of Orcs and Wolves to battle against Men, Elves and Dwarves.

BELAIN Within Arda since its beginning there was a race of guardians who were known as the VALAR in the High Elven tongue. The Grey-elves of Beleriand knew them as the Belain, which means the "powers".

BEORNINGS In the Third Age of Sun there was a race of solitary Northmen who guarded the Ford of Carrock and the High Passes in Rhovanion from the Orcs and Wargs. These people were the Beornings, and they were black-haired, black-bearded Men clothed in coarse wool garments. They carried the woodman's axe and were gruff, huge-muscled, but honourable. They were named after a fierce warrior called Beorn, who was a mighty man and a skin-changer. By some spell he could shift form and become a great bear. In terror of this bear-man the Orcs and Wargs of the Misty Mountains kept from his road.

Where Beorn learned the trick of form-shifting is not known, but he was a distant blood relation of the Edain of the First Age, and the "Quenta Silmarillion" relates how some of that race were skin-changers. Greatest of them was Beren, who, like Beorn, lived long alone in the forest and ate no flesh. As with Beorn, the beasts and birds came to Beren and aided him in his war with the Orcs and Wolves. In the Quest of the Silmaril it is told how Beren learned from the Eldar the art of form-shifting: presenting himself first in the shape of an Orc, and then as a great Wolf. So perhaps some of that magic was inherited by Beorn and his people, or perhaps it was as a result of living with bears for so long that Beorn learned this skill. Whatever the source, it is said that this trick of skin-changing was passed on to the heirs of Beorn through many generations. In the War of the Ring the Beornings led by Grimbeorn, son of Beorn, advanced fiercely with the Woodmen and the Elves of Mirkwood, and drove evil from that place for ever. Because of the terrible strength and the berserk rage of the Beornings in battle, the legend of the bear-skin warriors lived long in the memory of Men.

BIG FOLK To the small, shy race of the Hobbit, the ways of other races, except Elves, are thought to be coarse, loud and without subtlety. And though the affairs of other races might often threaten Hobbit lives, they seem little interested in the great nations of MEN, and so Men of whatever origin are simply called Big Folk.

BLACK NÚMENÓREANS In the "Akallabêth" is told the story of the land of the Númenóreans, which flourished as the mightiest kingdom of Men upon Arda during the Second Age of Sun. But in the year 3319 it was cast down beneath Belegaer, the Western Sea, for ever. Although most of the Númenóreans perished, some had departed to Middle-earth before the Downfall and so survived.

One part of those who were saved from disaster was named the Black Númenóreans. These people made a great haven in a place named Umbar, which lay on the coastlands in the South of Middle-earth. The Black Númenóreans were a great sea power and for many centuries they raided and pillaged the coastlands of Middle-earth. They were allies of Sauron, for he came among them and corrupted them through their overweening pride and gave them many gifts. To three of the Black Númenóreans he gave Rings of Power, and these three were numbered among the wraiths who were called the Nazgûl. To two others, who were named Herumor and Fuinur, he gave other powers and they became lords among the Haradrim.

The Black Númenóreans often came north into the lands of Gondor and Arnor to test their strength against that other noble remnant of the Númenórean race, the Elendili, the Elf-friends. For as allies of Sauron the Black Númenóreans opposed things Elvish and, above all, they hated these Men who they believed had betrayed Númenor and its king. The Black Númenóreans proved to be immensely strong and for more than a thousand years their pillaging was endured. But at last, in the tenth century of the Third Age, King Eärnil I arose in Gondor and reduced the sea power of the Black Númenóreans of Umbar to nothing and took the havens. Umbar became a fortress of Gondor, and, though in the years that followed the Black Númenóreans rose again, they were finally broken by Hyarmendacil of Gondor in the year 1050 and never again were they rulers of Umbar.

Thereafter the wandering people of this strong race merged with the Haradrim and the Corsairs, and others lived in Morgul and Mordor. As is told in the "Red Book of Westmarch", one became the spokesman of the Dark Lord and was named the Mouth of Sauron. But the end of the Third Age was also the end of the Black Númenóreans, for the gifts of power that Sauron gave them vanished with his fall, and the annals of the Fourth Age speak of these people no more.

VISION AND CREATION OF ARDA

In the beginning, the great spirits called the Ainur were bidden by Eru, the One, to create a Great Music, and out of the Music came a Vision like a globed light in the Void. Eru Ilúvatar gave this Vision life, and it became Eä, the "World that Is". The Ainur looked on it and were amazed and many for love of this new place entered it. They became the powers that were named the Valar and the Maiar; Men later thought of them as gods. These were the beings that shaped the World, which was called Arda. Into Arda the Valar and Maiar brought many things of beauty but also there was strife: one of the mightiest among them rebelled against Ilúvatar and his brethren and there was war.

DESTRUCTION OF THE GREAT LAMPS

When the Shaping of the World was complete,
the mighty Valar and Maiar spirits chose to light
all Arda with two Great Lamps. Aulë the Smith
forged these golden vessels and, with the skills of
other Valar, they were made radiant with light.
One Lamp was placed in the North and was
called Illuin and the other, called Ormal, was set
in the South. Each rested on a great pillar.
Yet after a time the evil Vala Melkor made war
and cast down the pillars, so the mountains
were broken and the consuming flame of the
Lamps spread over the World. Almaren, the first
kingdom of the Valar, was destroyed and the
Ages of the Lamps were ended.

TREES OF THE VALAR

After the destruction of Almaren, the Valar went into the West to the Undying Lands, where they built a second kingdom called Valinor. There they created many mansions and gardens and founded the city of Valimar. They chose to light these lands with two magical Trees. These were the tallest trees that ever grew and they were called Laurelin the Golden and Telperion the White. They shone eternally with brilliant gold and silver Light, and in the Ages of the Trees there was bliss and contentment in the Undying Lands.

PITS OF UTUMNO

While Valinor and the Undying Lands were bathed in the Light of the Trees of the Valar, all the lands of Middle-earth were plunged into gloom. These were the Ages of Darkness of Middle-earth, when Melkor dug the great Pits of Utumno deep beneath the mountains of the North and built many dungeons and domed halls of black stone, fire and ice. Here were gathered all the evil powers of the World under this Lord of Darkness. Their numbers were legion and Melkor created many new and dreadful forms. All the serpents of the World were bred in this place, as were the ancestors of the Dragons, and the Werewolves, Vampires, Kraken, Winged Beasts, Great Spiders and innumerable blood-sucking beasts and insects. Cruel spirits, phantoms, wraiths and evil demons stalked the halls of Utumno and were commanded by the rebel Maiar: Gothmog the Balrog and Sauron the Sorcerer. Yet with the coming of the Ages of Stars, the power of Utumno was brought to an end.

In the First Age of Stars Melkor bred Orcs and Trolls: twisted life forms made from tortured Elves and Ents who fell into his hands. Amid the sounding of trumpets the Valar came out of the West against this new and dreadful evil. There followed the War of the Powers in which Utumno was destroyed and after which Melkor was chained for three long Ages.

AWAKENING OF THE ELVES

After many Ages of Darkness, Varda the Lady of the Heavens took the dew from the Silver Tree of the Valar and, crossing the skies, rekindled the bright Stars which shone down on Middle-earth. With this Rekindling of the Stars, there came the Awakening of the Elves in the Mere of Cuiviénen by the shores of Helcar, the Inland Sea beneath Orocarni, the Mountains of the East.

Thus begun the Ages of Stars, which saw not only the awakening of the Elves but also the arising of the Dwarves and Ents and the breeding of the evil Orcs and Trolls. In these Ages the Great Journey, the migration of the Elves, also took place. For the most part these were peaceful, glorious years for the Elves in both Middle-earth and the Undying Lands.

CITY OF TIRION

In the Undying Lands, the Noldor and
Vanyar Elves built the first and greatest city
in Eldamar. This was Tirion of the white towers
and crystal stair and it was set on the hill of
Túna in Calacirya, the Pass of Light. The city
was placed so that not only could the Elves live
in the Light of the Trees and look out on the sea
but also, from under the shadow of Túna and
the tall towers, could view the glittering Stars
that are so dear to their hearts.

HAVEN OF ALQUALONDË

Last of the Elves to reach the Undying Lands
were the Teleri, who were called Sea-elves.
They were the first people to build ships, and
for many Ages they lived on the shores of
Middle-earth and on Tol Eressëa, the "lonely
isle". Because of their great love for the sea and for
their fair ships, they would not enter Eldamar.
They chose instead to live on the shores of the
Undying Lands beneath the Stars. There they
built Alqualondë, which is "haven of Swans",
and the ships of these Elves were like Swans
with eyes and beaks of jet and gold. Beneath the
arch of sea-carved stone that is the gate of
Alqualondë, the Teleri still sail their Swan ships,
sing fair songs and listen to the murmuring sea
on the shore.

DARKENING OF VALINOR

After three Ages of Chaining, Melkor came before the Valar to be judged. He seemed to have changed and he claimed to have repented, so Manwë, the Lord of the Valar, ordered his chains to be removed. But the Valar were deceived for Melkor only seemed to be fair and good: in secret he plotted their downfall. First he sowed strife among the Elves, and then in alliance with the Great Spider Ungoliant he made open war on the Valar. He came with Ungoliant to the Trees of the Valar and struck them with a great spear, and the Spider sucked the Light and Life from the Trees so they withered and died. All of Valinor was made hideously black with the Unlight of Ungoliant, and Melkor laughed with evil joy because for a second time he had put out the great Lights of the World.

FLIGHT OF THE NOLDOR

After the destruction of the Trees of the Valar,
Melkor slew Finwë, the Noldor king, and took
the Silmarils from him. In great wrath the
Noldor pursued the evil Vala, and, despite the
warning by the Valar, they made their way back
to Middle-earth. Some went in ships, which
they took from the Teleri, but a great number led
by Fingolfin crossed Helcaraxë, the Grinding Ice.
This was the northern narrow gap of sea
and ice between the Undying Lands and
Middle-earth. In that crossing many an Elf lord
and lady fell into the sea or perished beneath
collapsing towers of ice.

BLACK RIDERS In the centuries that followed the forging of the Rings of Power by the Elven-smiths and Sauron the Maia, nine Black Riders on swift black Horses appeared in Middle-earth. Few knew what manner of beings the Black Riders were, but the wise learned that they had once been Men, who by the power of the Rings had been turned to deathless wraiths. These Black Riders were the mightiest of the Ring Lord Sauron's servants; in the Black Speech of Orcs their name was NAZGÛL.

BOARS The hunting of Boars was always a sport among Elves and the Men of Arda. Even Oromë the Valarian huntsman, who was Lord of the Forest, would chase these tusked beasts of the woodlands with hounds and Horse.

Most famous of the tales of the hunted Boar is the one recorded in the "Annals of the Kings and Rulers", which tells how a king of Rohan died on a wild Boar's tusks. Folca of the Rohirrim was a mighty warrior and hunter, and thirteenth in the line of kings, but the beast named the Boar of Everholt that he pursued was fierce and huge. So, when the contest was joined in the Firien Wood beneath the shadow of the White Mountains, there was loud battle in which both hunter and hunted were slain.

BRAMBLES OF MORDOR In the Black Land of Mordor was Gorgoroth, where the furnace and forge of the Ring Lord Sauron were housed. It was boasted that nothing grew upon that poisoned land, but as the "Red Book of Westmarch" tells some life did in fact dare to come forth from the harsh ground. In sheltered places twisted tree-forms and stunted grey grasses haltingly grew and though the leaves were shrivelled with sulphur vapour and maggot hatchings, nowhere on Middle-earth did brambles grow so large and fierce. The Brambles of Mordor were hideous with foot-long thorns, as barbed and sharp as the daggers of Orcs, and they sprawled over the land like coils of steel wire. They were truly the flowers of the land of Mordor.

BRETHIL In the lost land of Beleriand, there were once wide forests of birch trees. In the Sindarin language of the Grey-elves of that land these trees were called Brethil, and their beauty was much admired by those Elves.

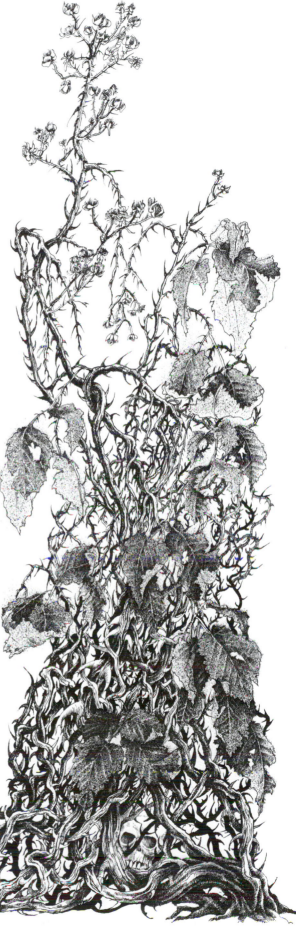

CALAQUENDI The "Quenta Silmarillion" tells how those Elves who arose in Middle-earth came to the Undying Lands in the time of the Trees of the Valar. These people were called the Calaquendi or LIGHT ELVES. For many Ages they lived in the Eternal Light of the Two Trees, and they were ennobled by that Light, strengthened in body, and filled with great knowledge by the teaching of the Valar and Maiar.

To compare the Calaquendi with the lesser Elves of Middle-earth was to compare diamonds with coal. The spirits of the Calaquendi were bright as the blades of their swords, and their souls strong and fierce as the naked flames that seemed to shine from their eyes. Before them, all but the mightiest of Melkor's servants stood in awe.

COLD-DRAKES Of the Dragons that Morgoth brought forth from Angband during the First Age of Sun, there were many breeds. Some were breathers of fire, others had mighty wings, but the most common were the Cold-drakes, who had no power of fire or flight but had great strength of tooth and claw and a mighty armour of iron scales. The Cold-drakes were a terror to all races who opposed them in that First Age, and they wrought untold destruction on the lands of Middle-earth. At the end of the Age nearly all the Dragon race and most of Morgoth's servants perished during the Great Battle in the War of Wrath.

In the Third Age of Sun, the histories of the Westlands tell how many Cold-drakes arose once again in the wastelands of the North and went to the Grey Mountains. Dwarves had come to these mountains for they were rich in gold, and in the twentieth century of this Age the Cold-drakes followed, seeking the Dwarf-hoards and prepared for war, and though the Dwarves battled bravely they were outmatched and the Cold-drakes wantonly stalked and slaughtered their foes. A prince of the Men of Éothéod – one named Fram, son of Frumgar – came and slew Scatha the Worm, the greatest Dragon of that land and the Grey Mountains were cleared

of Dragons for five centuries. Yet the Cold-drakes came again to the mountains in the year 2570. One by one the Dwarf-lords fell to them: the last was the Dwarf-king named Dáin I of Durin's Line, and he and his son Frór were slain by a great Cold-drake within their very halls. So the last of the Dwarves fled from the Grey Mountains, leaving most reluctantly all their gold as the Dragon's prize.

CORSAIRS In the Third Age of Sun the dreaded Corsairs of Umbar tyrannized the coastlands of Middle-earth for many centuries. The sight of their black-sailed dromunds always filled the peoples of Middle-earth with fear, for they held many warriors and were driven by the power of slaves pulling many oars.

The Númenóreans first came to Umbar in the Second Age of Sun, but in time they succumbed to evil and, after the Downfall of their land into the Western Sea, some remained in Umbar and were named the Black Númenóreans. They were an evil sea power. Yet in time the kings of Gondor came against them, and in 1050 of the Third Age the power of the Black Númenóreans was broken for ever and Umbar became a fortress in Gondor's realm.

But there was always strife with the Haradrim, who often attacked Umbar, and also there was rebellion within Gondor itself, until finally the rebels of Gondor, the Haradrim and those few of the scattered Black Númenóreans who remained, retook Umbar with many great ships and restored its power. So it was, from the fifteenth century until the War of the Ring, that these people were named the Corsairs of Umbar and they were always counted among the chief enemies of the Dúnedain of Gondor.

The "Red Book of Westmarch" tells how, in the last century of the Third Age, the Dúnedain chieftain Aragorn, son of Arathorn, proved to be the chief architect of the downfall of the Corsairs. For this fierce warrior led the Dúnedain of Gondor into the havens of Umbar. There he slew their captain and set a torch to their fleet. In the year of the War of the Ring itself, Aragorn brought a phantom army out of Dunharrow to the Corsairs' black ships at Pelargir. And with these Dead Men of Dunharrow Aragorn once again routed the Corsairs in what was their final defeat, for the chieftain took all their ships from them.

And with this action he both broke the power of the Corsairs and turned the tide of the War of the Ring. For Aragorn used the black ships of the Corsairs to bring the allies of the Dúnedain victoriously into the Battle of Pelennor Fields.

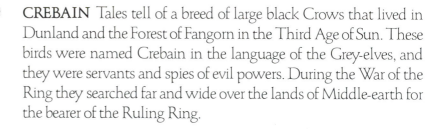

CREBAIN Tales tell of a breed of large black Crows that lived in Dunland and the Forest of Fangorn in the Third Age of Sun. These birds were named Crebain in the language of the Grey-elves, and they were servants and spies of evil powers. During the War of the Ring they searched far and wide over the lands of Middle-earth for the bearer of the Ruling Ring.

CROWS Crows were always the chief carrion birds of Middle-earth and they carried a reputation of being allied with Dark Powers. Men called them birds of ill-omen, for it was thought they spied over the land and brought tales to evil beings, who plotted deeds of ambush and slaughter. So it was that these carrion birds profited by bearing tales, for on the bloody work of these evil armies the Crows often feasted.

As was common among birds of Middle-earth, the Crows spoke a dialect of bird-tongue, although it was the opinion of Dwarves, who knew the language, that their discourse was as ill-disposed as that of the evil race of Orcs.

CULUMALDA In the wooded province of North Ithilien, in the realm of Gondor, is the Isle of Cair Andros, which like an anchored ship rests in the River Anduin. On this island grow the fairest of the trees of Ithilien. They are named Culumalda, which is "golden-red", for such is the hue of their foliage. To the Elven people their beauty is as a faint memory of Laurelin, that great Tree of the Valar in the Undying Lands, which was brilliant beyond imagining and which also bore the name Culúrien meaning both "gold" and "red".

DARK ELVES Those numbered among the Dark Elves were all the Elven-folk who never beheld the ennobling Light of the Trees of the Valar. These were the Avari – the Silvan Elves of the East and those of Mirkwood and Lothlórien – and the Eldar who never completed the Great Journey to the Undying Lands – the Nandor, the Laiquendi (Green-elves), the Falathrim and also the Sindar (Grey-elves) – who inhabited Beleriand until the end of the First Age of Sun, when all the Elf-realms of that place were lost in the sea.

The Dark Elves, or "Moriquendi" in the Elven tongue, were counted a lesser people than the High Elves of Eldamar, who were the Vanyar, Noldor and Teleri. Yet by the reckoning of Men these Dark Elves were magical and brilliant beings. For they were immune to pestilence and aged not with the passage of time. They were wiser, stronger and fairer than Men and their eyes always shone with the light of the Stars. In the first years of Sun, it was these Elves who taught all Men speech and many other arts and skills, that they might live in Middle-earth and raise themselves above the station of beasts.

The Nandor and the Laiquendi both were said to have learned powers of woodlore greater than any other living creatures. The Falathrim were the first shipbuilders of Middle-earth and the finest mariners. The Sindar, who were ruled by a High Eldar king and a Maia queen, built the fairest kingdom on Middle-earth and performed noble deeds counted great even by the measure of the High Elves.

In the Second Age of Sun, after the sinking of Beleriand new Elf-realms were created by the High Elves of Middle-earth and many Silvan Elves came to them out of the East and the North. Of these new realms, those of Lindon, Rivendell, Mirkwood and Lothlórien survived until the Fourth Age. But, as the "Red Book of Westmarch" tells, the High Elves in the Fourth Age took the white Elven-ships to the Undying Lands. And though Dark Elves long remained in Middle-earth, all their realms faded and they became a wandering folk of ever diminishing power.

D

DEAD MEN OF DUNHARROW In Mortal Lands of Arda there were many spirits who, because of some righteous curse or evil act of sorcery, were bound to Arda longer than was their right. The Barrow-wights and the mighty Ringwraiths were such beings; other unquiet souls inhabited the Dead Marshes, where floods disturbed the graves of Men and Elves who had fallen at the Battle of Dagorlad near the Black Gate of Mordor.

The "Red Book of Westmarch" also tells of those known as the Dead Men of Dunharrow, who haunted the labyrinths of the ancient citadel of Rohan. These were once Men of the White Mountains who in the Second Age of Sun had sworn allegiance to the king of the Dúnedain but, in time of war, broke that oath and betrayed the Dúnedain to the Dark Lord Sauron. Thereafter all the warriors of the Men of the White Mountains were cursed as oath-breakers and became wandering ghosts who could find no rest.

For all the years of the Third Age of Sun these Men haunted the Paths of the Dead above the mighty Hold of Dunharrow, and all who entered the corridors were driven mad with fear and were lost. But in the last years of that Age one who could command them came from the northern wilderness. He was Aragorn, son of Arathorn, the rightful heir of the king of the Dúnedain. He summoned the Dead to fulfil the oath they had broken long ago. And indeed they appeared, pale riders on pale Horses, yet they proved to be a mighty battalion of mighty Men. They rode with Aragorn to Pelargir and made war on the Corsairs of Umbar on land and sea, and they slew them and made them flee in terror. Thus the Dead Men of Dunharrow gave total victory to Aragorn and were redeemed by this act. Their souls were released and, before the eyes of amazed living Men, the vast form of a great pale army faded as mist in a wind at dawn.

DEEP ELVES Of all the Elves the most famous in the songs of Men are the NOLDOR, who are called Deep Elves because of their great knowledge of the crafts taught them in the Undying Lands by Aulë, the Smith of the Valar and Maker of Mountains.

In Eldamar, these Elves greatly loved to build with stone and they delved deep into the mountains for it. They were first to find the bright Earth-gems and they were first to devise the Elf-gems that were brighter still.

The Deep Elves were well known to Men, for alone of the Calaquendi they returned to Middle-earth after the coming of Men and performed great deeds, for both good and evil. These Elves wrought the Great Jewels – the Silmarils – and also made the Rings of Power. The greatest wars that ever were known to Men were fought over these works.

DORWINIONS On the western shore of the Inland Sea of Rhûn there lived the Dorwinions. Of all Northmen, the Dorwinions were the most easterly, and they were far-famed as makers of the finest and strangest of wines. By trading with many of the people of Middle-earth the Dorwinions became prosperous, for even the fine sensibilities of Elves were nourished by their wines.

DRAGONS The "Quenta Silmarillion" tells how, in the First Age of Sun, Morgoth the Dark Enemy hid himself in the Pits of Angband and wrought his masterpieces of evil from flame and sorcery. These dark jewels of Morgoth's genius were the Great Worms called Dragons. He made three kinds: great serpents that slithered, those that walked on legs, and those that flew with wings like the Bat. Of these kinds there were two types: the Cold-drakes, who fought with fang and claw, and the miraculous Urulóki Fire-drakes, who destroyed with breath of flame. All Dragons were the embodiment of the chief evils of Men, Elves and Dwarves, and so were great in their destruction of those races.

The Dragons were in themselves vast armouries that worked towards Morgoth's aims. The reptiles were of massive size and power and were protected by scales of impenetrable iron. Tooth and nail were like javelin and rapier, and their tails could crush the shield-wall of any army. The winged Dragons swept the land below them with hurricane winds, and the Fire-drakes breathed scarlet and green flames that licked the Earth and destroyed all in their path.

Beyond strength of arms, Dragons carried other more subtle powers. Their eyesight was keener than the hawk's and anything that they sighted could not escape them. They had hearing that would catch the sound of the slightest breath of the most silent enemy, and a sense of smell that allowed them to name any creature by the least odour of its flesh.

The intelligence of Dragons was renowned, as was their love of setting and solving riddles. Dragons were ancient serpents, and so were creatures of immense cleverness and knowledge but not of wisdom, for their intelligence had the flaws of vanity, gluttony, greed, deceit and wrath.

Being created chiefly of the elements of fire and sorcery, the Dragons shunned water and preferred darkness to the light of day. Dragon-blood was black and deadly poison, and the vapours of their worm-stench were of burning sulphur and slime. Their bodies

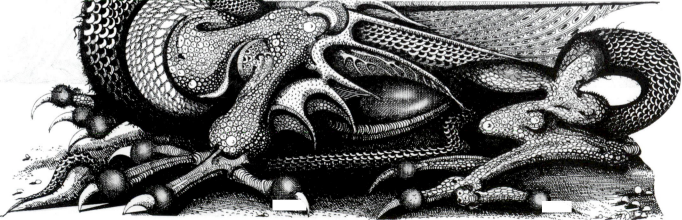

glowed always with a hard, gem-like flame. Their laughter was deeper than well-shafts and made the very mountains quake. The eyes of Dragons emitted rays of ruby light or in anger flashed red lightning. Their cruel reptilian voices were harsh whispers and, combined with the intensity of the serpent eye, invoked the Dragon-spell that bound unwary foes and made them wish to surrender to the beast's awesome will.

First of the Fire-drakes, the Urulóki created by Morgoth in Angband, was Glaurung, Father of Dragons. After only a century of brooding and growing in the caverns, Glaurung in fiery wrath burst out from Angband's gates and came into a startled World. Though he was not of the winged race that would later arise, Glaurung was the greatest terror of his time. He burned and savaged the land of the

Elves in Hithlum and Dorthonion before being driven back by Fingon, prince of Hithlum. Morgoth, however, was displeased with Glaurung for his impulsiveness, for he had planned that the Dragon should grow to full power before revealing him to an unsuspecting World. To Glaurung this attack was but mere adolescent adventure – a youthful testing of power. Terrible though it was to Elves, his strength was barely developed and his scale-armour was still tender to the assault of weapons. So Morgoth held Glaurung within Angband for another two centuries before he let the Urulóki loose. This was the beginning of the Fourth Battle in the Wars of Beleriand. It became known as the Battle of the Sudden Flame when Glaurung, the Great Worm, in full power led Morgoth's forces into battle against the High Elves of Beleriand. His great size and scorching fire cleared a path into the armies of the foe, and with Morgoth's demons, the Balrogs, and black legions of innumerable Orcs he broke the Siege of Angband and brought despair to the Elves.

In the Fifth Battle, called the Battle of Unnumbered Tears, Glaurung caused even more terrible destruction, as by now he had (in the mysterious way of Dragons) fathered a brood of lesser Fire-drakes and Cold-drakes to follow him in war. So a great army of Elves and Men fell before this onslaught, and none could withstand the Dragon-flame, except the Dwarves of Belegost, who had come to fight the common foe.

Morgoth used Glaurung as well to hold the territories he gained; but force in battle was not the only power this monster knew. He brought many under his sway with the binding power of his serpent eye and the hypnotic Dragon-spell.

Years after Glaurung had sacked and laid waste the kingdom of Nargothrond, the "Narn i Hîn Húrin" tells how he was slain by the mortal Túrin Turambar. For this son of Húrin came on the Fire-drake by stealth and drove the sword Gurthang deep into the beast's underbelly, but, by the poison of the black blood and the venom of the Dragon's last words, Túrin was also killed.

Though Glaurung was named Father of Dragons, the greatest Dragon that ever entered the World was one named Ancalagon the Black. "Rushing jaws" is the meaning of his name, and his ravening majesty devastated the army of the West in the Great Battle and the War of Wrath at the close of the First Age of Sun. Ancalagon was the first of the winged Fire-drakes, and he and others of that breed came out of Angband like mighty storm clouds of wind and fire as a last defence of Morgoth's realm was made. This was the first the World had seen of winged Dragons and for a time Morgoth's foes were in retreat. Yet Eagles and all the warrior birds of the Earth came out of the West together with the flying ship "Vingilot" and the warrior Eärendil. The battle of these beings of the air lasted a long time, but at last Eärendil was victorious, Ancalagon was cast down and the other Fire-drakes were slain or fled. So the War of Wrath ended and the power of Morgoth was broken for ever.

So great was the defeat of the Dragons in the Great Battle that it is not until the Third Age of Sun that the histories of Middle-earth speak again of the Dragons. In that time they inhabited the wastes beyond the Grey Mountains of the North. And, it is said, their greed led them to the hoarded wealth of the Seven Kings of the Dwarves.

Mightiest of the Dragons of the Grey Mountains was one named Scatha the Worm who drove the Dwarves from their halls in fear and dread, but a prince of Men stood and gave battle. This was the warrior Fram, son of Frumgar, chieftain of the Éothéod, and Scatha was killed by the hand of this Man. Yet this was but temporary release from the terror that lurked in the mountains,

for in time many Cold-drakes returned to the Grey Mountains. Though the Dwarves' defence was valiant and long, they were overwhelmed; one by one their warriors fell and the gold-rich Grey Mountains were left entirely to the Dragons.

In the twenty-eighth century of the Third Age, the chronologies of the Westlands tell how the mightiest Dragon of the Age came from the North to the great kingdom of Dwarves in Erebor, the Lonely Mountain. This Fire-drake called Smaug the Golden was vast and Bat-winged and a fearsome bane to Dwarves and Men. With consuming Dragon-flame Smaug ruined the city of the Men of Dale and broke the door and wall of the Dwarf-kingdom of the Lonely Mountain. The Dwarves fled or were destroyed and Smaug took the riches of that place: gold and gemstones, mithril and silver, elf-gems and pearls, the many-faceted crystals of emerald, sapphire and diamond.

For two centuries Smaug ruled Erebor unchallenged. Yet in the year 2941 a company of adventurers came to the mountain: twelve Dwarves led by the rightful king of Erebor, Thorin Oakenshield, and a Hobbit mercenary who was named Bilbo Baggins. They approached the Dragon by stealth and were amazed, for Smaug was huge beyond all that they had imagined and glowed golden-red with serpent rage. He was armoured as all of his race with scales of impenetrable iron, but in wariness he also protected his soft underbelly from assault: as he lay sprawled upon the wealth of his hoard he allowed diamonds and hard gemstones to imbed in his belly, and in this way armoured his only weakness. Yet, by cunning, the Hobbit Bilbo Baggins discovered one point upon the broad breast of the beast that was not sheathed in jewels, where sharp steel might cut.

When Smaug was aroused by the adventurers he came out in wrath and loosed his fire on the land. In vengeance he came to Esgaroth on the Long Lake, for the Lake Men had aided the adventurers. Yet there lived a Northman, valiant and strong, named Bard the Bowman who, guided by the secret of the Dragon's weakness, drove a black arrow into the beast's one vital place. Wondrously the Dragon screamed and fell flaming from the sky. So died Smaug the Golden, mightiest Dragon of the Third Age.

It was rumoured that Dragons continued for many centuries to inhabit the Northern Waste beyond the Grey Mountains, but no tale that has come to Men out of Middle-earth speaks again of these evil, yet magnificent beings.

DÚLIN The most loved bird song on Middle-earth is that of the nightingale, which the Grey-elves call Dúlin, the "night-singer", and TINÚVIEL "twilight-maiden". For, like the Elves themselves, the nightingales are delighted by starlight and bring forth song and joy into a dark World.

DUMBLEDORS In the playful Hobbit poem "Errantry," a part tells of a ferocious race of winged insects. They are named Dumbledors, but nothing has come to Men of the origin and history of these vanished creatures.

DÚNEDAIN The histories of the Dúnedain, the Men of Westernesse, begin at the start of the Second Age of Sun, for the Dúnedain were the remnant of the Edain of the First Age. These people were honoured by the Valar and given a land that lay in the Western Sea between Middle-earth and the Undying Lands. This place was named Númenórë, Westernesse in the common tongue of Men. The history of the Dúnedain of that time is told in the "Akallabêth" and in the tale of the Númenóreans, for the Dúnedain of Númenórë were known by that name. These people were mighty and their downfall was terrible when their land was plunged beneath the sea and the belly of the World was torn out. In that holocaust all the Númenóreans were lost, except those known as the Black Númenóreans, who in earlier times had gone to the southern haven of Umbar, and those known as the Elendili, who made the realms of Arnor and Gondor. So when the histories speak of the Dúnedain they most often mean the Elendili, the "faithful".

The histories of Middle-earth tell how, in the year 3319 of the Second Age of Sun, nine ships came upon a great wave out of the Western Sea. These were the ships of Elendil the Tall who, with his

sons, brought the faithful Dúnedain to Middle-earth. Elendil then made Arnor, the North Kingdom of the Dúnedain, and built Annúminas as its first city near the Elven lands of Lindon, while Anárion and Isildur went to the South, and made Gondor, the South Kingdom of the Dúnedain, and built Osgiliath as its first city. In Arnor were the extensive provinces of Rhudaur, Cardolan and Arthedain; whereas in Gondor were the fiefs and territories of Anórien, Ithilien, Lebennin, Lossarnach, Lamedon, Anfalas, Tolfalas, Belfalas and Calenardhon.

The Dúnedain prospered peacefully for a century of that Age while they strengthened their new kingdoms, but another power was also growing. Out of Mordor came Sauron and the Nazgûl, and Orcs and Men of many races who were his thralls. So there was war once again, but a pact was made that in later times was named the Last Alliance of Elves and Men; Gil-galad, the last High King of the Elves on Middle-earth, led the Elves of Lindon, and Elendil commanded the Dúnedain. Sauron's servants fell before their strength and Sauron himself was forced into battle at last. And although Elendil, Anárion and Gil-galad were all killed, so too was the power of the Ringwraiths and Sauron ended. Isildur cut the Ring from Sauron's hand and Sauron, the Ringwraiths and all his servants went into the shadows.

This was the war that ended the Second Age of Sun. With Sauron gone a time of peace was anticipated, but the Third Age was also doomed to end in bloody war, for Isildur did not destroy Sauron's Ring and within the Ring a terrible power remained. In the second year of the Third Age, Isildur was ambushed upon Gladden

Fields, slain by black Orc arrows, and the Ring was lost in the River Anduin. So, as the "Red Book of Westmarch" and the "Annals of the Kings and Rulers" tell, though there was peace for a time, strife was doomed to return to the Westlands. The Dúnedain were attacked from all sides: Balchoth and Wainriders out of Rhûn; Black Númenóreans and Haradrim from the South; Variags from Khand; Orcs and Dunlendings from the Misty Mountains; Hillmen and Trolls from the Ettenmoors; and Ringwraiths risen once again in Mordor, Angmar, Morgul and Dol Guldur. So did the Third Age pass, with the Dúnedain warring with those who were driven by a single force that had at last regained a form and resided in the mighty tower of Barad-dûr in Mordor: Sauron the Ring Lord.

At times the Dúnedain grew still more powerful in those years and their lands increased far into Rhûn and Harad. But through the centuries they were like sea-cliffs, worn down by the tides: Arnor as a kingdom was broken apart, and in 1975 the last city of Arnor fell; though an heir to the throne remained hidden in the land this Dúnedain kingdom was completely lost. After that time, in the North those who were rightful kings of the Dúnedain were only chieftains. In the South, though frequently besieged and threatened, most of the Dúnedain kingdom of Gondor remained intact and strong, yet the royal line was broken and the kingdom was ruled by Stewards.

Through the Third Age Sauron's power increased, until at last he came forth openly in war, determined to drive the Dúnedain and the Elves from the World and make Middle-earth his domain for ever. This was the War of the Ring, which ended the Third Age; and its history is told in the "Red Book of Westmarch".

In that War, among the Dúnedain of the North rose Aragorn, son of Arathorn, the one true heir of Isildur and rightful king of all the Dúnedain of Middle-earth. His knights were the Rangers of the North: horsemen armed with sword and spear in hooded travellers' cloaks of forest-green and high leather boots. Aragorn himself went about the land in this guise, weather-worn, yet strong, brave and keen of eye.

In that time he was called Strider, but in the many adventures of his long life he went by other names: he was Estel among the Elves of Rivendell in his youth, and Thorongil as the captain of Gondor who went to the South and destroyed the fleets of Umbar. During the War of the Ring he fought at the Hornburg, Pelargir, Pelennor Fields and before the Black Gate of Mordor itself.

He proved to be a true leader of Men, and as the heir of Isildur was crowned King Elessar Telcontar, ruler of all the Dúnedain of the twin realms of Gondor and Arnor, after the War of the Ring.

Upon his succession Aragorn was totally transformed from rugged Ranger into a king, fierce and lordly yet glad, wise and

Elven-eyed. He was enthroned and crowned beneath three banners, green, blue and sable: Rohan, Dol Amroth and Gondor. He wore the White Crown of the Dúnedain, the tall warrior's helm of mithril with white seabirds' wings of pearl and silver. A circlet of seven adamant gems was set around it, and a single Elf-gem on the crown glowed with a bright, clear light. Aragorn was compared with the noblest of the Númenóreans of old and even with the Elven-lords. Indeed he took the Elf-princess Arwen Undómiel as his queen, and they ruled wisely over the Westlands long into the Fourth Age and brought peace to all the people of Middle-earth.

DUNLENDINGS In the Second Age of Sun, before the Dúnedain came to Middle-earth and made the kingdoms of Gondor and Arnor, there lived a tall dark-haired people in the fertile valleys below the White Mountains. For many centuries, it is said, they developed a civilization apart from other people and built many great fortresses of stone. No history tells of the fate of these Men of the White Mountains, yet they vanished and only those descendants named Dunlendings remained in their lands.

Long before the Dúnedain made the kingdoms of Gondor and Arnor, Dunlending power had dwindled. The people had become divided. Those who had remained in Dunharrow became allies of the Men of Gondor; others had wandered North and settled peaceably in the land of Bree. Yet most of the Dunlendings had retreated to the hills and plains of Dunland and had become a tribal herding people. Though they kept their language and remained fierce warriors, they became a barbaric folk.

In the twenty-sixth century of the Third Age the Men of Gondor granted the Rohirrim a province called Calenardhon but the Dunlendings considered it theirs by right. So these two people grew to hate one another, and in the year 2758 a Dunlending named Wulf led a great invasion of his people against the Rohirrim and was victorious. But this was at great cost, for in the next year the Rohirrim arose and drove the Dunlendings back into the hills, and Wulf himself was slain.

So it was that for nearly three centuries the Dunlendings remained in the hill lands and left the fertile valleys to the Rohirrim. Yet they did not forget their hurt, and the tall, dark Men of Dunland made an evil pact with the rebel Wizard Saruman who had brought vast numbers of the Great Orcs called Uruk-hai into Isengard. And it is recorded that by some evil act of sorcery the Dunlendings were bred with the Uruk-hai, and evil offspring called Half-orcs were the result of this union. Half-orcs were black, lynx-eyed Men with evil Orkish features; combined with the Dunlendings and Great Orcs, the Half-orcs made a huge army of terrifying strength.

When the power of Gondor and Rohan seemed to wain, this army gathered in Isengard about the banner of Saruman's White Hand to fight against the Rohirrim. The "Red Book of Westmarch" tells how the fierce Dunlendings in tall helms and sable shields advanced to the Battle of the Hornburg at Helm's Deep with the Uruk-hai and Half-orcs.

But the Battle of the Hornburg was a great disaster for the Dunlendings; they were overthrown and the fierce Uruk-hai and Half-orcs were annihilated. Those who were not slain could only sue for peace, promising never again to arise against their Rohirrim conquerors.

DWARVES In a great hall under the mountains of Middle-earth Aulë, the Smith of the Valar, fashioned the Seven Fathers of Dwarves during the Ages of Darkness, when Melkor and his evil servants in Utumno and Angband held sway over all Middle-earth. Therefore Aulë made Dwarves stout and strong, unaffected by cold and fire, and sturdier than the races that followed. Aulë knew of the great evil of Melkor, so he made the Dwarves stubborn, indomitable, and persistent in labour and hardship. They were brave in battle and their pride and will could not be broken.

The Dwarves were deep-delving miners, masons, metal-workers and the most wondrous stone-carvers. They were well suited to the crafts of Aulë, who had shaped the mountains, for they were made strong, long-bearded and tough, but not tall, being four to five feet in height. As their toil was long, they were each granted a life of about two and a half centuries, for they were mortal; they could also be slain in battle. Aulë made the Dwarves wise with the knowledge of his crafts and gave them a language of their own called Khuzdul. In this tongue Aulë was called Mahal and the Dwarves Khazâd, but it was a secret tongue unknown but for a few words to all but Dwarves, who guarded it jealously. The Dwarves always gave thanks to Aulë and acknowledged that by him they were given shape. Yet they were given true life by Ilúvatar.

It is said that once Aulë had made the Dwarves, he secretly hid them from the other Valar and thought himself and them hidden

as well from Ilúvatar. Yet Ilúvatar was aware of Aulë's deed and judged that Aulë's act was done without malice, and thus He sanctified the Dwarves. Yet He would not permit that this race should come forth before His chosen children, the Elves, who were to be the Firstborn. So, though the Dwarves were full-wrought, Aulë took them and laid them deeply under stone, and in this darkness the Seven Fathers of Dwarves slept for many Ages before the Stars were rekindled and the Time of Awakening drew near.

So it was that the Elves awoke in Cuiviénen in the East in the First Age of Stars. In the years that followed the Seven Fathers of Dwarves stirred, and their stone chamber was broken open, and they arose and were filled with awe.

It is said that each of these Seven Fathers made a great mansion under the mountains of Middle-earth, but the Elven histories of these early years speak only of three. These were the Dwarf-realms called Belegost and Nogrod in the Blue Mountains and Khazad-dûm in the Misty Mountains. The tale of Khazad-dûm is longest for this was the House of the First Father called King Durin I and Durin the Deathless.

To the Elves of Beleriand in the Age of Stars the Dwarves of Belegost and Nogrod were a boon indeed. For they came into the realm of the Grey-elves with weapons and tools of steel and displayed great skills in the working of stone. And though the Grey-elves had not previously known of these people, whom they thought unlovely, calling them the Naugrim, the "stunted people", they soon understood the Dwarves were wise in the crafts of Aulë, and so they also called them the Gonnhirrim, "masters of stone". There was much trade between Elves and Dwarves, and both peoples prospered.

And though an ungainly people without graceful form, the Dwarves brought forth much beauty. Their mansions had grand halls filled with bright banners, armour, jewelled weapons and fine tapestries. Starlight shone down great light-wells and played upon mirroring pools and sparkling silver fountains. In echoing domes, by the light of crystal lamps, bright gemstones and veins of precious ores might be seen. In walls of jet polished like glass, dreaming marble forms were visible, and winding stair or twisting avenue might lead to tall, fair tower or court of many-coloured stone. Tunnels led to courtyards and grottos with columns of alabaster, fluted by Time and the gentle promptings of Dwarf chisels.

In the Ages of Starlight, the Dwarves of the Blue Mountains fashioned the finest steel that the World had ever seen. In Belegost, which was also named Gabilgathol and Mickleburg, the famous Dwarf-mail of linked rings was first made; while in Nogrod, which was called Tumunzahar and Hollowbold, resided Telchar, the greatest Dwarf-smith of all time. At this time these Dwarves forged the weapons of the Sindar and built for the Grey-elves of King Thingol their citadel of Menegroth, the Thousand Caves, reputed to be the fairest of mansions on Middle-earth.

The War of the Jewels came in the First Age of Sun and in it most of the Dwarves fought with the Elves against the servants of Morgoth. Of all Dwarves of that Age, greatest fame was won by King Azaghâl, the lord of Belegost. In the Battle of Unnumbered Tears only the Dwarves could withstand the blaze of Dragon-fire, for they were a race of smiths used to great heat, and on their helms they wore masks of steel that protected their faces from flames. Thus the Dwarves of Belegost could stop the advance of the Dragon-horde, and, though slain in the act, King Azaghâl drove his sword into the belly of Glaurung, the Father of Dragons, and so Glaurung and his brood fled from the battle field.

Not all the deeds of the Dwarves in that Age were praiseworthy. For, it is told, the Dwarves of Nogrod desired the Silmaril, and for it they murdered King Thingol and sacked the citadel of Menegroth. In turn the Dwarves were caught by the Laiquendi at the Ford of Gelion and the Silmaril was taken from them, and those who escaped the ambush were attacked by Ents and utterly destroyed.

From the ending of the First Age of Sun the histories of Elves and Men that speak of Dwarves tell primarily of those of Durin's Line who lived in Khazad-dûm. When the destruction of Beleriand came with the War of Wrath, the mansions of Nogrod and Belegost were broken and lost. The Dwarves of those kingdoms came into the Misty Mountains in the Second Age and made Khazad-dûm, that greatest mansion of Dwarves on Middle-earth, greater still. The vast halls filled with these prosperous people, whose craftsmen achieved matchless deeds and whose miners delved deep and long into the mountains' heart. In the Second Age many of the Noldorin Elves of Lindon entered into Eregion near the West Door of Khazad-dûm and made a kingdom so they might trade with the Dwarves for the precious metal mithril, which was found in abundance there. These Elves were the Gwaith-i-Mírdain, who were called the Elven-smiths in later times. By the wisdom of these Elves and Sauron's deceit, the Rings of Power were forged in this place. And though Dwarves were given seven of these Rings, they were not drawn into the terrible wars that followed for all the years that remained in the Second Age. In Khazad-dûm, the Dwarves closed the doors of their mansions to the troubles of the World. None could force an entry into their realm; but ever after it was thought to be a closed and dark kingdom, and so Khazad-dûm was renamed Moria.

Thus the Dwarves of Durin's Line survived into the Third Age of Sun, though by then they had seen their greatest days and the Dwarvish people had begun to dwindle. Yet Moria stood for five

Ages of Stars and three of Sun and until the twentieth century of the Third Age was still wealthy and proud. But in the year 1980, when Durin VI was king, the delving Dwarves quarried too deep beneath the mountains, because they released a great demon. This was one of Morgoth's Balrogs, and it came in wrath and slew King Durin and his son Náin and drove the Dwarves of Moria out for ever.

Durin's people were made a homeless, wandering folk, but in the year 1999 Náin's son Thráin founded the kingdom under the Mountain in Erebor. For a while Thráin and some of the people of Moria prospered, for Erebor, the Lonely Mountain, was rich in ore and stones. But Thráin's son, Thorin, left that place and in the year 2210 went to the Grey Mountains, where it was said the greatest numbers of the scattered Dwarves of Moria already lived. Here Thorin was accepted as king, and with his Ring of Power his people grew wealthy again. After Thorin his son Gróin ruled, then Óin and Náin II, and the Grey Mountains became famed for Dwarf-gold. And so, during the reign of Náin II's son Dáin, out of the Northern Waste there came many Cold-drakes of the deserts. Lusting for the wealth of the Dwarves, these Dragons came prepared for war and they slew the Dwarves and drove them out of the Grey Mountains.

In the year 2590 the heir of Dáin I, Thrór, took part of the survivors of the Grey Mountain realm back to the kingdom under the Mountain in Erebor, while in the same year his brother Grór took those others who remained to the Iron Hills. And again for a time all these people prospered, for there was great trade between Dwarves, Men of Dale and Esgaroth, and the Elves of Mirkwood. Yet for Durin's Folk the peace was short-lived, for in 2770, during the long reign of Thrór, the greatest Dragon of the Third Age, the winged Fire-drake called Smaug the Golden, came to Erebor. None could stand before this great Dragon. He slew wantonly, sacked Dale and drove the Dwarves from the Mountain. There for two centuries Smaug remained, lord of the Lonely Mountain.

So again the Dwarves were driven from their homes. Some retreated into the Iron Hills colony for shelter, but other survivors followed King Thrór and his son Thráin II and grandson Thorin II in wandering companies.

In this period Thrór was slain by the Orcs of Moria and his body was mutilated and his severed head was delivered to his people. The Dwarves, who had already suffered grievously from various evil hands, felt they could not bear this last insult. All the Houses of Dwarves gathered together and they decided to wage a great war.

This was the terrible and bloody War of the Dwarves and Orcs. It raged for seven long years, and through all the Westlands the Dwarf army hunted out every Orc cavern and slew every Orc band, until at last it reached Moria's East Gate in the year 2799. Here was fought the Battle of Azanulbizar, which is famous even in the histories of the Elves. In that battle the Orcs of the North were all but exterminated by the Dwarves. Yet the Dwarves had little joy in their victory, for half of all their warriors perished in that war. Such a loss could never be regained by this already dwindling folk. Even in spoils and territory they gained little from this war, for, though the Orcs were slain, the Balrog still held Moria and Dragons occupied the kingdom under the Mountain in Erebor and the Dwarf-realms of the Grey Mountains.

The Dwarves returned to their kingdoms filled with sadness. The grandson of Grór, Dáin Ironfoot, returned to rule in the Iron Hills, while Thráin II with his son Thorin II (now called Oakenshield) went west to the Blue Mountains and made a humble kingdom there. Yet Thráin II did not rule long, because while travelling he was captured by Sauron near Mirkwood and imprisoned in Dol Guldur. The last Ring of the Dwarves was taken from him and he was tortured to death.

Yet Thorin Oakenshield remained in the Blue Mountains, for he did not know the fate of his father. Many wandering Dwarves

came to the Blue Mountains and his halls grew, but he was unhappy and desired to return to Erebor to the kingdom under the Mountain, which had been his grandfather's. With such thoughts in mind, Thorin Oakenshield approached the Wizard Gandalf in the year 2941 and they immediately fell to a plan of great adventure, which is told by the Hobbit Bilbo Baggins in the "Red Book of Westmarch". This one Hobbit and twelve Dwarves accompanied Thorin in his mission to regain his kingdom. The twelve were: Fíli, Kíli, Dori, Ori, Nori, Óin, Glóin, Balin, Dwalin, Bifur, Bofur and Bombur. As is well told in the Hobbit's tale, Thorin more or less achieved his aim. For, in the end, the Dragon Smaug the Golden was slain and Thorin II took possession of his rightful kingdom, yet his grasp of it was brief. There followed the Battle of Five Armies, in which Orcs, Wolves and Bats battled against Dwarves, Elves, Men and Eagles. And though the Orkish legions were destroyed, so too was Thorin's life ended.

This was not, however, the end of Durin's Line, for Dáin Ironfoot had come to the Battle of Five Armies with five hundred warriors out of the Iron Hills and he was Thorin's rightful heir, being like Thorin a great-grandson of Dáin I. So Dáin Ironfoot became Dáin II and he ruled wisely until the last days of the War of the Ring, when he fell with King Brand of Dale before the gates of the kingdom under the Mountain. Yet this Dwarf kingdom withstood the attack by Sauron's minions, and Dáin's heir Thorin III, who was also called Thorin Stonehelm, ruled there long and prosperously into the Fourth Age of Sun.

Yet the kingdom under the Mountain was not the last and only home of Durin's Folk in the Fourth Age. Another noble Dwarf descended from Borin, brother of Dáin I, had founded a kingdom of Dwarves at the beginning of the Fourth Age, after the War of the Ring. This Dwarf was Gimli, son of Glóin; he had won great fame in the war and he had been one of the Fellowship chosen for the Quest of the Ring. He had acquitted himself well in all tasks and the song of his axe had been a terror to his foes at the Battles of the Hornburg, Pelennor Fields and before the Black Gate. At the War's end, Gimli had taken many of the Dwarves out of the kingdom under the Mountain into the wondrous caverns of Helm's Deep, and by all he was named lord of Aglarond, the "glittering caves".

For more than a century Gimli the Elf-friend ruled Aglarond, but after the death of King Elessar he allowed others to govern and went to the realm of his great friend Legolas, Elf-lord of Ithilien. Here it is claimed Gimli boarded an Elven-ship and with his companion sailed over the Great Sea to the Undying Lands.

This is the last that the histories of Middle-earth tell of Dwarves. It is not known if their kingdoms survived the Fourth Age and the Dominion of Men. It is known that they dwindled further, but whether they still live within secret caverns of the World or have now gone to the Mansions of Aulë cannot be learned.

DWIMMERLAIK Middle-earth was a land that had seen many Ages of bloody war and strife. Multitudes had been laid to rest in its soil by sword, fire and pestilence. But then too there were those who, by reason of some act of sorcery or broken oath, remained with unquiet spirits in the mortal World. Of these the "Red Book of Westmarch" speaks of the Barrow-wights, the Dead Men of Dunharrow, the Phantoms of the Dead Marshes, and the terrible Ringwraiths who in Black Speech were named Nazgûl.

In the lands of Rohan in the time of the Riders of the Mark, all such haunting spirits were named Dwimmerlaik. Such were the superstitions of these Rohirrim horsemen that even the Elves of Lothlórien and the Ents of Fangorn were named Dwimmerlaik and were thought to be similar evil spirits.

EAGLES Noblest of the winged creatures of Arda were the Eagles, for they were brought forth by two mighty Valar: Manwë, Lord of the Air, and Yavanna, Queen of the Earth. The Eagles were numbered among the most ancient and wisest of races: they were made before the Stars were rekindled and the Elves awoke. In the Ages that followed, these birds were always messengers and servants of Manwë. On Taniquetil, the Great Mountain, the Eagles would rest, clasping the high crags with crooked hands. Over all the azure World they flew, for they were the eyes of Manwë and like thunderbolts fell on his foes.

In the First Age of Sun a mighty breed of this race lived in Beleriand. They were called the Eagles of the Encircling Mountains and they lived in high eyries on the peaks called Crissaegrim. These Eagles were far-famed for their deeds in the War of the Jewels. Their lord was Thorondor and he was largest and most majestic of all Eagles. The wing-spread of Thorondor was thirty fathoms and the speed of the bird out-stripped the fastest storming wind. Thorondor was strong and fearless and he perpetually fought the evil creatures of the Earth.

It was Thorondor who rescued Maedhros the Noldor lord from a pinnacle of Thangorodrim. He also brought the broken body of King Fingolfin back from Angband and scarred the face of Morgoth with his long talons. In the Quest of the Silmaril both Beren and Lúthien were rescued from Angband by Thorondor. And, though Gondolin finally fell through treachery, the Eagles guarded that hidden Noldor kingdom for many centuries.

Thorondor and his people earned their greatest glory in the War of Wrath. The "Quenta Silmarillion" tells how the Eagles were victorious in the Great Battle against even that most terrible evil — the winged Fire-drakes.

In the Third Age of Sun Gwaihir the Windlord ruled over the Eagles of Middle-earth. Though he was not the size of even the least of the Eagles of the First Age, by the measure of the Third Age he was the greatest winged being in that day. Gwaihir's people, the

Eagles of the Misty Mountains, were fierce and much feared by Dark Powers. The long tale of the Quest of the Ring and the War tells how Gwaihir with his brother Landroval and one named Meneldor the Swift often advanced in battle with the Eagle host. The Eagles of the Misty Mountains did many great deeds. They helped to achieve the death of the Dragon of Erebor and, later, the defeat of the Orcs in the Battle of Five Armies. They also rescued the Wizard Gandalf and the Hobbit Ringbearers and fought in the last battle of the Ring War before the Black Gate of Mordor.

EAST ELVES At the time of the Rekindling of the Stars, all Elves lived in the East of Middle-earth, under the shadow of the Orocarni, the Mountains of the East, beside the shore of the Great Inland Sea of Helcar. But in time the Lord of Forests, the huntsman Oromë of the Valarian race, came to the Elves and brought the summons to leave that land of starlight and crystal water and come to a land beyond many mountains and across the great sea which promised to be of eternal light and great joy.

Many heeded his call and travelled to the West and were variously called West Elves, the People of the Great Journey and Eldar. Those who remained were named East Elves or the AVARI, the "unwilling" who feared the Great Journey. Later still they were called the Silvan Elves or Wood-elves. They loved starlight and the sound of the waters of Cuiviénen and, though many evil things might lurk in the shadows of the forest, they cared greatly for the

Kelvar and Olvar of the lands and did not wish to leave them for a brilliant vision.

So they remained and dwindled, or so it seemed to the eyes of Men who came later, for they seldom saw these Elves, and what power they had remained closely linked to the power of growing things. They hid themselves, for as long as the power of Melkor in the East remained unchecked the only chance for these people lay in living secretly on the land.

EASTERLINGS In the First Age of Sun, all Men arose first in the eastern lands of Middle-earth. Some went to the West, but those who remained in the East lived under the dark shadow of Melkor the Enemy and turned to evil ways. These people were called the Easterlings and their land was called Rhûn.

After a time, some of these Men left the East and went to the Elf-lands of Beleriand. These Easterlings were not a tall people, but broad, strong of limb, and swarthy skinned with dark eyes and hair. They mostly proved untrustworthy and in war betrayed their allies the Elves to Morgoth. Few names of these Men were passed on in histories, but Ulfang the Black, and his sons Ulfast, Ulworth and Uldor, earned fame by virtue of committing the greatest treachery. For in the Battle of Unnumbered Tears, Ulfang and his people turned upon their Elf allies in the midst of battle and slew them from behind, and by this act the tide of battle was turned and the Elves were broken. However not all Easterlings were unfaithful and one named Bór, and his sons Borlad, Borlach and Borthand, fought nobly to the death on behalf of Elves in that Age.

Yet ever after the Easterling people kept this alliance with Morgoth or his mighty servant Sauron, and came always in war against the noble descendants of the Edain. Through the Ages of

Sun the Easterlings became a confederacy of many kingdoms and races. In the Third Age many Easterling people came out of Rhûn. Among them were the fierce Balchoth and the chariot warriors called Wainriders. Then too, farther south in Harad, there lived many war-like Men who had come from the East long before.

At Sauron's command the Easterlings sent warriors into the War of the Ring. Upon Pelennor Fields innumerable companies of armoured Easterlings, bearded like Dwarves and armed with great two-handed axes, battled fiercely and died. Others too met their end when the Black Gate was broken and Sauron's kingdom of Mordor was destroyed.

The War of the Ring broke the hold of the Dark Power over the Easterlings for ever. So when King Elessar was crowned in Gondor, and in the Fourth Age came to Rhûn, the Easterlings sued for peace. This Elessar granted, and for long years after that treaty there was peace in the Westlands and in the lands of Harad and Rhûn.

EDAIN Of the Men of the First Age those counted greatest were named the Edain. They were the first Men to come out of the East into Beleriand, where the High Elves had made many kingdoms. Most were strong and brave Men, and the tales of that time tell of many great deeds.

These Men first entered Beleriand in three hosts led by the chieftains Bëor, Haldad and Marach, and these hosts became the Three Houses of Edain. Because the Elves were called the Firstborn Children of Ilúvatar, the Noldor in Beleriand called these Men the Atani, meaning the "Secondborn", and filled them with immense knowledge; much that is counted great and noble in all Men had its beginning in the Noldor masters. In the space of quite a short time the common tongue of Beleriand became Sindarin, the language of the Grey-elves, and Quenya words were little used. This is why the Atani are called the Edain in all the written lore of Beleriand, for such is the Sindarin form of Secondborn.

Of the Three Houses, the House of Bëor (which was later named the House of Húrin) was the first to meet the Noldorin Elves. Of all Men they were most like the Noldor, who loved them greatly. Their hair was dark and their bright eyes were grey. They were eager-minded, swift to learn and great in strength. Those of the Second House were named the Haladin and the People of Haleth; they were a forest-dwelling people, smallest in number and in stature of the Three Houses. The Third House was the House of Hador, whose people were golden-haired and blue-eyed and they were the most numerous of the Edain.

Many heroes arose among the Edain. Hador Lórindol, which is "goldenhead", was named peer of Elf-lords and lord of Dor-lómin. Húrin the Steadfast was the mighty warrior who slew seventy

Trolls in battle. As is told in the "Narn i Hîn Húrin", Húrin's son was Túrin Turambar, who wore the heirloom of his people, the Dwarf-wrought Dragon-helm of Dor-lómin, and carried the Black Sword called Gurthang. With these weapons, and by strength and stealth, Túrin slew Glaurung, the Father of Dragons.

Of all the deeds of Men within the Spheres of the World the greatest were those of Beren Echamion, who was married to the Elven-princess Lúthien Tinúviel, the fairest daughter of the World. For Beren was the hero who, with the knife Angrist, cut a Silmaril from Morgoth's Iron Crown.

In the histories of Elves there were but two other unions of Edain and Elves. Tuor wed Idril, daughter of Turgon, Noldor lord of Gondolin. Because of this, it is claimed that Tuor is the only Man to have been taken into the Undying Lands and permitted to dwell there. The son of Tuor and Idril, Eärendil the Mariner, wed the Sindar princess Elwing. It was Eärendil who sailed the flying ship "Vingilot" and carried the Silmaril, the flame of the blue star of twilight. In the Great Battle, Eärendil in his ship "Vingilot" also slew the winged Fire-drake Ancalagon the Black.

The remnant of the Edain were led out of Middle-earth by the guiding light of Eärendil in the Second Age, for the Edain were rewarded by the Valar for their suffering. Strengthened in body and mind and granted long life, they were led to the land of Númenor, which lay in the Western Sea between Middle-earth and the Undying Lands. At this time they were renamed the Dúnedain, the "Edain of the West", and they lived there for the Second Age of Sun and were counted the wisest and greatest of Men ever to walk upon Earth.

EDHIL In the dialects of the Elven peoples, there arose various names by which they knew themselves. Among these was the term Edhil, by which the Sindar called all ELVES.

EGLATH In the story of the Great Journey of the Elves in the Ages of Stars, there is the tale of how the Third Kindred, the Teleri, lost their king, Elwë Singollo. In the Forest of Nan Elmoth in the lands of Beleriand he fell under an enchantment. And though they searched for the king for many years the Teleri could not find him and finally took Elwë's brother as king and went again westwards towards the Undying Lands. But many would not leave Nan Elmoth and stayed for love of Elwë Singollo, though many more years passed. These were the Elves called the Eglath; they were divided from their kindred for ever and their name was Elvish for the "forsaken". In the end, their faithfulness had its reward, for their king did return. Where once he was named Elwë Singollo, he was now called Elu Thingol or King Greymantle, and he was greatly changed. A great light shone about him, and with him he brought the source of his enchantment, his queen, Melian the Maia. With the return of the king and the blessing of the new queen a great destiny came to the Eglath. Ever afterwards they were named the Sindar, the Grey-elves, and in the years of Stars they were held to be mightiest of people in Middle-earth.

ELANOR In the Third Age of Sun, there grew a fair winter flower in the land of Lothlórien. This flower was called Elanor, which means "star-sun", and its bloom was Star-shaped and golden. The histories of Middle-earth link Elanor to the "Tale of Aragorn and Arwen". Both Elanor the gold Star and Niphredil the white Star grew thickest on Cerin Amroth, the mound on which Aragorn, the mortal lord of the Dúnedain, and Arwen Undómiel, the daughter of Elrond Half-elven, plighted their troth. Arwen cast her lot with the race of mortal Men and, after the War of the Ring, Aragorn and Arwen were wed. Though her life was happy, soon after Aragorn died Arwen too perished, choosing the hill of Cerin Amroth as the place of her final rest.

ELDALIË After a time spent in the great Mere of the East called Cuiviénen in Middle-earth, the Elves were given a great choice. Either they must continue to abide in the East and know only starlight or they must make a Great Journey and come to the Land of Eternal Light in the Uttermost West. The Elves who in the First Age of Starlight chose the Great Journey out of Middle-earth to the Undying Lands were named the Eldalië, the people of the Eldar. They were of Three Kindred: the Vanyar, the Noldor and the Teleri, and much is told of these Eldalië in song and tale.

ELDAR According to the tales that have reached the ears of Men, and by what is written in books that Men might read, the history of the Eldar is largely the history of the Elven race. In the First Age of Stars, when Oromë the Huntsman of the Valar discovered the Elves in the east lands of Middle-earth, he looked at them in wonder and named them the Eldar, the "people of the Stars". At this time all Elves were named Eldar, but later this name was taken only by those who had accepted the summons of the Valar to the West and undertook the Great Journey to the Undying Lands. Those who remained were named the Avari, the "unwilling", and they stayed for love of Middle-earth, or because they distrusted the promise of the Land of Eternal Light.

So the Eldar were a chosen people and they were divided into Three Kindred: the Vanyar, the Noldor and the Teleri. The Journey was, however, long and perilous and many Eldar did not reach the Undying Lands; they were named the Úmanyar, "those not of Aman". Among them were the Nandor, the Sindar, the Falathrim and the Laiquendi. But the greater number did reach the Journey's end and came to the Undying Lands in the days of the Trees of the Valar. There they took that land named Eldamar, which had been set apart for them, built fine cities and became a great people.

Even in the years of strife and darkness that came with their Hopeless War against Morgoth the Enemy, the "Quenta Silmarillion" tells of their great deeds, which blaze in that dark history, and for many Ages the kingdoms of the Eldar flourished in both Middle-earth and the Undying Lands. Much of this is told in the tale of the Elves, the histories of the many sundered Teleri, and in the "Noldolantë" which Maglor sang.

ELENDILI The "Akallabêth" tells how when the Númenóreans foolishly went to war against the Powers of Arda in the Undying Lands, all their country was cast down and destroyed. However before the Downfall, nine ships sailed away from that doomed land. These were the ships of the Elendili, the "faithful" and the Elf-friends, who repudiated the ways of the Númenóreans and sailed to Middle-earth. There Elendil the Tall and his two sons made the kingdoms of the DÚNEDAIN in the North in Arnor and in the South in Gondor.

ELVEN-SMITHS In the Third and Fourth Ages of Sun, legends of Men and Dwarves spoke widely of the Elven-smiths, a vanished race that once lived in Eregion, to the west of the Mountains of Mist. These were Noldorin Elves who were more properly named the GWAITH-I-MÍRDAIN. It was they who forged the great Rings of Power which for two Ages of Sun loosed so much terror upon the lands of Middle-earth.

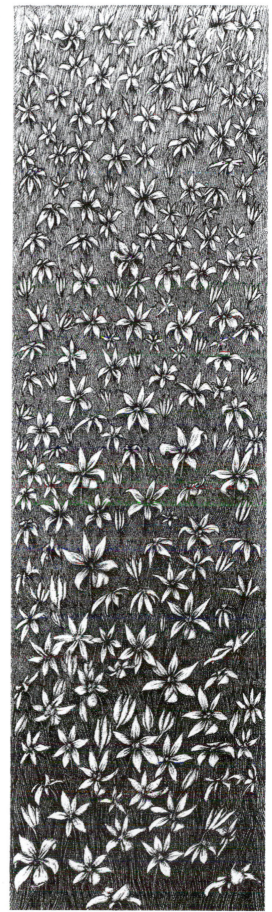

ELVES In the very hour that Varda, the Lady of the Heavens, rekindled the bright Stars above Middle-earth, the Children of Eru awoke by the Mere of Cuiviénen, the "water of awakening". These people were the Quendi, who are called Elves, and when they came into being the first thing they perceived was the light of new Stars. So it is that, of all things, Elves love starlight best and worship Varda, whom they know as Elentári, Queen of the Stars, over all Valar. And further, when the new light entered the eyes of Elves in that awakening moment it was held there, so that ever after it shone from those eyes.

Thus Eru, the One, whom the Earthborn know as Ilúvatar, created the fairest race that ever was made and the wisest. Ilúvatar declared that Elves would have and make more beauty than any earthly creatures and they would possess the greatest happiness and deepest sorrow. They would be immortal and ageless, so they might live as long as the Earth lived. They would never know sickness and pestilence, but their bodies would be like the Earth in substance and could be destroyed. They could be slain with fire or steel in war, be murdered, and even die of great grief.

Their size would be the same as that of Men, who were still to be created, but Elves would be stronger in spirit and limb, and the Elves would not grow weak with age, only wiser and more fair.

Though far lesser beings in stature and might than the god-like Valar, Elves share the nature of those powers more than the Secondborn race of Men do. It is said that Elves always walk in a light that is like the glow of the Moon just below the rim of the Earth. Their hair is like spun gold or woven silver or polished jet, and starlight glimmers all about them on their hair, eyes, silken clothes and jewelled hands. There is always light on the Elven face, and the sound of their voices is various and beautiful and subtle as water. Of all their arts they excel best in speech, song and poetry. Elves were the first of all people on Earth to speak with voices and no earthly creatures before them sang. And justly they call themselves the Quendi, the "speakers", for they taught the spoken arts to all races on Earth.

In the First Age of Starlight, after the Fall of Utumno and the defeat of Melkor the Dark Enemy, the Valar called the Elves to the Undying Lands of the West. This was before the Rising of the Sun and the Moon when only the Stars lit Middle-earth, and the Valar wished to protect the Elves from the darkness and the lurking evil that Melkor had left behind. They also wished to have the companionship of these Fair Folk and wanted them to live in the Everlasting Light of the sacred Trees of the Valar in Valinor.

And so, in the Undying Lands, which lie beyond the seas of the West, the Valar prepared a place named Eldamar, "elvenhome", where it was foretold that in time the Elves would build cities with

domes of silver, streets of gold and stairs of crystal. The land would be bountiful with fruit and grain, and the Elves would be happy, resourceful and wealthy. The shores of Eldamar would be strewn with diamonds, opals and pale crystals that the Elves themselves would work for the simple joy of making wondrous objects of beauty.

In this way the Elves were first divided, for not all the Elven people wished to leave Middle-earth and enter the Eternal Light of the Undying Lands. At the bidding of the Valar a great number went to the West, and these were called the Eldar, the "people of the Stars", but others stayed for love of starlight and were called the Avari, the "unwilling". Though they were skilled in the ways of

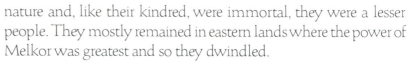

nature and, like their kindred, were immortal, they were a lesser people. They mostly remained in eastern lands where the power of Melkor was greatest and so they dwindled.

The Eldar were also known as the People of the Great Journey for they had travelled westwards across the pathless lands of Middle-earth towards the Great Sea for many years. Of these Elven people there were Three Kindred, ruled by three kings. The first was the Vanyar, and Ingwë was their king; the second the Noldor, with Finwë as their lord; and the third was the Teleri who were ruled by Elwë Singollo. The Vanyar and Noldor reached Belegaer, the Sea of the West, long before the Teleri, and Ulmo, Lord of the Waters, came to them and set them on an island that was like a vast ship. He then drew the two hosts over the sea to the Undying Lands, to Eldamar, the place that the Valar had prepared for them.

The fate of the Teleri was different from their kindred and they separated into various races. Because the Teleri were the most numerous of all the kindred, their passage was slowest. Many turned back from the Journey, and amongst these were the Nandor, the Laiquendi, the Sindar and the Falathrim. Elwë the High King was himself lost and he remained in Middle-earth. However most of the Teleri pushed westwards, taking Olwë, Elwë's brother, as their king, and they reached the Great Sea. There they awaited Ulmo, who at last took them to Eldamar.

So it was that most of the Eldar came to the Undying Lands in the days of Eternal Light when the Trees of the Valar lit all the lands. In that Light the Elves were ennobled and grew wise and powerful beyond the imagining of those in Mortal Lands. Their tutors were the Valar and the Maiar, from whom they learned great skills and untold knowledge.

In Eldamar, the Vanyar and Noldor built a great city named Tirion on the hill of Túna, while on the shore the Teleri built the Haven of Swans, which in their language was Alqualondë. These cities of the Elves were the fairest in all the World and to compare them in beauty was to compare the silver Tree of Telperion to the gold Tree of Laurelin. During that time called the Peace of Arda and the Chaining of Melkor, the Eldar grew in body and spirit as the fruit and flower of the Trees. They created many objects of a great skill and beauty that have never been surpassed and since the Dying of the Light shall never again be achieved.

In Middle-earth, the Sindar (who were called Grey-elves), through the teachings and the light of Melian the Maia, grew mightier than all other Elves in Mortal Lands. An enchanted kingdom with great power was made in the Wood of Doriath, and it was the greatest kingdom amongst the Eldar who did not see the Trees of the Valar. With the help of the Dwarves of the Blue Mountains, the Sindar built Menegroth, a mighty city. It was called the Thousand Caves, for it was a city beneath a mountain. Yet it was like a forest hung with golden lanterns. Through its galleries could be heard bird song and the laughter of crystal water flowing in silver fountains. No fairer city was built by any race in Middle-earth.

These were the great Ages of the Eldar, both in Middle-earth and in the Undying Lands. Yet this time of peace was fated to end, soon after the Release of Melkor. All believed Melkor to have repented of his ways, and he had given much help and wisdom both to the Valar and to the Eldar, but he had secretly instilled strife in the lands. However for a while the Eldar grew greater still, and it was during this time that Fëanor rose among the Noldor and made a work that is named greatest of the deeds of the Elves in Arda. The genius of Fëanor wrought the Silmarils, three jewels like diamonds that shone with a flame that was a form of life itself and shone too with the living Light of the Trees of the Valar. At this time the lies that Melkor had spread bore fruit, and there was strife and war. With the Great Spider, Ungoliant, Melkor came and destroyed the Trees, and Light went from the Undying Lands for ever. During the Long Night that followed, Melkor stole the Silmarils and with Ungoliant fled across Helcaraxë, the "grinding ice", and returned to Middle-earth and the dark Pits of Angband, his great armoury.

Fëanor swore vengeance and, against the Will of the Valar, bound the Noldor to his purpose with an oath. The Noldor therefore pursued Melkor to Middle-earth. In doing this they became a cursed people, for they captured the Swan ships of the Teleri of Alqualondë and slew their Elven brothers. This was the first Kinslaying among Elves. With the ships of the Teleri the Noldor of Finwë crossed Belegaer the Great Sea, while the Noldor led by Fingolfin in an act of great courage dared to cross the Helcaraxë, the bridge of ice, on foot.

As the "Quenta Silmarillion" tells so began the War of the Jewels, which caused the downfall of the Noldor and Sindar in the lands of Beleriand in Middle-earth. For the Noldor pursued Melkor and made war on his kingdom for all the First Age of Sun. Melkor they named Morgoth the "dark enemy of the World". The war was bitter and terrible and, of those Eldar who were in Middle-earth, few survived that struggle, though great deeds were done and mighty kingdoms rose and fell. Finally the Valar and many Eldar in the Undying Lands came and, in the War of Wrath, crushed Morgoth the Enemy for ever. But in that war Beleriand was destroyed and was covered by the waves of the vast sea. The great kingdoms of that place disappeared for ever, as did the Elven cities of Menegroth, Nargothrond and Gondolin. Only one small part of Ossiriand, which was named Lindon, survived the deluge. There the last Eldar kingdom in Middle-earth remained in the first years of the Second Age of Sun. Most of the Eldar who survived the War of Wrath returned West and were brought by the white ships of the Teleri to Tol Eressëa in the Bay of Eldamar. There they built the haven of Avallónë, including a tower that sent light over the Shadowy Seas. Meanwhile those of the Secondborn race of Men who had aided the Eldar against Morgoth went to an island named Númenórë in the centre of Belegaer, the Great Sea.

Little is told after that time of those Eldar in the Undying Lands, except that, though the Light of the Trees had gone, there never was anything on Middle-earth, in even its greatest days, to compare with the twilight years of Eldamar. The Eldar grow still wiser on the Blessed Shores, but none have returned to tell the tales of that place and the deeds of those people.

Yet still for a while some Eldar remained in Mortal Lands, for their doom was not fulfilled. Some who were great among the Noldor and Sindar had remained. One was Gil-galad and he was last of all the High Kings of the Eldar in Middle-earth. His reign lasted as long as the Second Age of Sun and his kingdom of Lindon survived until the Fourth Age. There was peace in the years of the Second Age. The Elves again prospered and wandered into the East. Some Noldor and Sindar lords joined the Silvan Elves and made themselves kingdoms: Thranduil made Greenwood the Great his Woodland Realm and Celeborn and Galadriel ruled Lothlórien, the Golden Wood. In that Age the greatest of the Eldarin colonies was Eregion, which Men named Hollin, where many great nobles of the Noldor went. As a people they were named the Gwaith-i-Mírdain, but in later days they were called the Elven-smiths. And it was to these people that Sauron the Maia, greatest servant of Morgoth, came in disguise. Celebrimbor, the greatest Elven-smith of Middle-earth and grandson of Fëanor, who made the Silmarils, lived in Hollin. At his order and with his skill the Rings of Power were made, and because of them and the One Ring that Sauron forged the War of Sauron and the Elves was waged and many other wars both in that Age and the next.

The evil battles of Sauron's War were terrible. Celebrimbor perished and his land was ruined, and Gil-galad sent Elrond and many warriors from Lindon to the aid of the people of Eregion.

Those Elves who survived the destruction of Eregion fled to Imladris (which in the Third Age was called Rivendell) and hid from the terror, and they took as their lord Elrond Half-elven. But though the Elves were not strong enough to break the power of the Dark Lord as long as he held the One Ring, their allies, the Númenóreans, had grown mighty in the West and even by the reckoning of Elves were god-like in power though they were but mortals. The Númenóreans came in their ships to Lindon and drove Sauron from the lands of the West. In a later time still, they came again, and to the amazement of the World they captured the Dark Lord himself and in chains took him to their lands.

Even in defeat the Dark Lord Sauron was filled with cunning. Indeed by treachery he achieved what he never could in war. The "Akallabêth" tells how the Númenóreans were deceived by Sauron and a terrible doom fell on them. All the lands of Númenórë were

swallowed up by the Sea of Belegaer, and all but a chosen few of that race vanished from the Earth for ever. The Change of the World also occurred, and at that time the Undying Lands of Valinor and Eldamar were removed from the Circles of the World. Mortal Lands became closed in on themselves and the Undying Lands were set apart. They were unreachable except by the white Elven-ships that sailed by what was named the Straight Road, which reached beyond the Spheres of the mortal World to that Undying Blessed Shore.

But in that Second Age of Sun there was still Sauron, Lord of the Rings, to deal with. For he had escaped the Downfall of Númenor and had returned to his kingdom of Mordor. Therefore the Last Alliance of Elves and Men was made, and all who were great among Eldar and Númenóreans made war on the Ring Lord. They broke Mordor and Barad-dûr, his tower, and took his Ring from him. He and his servants perished and went into the shadows, but Gil-galad, the last High King of Elves in Middle-earth, was also killed, as were nearly all the great lords of the Númenóreans. And again there was peace for a time and many Eldar went into the West from the Grey Havens.

There still remained a few Eldar to watch over the lands that slowly the race of Men were coming to possess. In the Third Age, the Eldar in Middle-earth were but a shadow of their former presence. Lindon remained but stood mostly apart from the strife of Middle-earth, and Círdan, lord of the Grey Havens, was held highest among them. East of the Blue Mountains the Eldar ruled only the lands of Lothlórien, the Golden Wood, Imladris, which was called Rivendell, and the Woodland Realm of Greenwood, which was renamed Mirkwood. All of these were in some way hidden and kept apart from the World of Men. The concerns of Elves seemed largely their own in all but one matter: that of the Lord of the Rings, who came to Mordor once again and sent his servants, the Nazgûl, out over the land. Then the Elves and the descendants of the Númenóreans once more fought in that which is called the War of the Ring. The One Ring in that time was destroyed. Mordor fell again, and finally, and Sauron vanished for ever, as did his servants; and his hold on all evil in the World was broken. However, the power of the Ring was also bound to the power of the Eldar in Mortal Lands, and, when the One Ring was unmade, the glory of the Eldar faded. The Ringbearers and many of the kin were then called to the Undying Lands. In the Fourth Age in the time of the Dominion of Men, the last of the Eldar sailed the last white ship that Círdan of the Grey Havens made out upon the Straight Road. And thus these People of the Stars passed away for ever to that place beyond the reach of mortals save in ancient tale and perhaps in dream.

ENGWAR At the time the race of MEN first came into the World, the Elves were much amazed. Compared with Elves, Men were a frail race unable to withstand the harsh elements. So the Avari, the Elves of the East, taught skills to many of these Men that they might live without deprivation and fear. However, the Elves still found that these people faded quickly, as they were mortal beings; the Elves could hardly learn the worth of a Man before he would be dead with the frost of age. Most terrible and mysterious to Elves were the sicknesses of the body that swept through the race of Men like flames in a wheat field. When these plagues came to Men they perished, while no Elf could ever know such evil. One of the names therefore that Elves called Men was given with great pity: the Engwar, which means the "sickly".

ENTS During the War of the Ring the strange forest giants called Ents came in battle against the Orcs and Men of Isengard. Half Men, half trees, the Ents were fourteen feet tall, and the eldest had lived in Middle-earth for nine Ages of Stars and Sun.

Lord of the Ents was Fangorn who in the common tongue was called Treebeard. He was huge and ancient, for he belonged to the tallest and strongest race born into the World. Like oak or beech was the huge rough-barked trunk of Treebeard, while his branch-like arms were smooth and his seven-fingered hands were gnarled. Treebeard's peculiar, almost neckless head was tall and thick as his trunk. His brown eyes were large and wise and seemed to glint with a green light. His wild grey beard was like a thatch of twigs and moss. He was made of the fibre of trees, yet he moved swiftly on unbending legs with feet like living roots, swaying and stretching like a long-legged wading bird.

Elvish histories tell how, when Varda, Queen of the Heavens, rekindled the Stars and the Elves awoke, the Ents also awoke in the Great Forests of Arda. They came from the thoughts of Yavanna, Queen of the Earth, and were her Shepherds of Trees. Shepherds and guardians they proved to be, for if roused to anger Entish wrath was terrible and they could crush stone and steel with their hands alone. Justly they were feared, but they were also gentle and wise. They loved the trees and all the Olvar and guarded them from evil.

At the time of their awakening Ents could not speak, but the Elves taught them that art, and they loved it greatly. They delighted in learning many tongues, even the short chirping languages of Men. Dearest of all they loved the language they had devised themselves, that none but Ents ever mastered. It rolled deep and full from their tongues as slow thunder or the timeless booming of waves on forgotten shores. In the slow passing of Entish time they formed their thoughts in unhurried meditation, and framed them into speech as undisturbed and rolling as the changing seasons.

92

Though Ents at times had great gatherings called Entmoots, for the most part they were a solitary folk living apart from one another in isolated Ent houses in the great forests. Often these were mountain caverns plentifully supplied with spring water and surrounded by beautiful trees. In these places they took their meals, not solid food but clear liquid stored in great stone jars. These were Ent-draughts and the magical fluid glowed with gold and green light. And in the Ent houses they took their rest, often finding refreshment in standing beneath the crystal coolness of a waterfall throughout the night.

So the Ents lived out their wise, almost immortal lives, and the many races of the Earth thrived and declined around them without troubling their greatness. Only when the foul Orcs came armed with weapons of steel were the Ents roused in wrath. The Dwarves too were not loved by Ents, for they were axe-bearers and hewers of wood. And it is said that in the First Age of Sun the Dwarf-warriors of Nogrod, who had sacked the Grey-elven citadel of Menegroth, were caught by Ents and utterly destroyed.

Ents, in the years of Starlight, had been both male and female, yet in the Ages of Sun the Entwives became enamoured of the open lands where they might tend the lesser Olvar – the fruit trees, shrubs, flowers, grasses and grains; whereas the male Ents loved the trees of the forests. So it was that the Entwives went to the open Brown Lands, where they were worshipped by the race of Men who learned from them the art of tending the fruits of the Earth.

Yet before the end of the Second Age of Sun, the gardens of the Entwives were destroyed, and with the gardens went the Entwives. Among them was the spouse of Treebeard, Fimbrethil, who was called Wandlimb the Lightfooted. No tale tells of their fate. Perhaps the Entwives went to the South or East; but, wherever it was, it was beyond the knowledge of the Ents of the forests, who wandered in search of them for many long years.

So, though Ents could not die in the manner of Men through age, they became a dwindling race none the less. They were never numerous, and some were slain with steel and fire, and no new Entings came after the departure of the Entwives. As well, the vast forests of Eriador where many once roamed had by the Third Age been hewn down or burnt, so only the Old Forest, which bordered the Shire, and the great Entwood of Treebeard remained.

By the War of the Ring Treebeard was counted among the three eldest Ents who had come forth under the Stars at the Time of Awakening. Besides Treebeard, there was Finglas, which means "leaflock", and Fladrif, which means "skin-bark", but the latter two had withdrawn even from the affairs of other Ents. Finglas had retreated in Ent fashion into the nature of his being and had become "treeish". He moved but little and few could tell him from the trees. Fladrif had battled alone against Orcs, who had captured his birch groves, slain many of his Entings, and had wounded him with axes. He eventually fled to live alone on high mountain slopes.

Though only Treebeard of the elders remained limb-lithe and active, there were many young Ents. Throughout the Entwood there was discontent because the Ents were being harassed by the servants of Saruman, who inhabited neighbouring Isengard. So the Ents entered the War of the Ring, and this was the great March of the Ents. Rank upon rank of the Ents marched on the stronghold of Isengard. With them came the Huorns, the Tree-spirits whom the Ents commanded and whose strength was nearly as great as their own. The very walls of Isengard were torn down and destroyed by Entish wrath and the power of Saruman was shattered. The Huorns advanced into the Battle of the Hornburg like a great forest, and the Orc legions of Saruman were exterminated.

After the War of the Ring, the Ents again lived on peacefully in the Entwood, yet they continued to wane and the Fourth Age was believed to be their last.

EORLINGAS In the fair and rolling grasslands that, in the Third Age of Sun, lay north of the White Mountains, there lived a race of Men who were named the ROHIRRIM, the "horse-lords". They often called themselves the Eorlingas in honour of Eorl the Young, the first in their line of kings. It was he who first tamed the Mearas, the "horse-princes", and led his people in victory against the Easterlings. Five centuries of rulers of Rohan descended from this one great king.

ÉOTHÉOD Among those Northmen who lived east of the Mountains of Mist there arose a strong and fair race that entered the histories of the Westlands in the twentieth century of the Third Age of Sun. They were led into the Vales of Anduin between the Carrock and Gladden by a chieftain named Frumgar. These people were named the Éothéod and they were great horsemen and men-at-arms. The son of Frumgar was named Fram and he slew Scatha the Worm, a Dragon of the Grey Mountains. Of Frumgar's line was Léod and his son Eorl the Young, who first tamed the Horse Felaróf, sire of the Mearas, the princes of Horses. Eorl led the Éothéod cavalry into the Battle of the Field of Celebrant and crushed the Balchoth and the Orcs who had broken the shield-wall of Gondor's army. For that rescue Cirion, Ruling Steward of Gondor, made a gift of the southern province of Calenardhon (which was called the Mark) to the Éothéod, who came south willingly and afterwards were known as the Rohirrim, the "horse-lords". Eorl became the first in the line of kings of the Mark, who were rulers of that land for five hundred years and more.

ERUHÍNI The "Ainulindalë" tells that in the time of the Ordering of the World, it was Eru, who is called Ilúvatar, who brought into being the races of ELVES and MEN. So it is that these races were in the Elvish tongue called the Eruhíni, which in Westron would be the "children of Ilúvatar".

ERUSËN The races of ELVES and MEN were made by Eru and were given life with the Flame Imperishable. The Elves therefore called these races His children and named them the Erusën.

EVERMIND The fair white flowers that in the Westron tongue of common Men were called Evermind grew over the grave barrows of the kings of the Mark near Edoras in the land of Rohan. These flowers, which were called SIMBELMYNË in the Rohirric tongue, were like glittering crystals of snow that fell in all seasons on the tombs of these kings. And to the Rohirrim and common Men alike these white flowers on the green swards were always a reminder of the power of the strong kings of the Mark.

AWAKENING OF MEN
Although the Trees of the Valar had been destroyed, the Valar Yavanna and Nienna coaxed from their scorched ruins a single flower of silver called Isil the Sheen and a single fruit of gold called Anor the Fire-golden. This flower and this fruit were placed in great vessels that became the Moon and the Sun which were carried across the skies by Maiar spirits. It is said that with the Rising of the Sun there came the Awakening of Men in the eastern land of Hildórien on Middle-earth. So began the Ages of Sun in which the race of mortal Men flourished and spread over all the lands of Middle-earth.

THOUSAND CAVES OF MENEGROTH

Through the Ages of Stars, while the High Elves
of Eldamar flourished in the Light of the Trees,
on Middle-earth the Sindar Grey-elves became a
great race. Their king was Elu Thingol and their
queen was Melian the Maia. The Sindar were
lords of all Beleriand and they lived in the
citadel of Menegroth, the Thousand Caves.
This place was a wonder to all the World:
because the Sindar loved the forests so greatly, the
halls and caverns of Menegroth were carved
with trees, birds and animals of stone and filled
with fountains and lamps of crystal. Through
these halls walked the Sindar lords, the greatest
Elves of Middle-earth in the Ages of Starlight.

DWARF-KINGDOM OF BELEGOST

Belegost was one of the seven great kingdoms of
Dwarves. With her sister realm of Nogrod,
Belegost was dug deep under Mount Dolmed in
the Blue Mountains in the Ages of Stars. Among
the Dwarves of Belegost were the finest smiths
and stone-carvers on Middle-earth. In their
Armourers' Halls, which were next only to
Khazad-dûm in grandeur, they made many
bright weapons and were the first people to forge
chain-mail. The Dwarves of Belegost traded
with the Sindar of Beleriand and supplied these
Elves with weapons of incomparably tempered
steel; furthermore these Dwarves carved the
stone chambers of Menegroth.

In the First Age of Sun, the Dwarves of
Belegost and their lord Azaghâl won great fame
in the War of the Jewels. For in the Battle of
Unnumbered Tears the Dwarves alone could
withstand the blaze of Dragon-fire because they
were a race of smiths used to great heat and on
their helms they wore masks of steel that
protected their faces from flames. The axes too
that they forged were strong enough to hold the
Dragons in check. Though Lord Azaghâl was
slain in the battle, he wounded Glaurung, the
Father of Dragons, and the Dragon brood fled
from the battle-ground.

Yet valiant as the Dwarves were, neither
Belegost nor Nogrod survived the First Age of
Sun. For when the Great Battle was fought at the
end of the Age, Beleriand and the Blue
Mountains were broken apart in the struggle
and all the land and the mountains shifted and
collapsed into the sea. So Belegost and Nogrod
were destroyed and those Dwarves who did not
perish at that time fled East to the great
mansions of Khazad-dûm.

QUEST OF THE SILMARIL

The War of the Jewels dominated the First Age of Sun. In the war there was much tragedy and sorrow but there were also many deeds of valour. In this time the Balrogs were defeated, Orc legions were destroyed and Dragons were slain, yet the greatest of deeds was performed in the Quest of the Silmaril. A single Elven-princess and one mortal warrior achieved what all the armies of Middle-earth could not. In that Quest, Lúthien the Fair took on the form of a mighty Vampire and her lover Beren the Edain took on the shape of a great Wolf. In such disguises they entered the very throne room of Morgoth in the deep Pits of Angband. There Lúthien cast a great enchantment of sleep over Morgoth and his servants. In fulfilment of the Quest, Beren arose from the sleeping shape of the great Wolf and with the knife Angrist cut a Silmaril from Morgoth's Iron Crown.

FALL OF GONDOLIN

The most beautiful Elven city built on Middle-earth was said to be Gondolin, the Hidden Kingdom. This was the last Elf-kingdom to survive the War of the Jewels. Its king was Turgon, the Noldor lord, who wisely chose to conceal this city in the Encircling Mountains. But in the end the servants of Morgoth discovered it; Orc legions appeared before its gates, together with Trolls and fire-breathing Dragons driven on by the Balrog demons. Though the Elves battled valiantly Gondolin was sacked, and with its destruction the Elf-realms of Beleriand were brought to an end.

DESTRUCTION OF ANGBAND

After watching the defeats and sufferings of the Elves and Men of Beleriand, the Valar could no longer tolerate the evil dominion of Morgoth over the lands of Middle-earth. So the Valar and Maiar joined in the War of Wrath against Morgoth's evil kingdom of Angband. All the World was rent by this great war. The Iron Mountains were broken open and the dungeons and great chambers of torture were destroyed. Morgoth's Dragons and demons came into battle but were slain by the Valarian host. The servants of Morgoth were scattered and he himself was cast into the Void. So ended the First Age of Sun, and with it the chief architect of evil vanished for ever, though much that Morgoth had made remained within the Spheres of the World.

EREGION AND THE WALLS OF KHAZAD-DÛM

Eregion was the land of the Gwaith-i-Mírdain, the Elven-smiths of the Second Age of Sun, and Ost-in-Edhil was their chief city. In Eregion trade between these Elves and the Dwarves of Khazad-dûm flourished for a thousand years. Here Celebrimbor, the greatest smith of the Age, directed the forging of the Rings of Power, over which the War of Sauron and the Elves was to be fought. In that War Eregion was destroyed and Khazad-dûm closed its doors to the World and was renamed Moria.

DOWNFALL OF NÚMENOR

The Second Age of Sun was accounted the Age of the Númenóreans: those Men who were descended from the Edain of the First Age and to whom the Valar had given Númenor, a land in the midst of the wide sea between Middle-earth and the Undying Lands.

The Númenóreans were granted a span of life far greater than ordinary Men, and through the centuries their strength and wealth increased and their navy sailed over all the seas of the mortal World. So great had their power become that they dared to challenge Sauron the Dark Lord, and indeed took him in chains to their country. But by guile Sauron achieved what he could not by strength of arms. For Sauron falsely counselled the proud Númenóreans and corrupted them, and so the Númenóreans made war on the Valar in the Undying Lands. And, for this act, Ilúvatar caused the fair land of Númenor to burst asunder. The mountains and cities fell; the sea arose in wrath and all Númenor collapsed into a watery abyss.

In that cataclysm also came the Change of the World. The Undying Lands were set beyond the Spheres of the mortal World and were for ever beyond the reach of Men.

DARK TOWER OF MORDOR

By the power of the Ruling Ring, Sauron made the foundations of Barad-dûr, the Dark Tower of Mordor. The Last Alliance of Elves and Men laid siege to that Tower for seven years at the end of the Second Age before finally forcing Sauron into open battle. Though many of the greatest Eldar and Dúnedain lords were slain, the Alliance was granted victory and the One Ring was cut from Sauron the Ring Lord's hand.

For more than a thousand years Sauron had no shape and wandered Earth as a powerless shadow. Yet because the One Ring was not destroyed, Sauron and his Tower were not ended. Both he and the Tower were to arise in the Third Age and once again Sauron the Ring Lord would seek to dominate the World.

FAIR ELVES Of all the Elvish race, those most favoured and loved are the First Kindred of the VANYAR, for they are the wisest Elves and they always sit at the feet of Manwë, High Lord of all the Powers of Arda. They are called Fair Elves and they have resided longest in the bright Light of the Trees of the Valar, and their eyes burn most brilliantly of all Elves with that Light. Furthermore, they are a blonde race, and their hair and skin is fairest of the Eldar. They seem golden and powerful, and their king, who is named Ingwë, has always been High King of all the Elves of the World.

FAIR FOLK From the beginning, before the Making of Arda and the Count of Time, Ilúvatar planned to bring the race of ELVES into the World. In his grand plan these were to be the first people to be born and the fairest of all races to come into being. And so ever afterwards, by all but their evil enemies, the Elves were usually called the Fair Folk.

FALATHRIM The Falathrim, the Elves of the Falas, lived on the coast lands of Beleriand in the years of Starlight and the First Age of Sun and were ruled by the lord Círdan. The Falathrim were of the Teleri kindred, but, when Ulmo the Ocean Lord came to the Teleri, Círdan and his people refused the final journey to the Undying Lands and so were divided from their kindred. The Falathrim lived by the sea for a long time and they were wisest of the sea-folk on Middle-earth. They were the first to build ships in Mortal Lands. The ships of Círdan were white and magical and they were able to make that far journey into the Undying Lands, even after the Change of the World, when Middle-earth and the Undying Lands were drawn apart for ever. Then only the Elven-ships of the Falathrim could make that lonely journey.

For a time after the departure of the Teleri to the Undying Lands, the Falathrim lived alone on the shores of Beleriand, and they built there two great havens named Eglarest and Brithombar. But after a period of peace under starlight, they discovered that another part of the Umanyar had become powerful in the Wood of Doriath just east of the Falas. The king of these Elves was Elwë Singollo, who had been lost, and with him was Melian the Maia, who was his queen. At this time Círdan and the Falathrim came to know these brethren, the Grey-elves, once again and after a while they became allied with these people, for they spoke the tongue of the Grey-elves and took all their causes to their hearts. In the years of strife that came with the Rising of the Sun, the Falathrim fought for them against Morgoth the Enemy, who arose in the North.

In that First Age of Sun, the Falathrim were beseiged by Orcs for a time, and later still their havens fell to Morgoth, but they took their ships and sailed to the Isle of Balar, and no power of Morgoth was able to come on the sea, for he greatly feared the Ocean Lord, Ulmo. There the Falathrim remained and were safe from strife, until the War of Wrath, when Beleriand itself was thrown down into the sea with the destruction of Angband. Again the ships of the Falathrim sailed and went south to the Gulf of Lune in the land of Lindon, the last of the Elf-realms of Beleriand to survive the holocaust of that Great Battle. Here Círdan built the last haven of the Elves on Middle-earth. This was called the Grey Havens and from this place the last Elven-ship sailed for ever from Mortal Lands.

FALLOHIDES Of the Halfling people called Hobbits there were said to be three strains: the Fallohides, the Stoors and the Harfoot.

The Fallohides were a woodland folk and were wisest in the arts of song and poetry. By Hobbit standards they were tall, fair-haired and fair-skinned. They numbered fewer than either of the other Hobbit strains but were more adventurous and inclined to commit acts of daring. Because of this, Fallohides often became leaders of their people and were known to seek the company and advice of Elves. The Fallohide brothers Marcho and Blanco in the year 1601 of the Third Age founded the Shire. And those of the families of Tooks, Brandybucks and Baggins who contributed famous heroes to the great conflict of the War of the Ring all had strong blood ties to the Fallohide strain.

FALMARI Of all people the Third Kindred, the TELERI, lived longest on the shores of Belegaer, the Great Sea of the West. These people were wisest in the ways of the sea and so they were named the Falmari and the Sea-elves. Their knowledge of the ways of Ulmo the Ocean Lord and his minions Ossë of the Waves and Uinen of the Calms perpetually increases. In the days when the Falmari travelled to the Bay of Eldamar on the Lonely Isle, Ossë came among them and because of his teaching they were the first people to know the skills of shipbuilding. The fleets of the Teleri were made, and the Falmari came in these ships to Eldamar, where they built Alqualondë, the "haven of Swans", and lived in mansions of pearl. In their ships the Falmari are always sailing in and out of the sea-sculpted archway of stone that is its gate on the Bay of Eldamar.

All races later came to know the arts of building ships and sailing from the Falmari, but they only learned a little of the Falmari's knowledge of the sea, for other peoples did not have the skill of language nor the subtlety of voice and ear to know the ways of the sea as well as the Falmari did.

FASTITOCALON In the fanciful lore of the Hobbits is the tale of a vast Turtle-fish that Men thought was an island in the seas. All seemed well when Men made a dwelling place on the beast's back until they lit their fires and in alarm the beast dived deep beneath the sea, drowning the encampment.

By Hobbits the beast was named the Fastitocalon, but whether the tale, like that of the Oliphaunt, was based on fact cannot be discovered from the histories that have passed on to Men. For though the creatures of Middle-earth were many, no leviathans are mentioned in the tales of other races.

It is likely that the story is in fact an allegory of the Downfall of the Númenóreans, as told in the "Akallabêth". For in the Second Age of Sun these most gifted of Men rose to the greatest power that was allowed them within the Spheres of the World, and the flame of passion and ambition overwhelmed them, and their great island, like the Fastitocalon, sank beneath the wide ocean and most of the Númenóreans perished in that Downfall.

FIRE-DRAKES Of all the creatures bred by Morgoth the Dark Enemy in all the Ages of his power the evil reptiles that were called Dragons were feared most. There were many breeds of these beings; the most deadly were those that vomited leaping flames from their foul bellies. These were called Fire-drakes, and among them were numbered the mightiest of Dragons. Glaurung, Father of Dragons, was first of the Urulóki Fire-drakes, and he had many offspring. The evil work of these Dragons on the kingdoms of Elves, Men and Dwarves in the First Age of Sun was terrible.

In the last days of that Age, when most of the Earth-bound brood of Glaurung had been put to death in the War of Wrath, the winged Fire-drakes appeared out of Angband. They are said to have been among the greatest terrors of the World, and Ancalagon the Black, who was of this breed, was said to have been the mightiest Dragon of all times.

In later Ages, the histories of Middle-earth all tell of one last winged Fire-drake that was almost as fearsome as Ancalagon. This was the Dragon of Erebor, which drove the Dwarves of Durin's Line from the kingdom under the Mountain. He was called Smaug the Golden, and in the year 2941 of the Third Age he was killed by Bard the Bowman of Dale.

FÍRIMAR In the First Age of Sun, the Elves of Middle-earth found a new race had arisen in the land of Hildórien far to the East. This was the race of MEN, whom Elves named Fírimar, which is the "mortal people". To the minds of immortal Elves, it was a frail race with little wisdom, for Men could at best but briefly learn the least murmur of knowledge before death took them.

FIRSTBORN As the "Ainulindalë" relates, in the Timeless Halls before the World was made, there was Music, and in it the Ordering of all things. In that Music came a theme that was made by Ilúvatar alone. This was the coming of the first race to awaken in Arda, an immortal race that was to last as long as the World itself. This was the race of ELVES, who awoke in the East when only starlight shone upon Middle-earth and thereafter in honour was called the Firstborn. Many Ages passed before the coming of the Sun heralded the time of the Secondborn, when that lesser race called Men arose, as had the Elves, in the eastern lands.

FLIES OF MORDOR In the Black Realm of Mordor it was said there lived only Orcs, Trolls and Men, who were thralls of Sauron the Dark Lord. The only beasts in Mordor were the evil swarms of bloodsucking flies. These were grey, brown and black insects; they were loud, hateful and hungry, and they were all marked, as Orcs of that land were marked, with a red eye-shape upon their backs. So the Dark Lord's power had spread to the smallest evil in his land.

FORGOIL Among the Northmen who resided east of the Mountains of Mist in the Third Age of Sun were the ROHIRRIM. These were a golden-haired people who boasted the fiercest cavalry of the Westlands. They were greatly feared and hated by their barbarous neighbours, the Dunlendings, who in contempt called them Forgoil, which in that tongue means the "strawheads."

FORODWAITH The "Annals of the Kings and Rulers" relate how after the Fall of Angband, the fortress of Melkor, a bitter cold descended on the northern desert land of Forochel. For a long time afterwards a people named the Forodwaith lived in that land. Little is told of these people except that they endured the icy colds of the North, and from them were descended the Lossoth who, in the Third Age of Sun, were called the Snowmen of Forochel by the Men of the West.

G

GALADHRIM The forest that in the Second Age of Sun was first named Laurelindórenan, "land of the valley of singing gold", and later Lothlórien, "land of blossoms dreaming", and even by some Lorien, "dreamland", was east of the Misty Mountains by the Silverlode, which flows into the Great River Anduin. It was the Golden Wood, where the tallest trees on Middle-earth grew. They were called the Mallorn trees and were the most beautiful of trees in Mortal Lands. Their bark was silver and grey, their blossoms golden and their leaves green and gold.

Within the forest was the concealed Elven kingdom of the Galadhrim, the "tree-people", who made their homes on platforms called telain, or flets, high in the branches of the sheltering Mallorn.

The Galadhrim did not build mighty towers of stone. Indeed to most people the Galadhrim lived invisibly in their forest kingdom, where they wore Grey-elven cloaks that were like a chameleon's coat. By use of ropes and woodlore they needed no bridges or roads. Deep within the Golden Wood, they did have one great city, which was named Caras Galadhon, the "city of the trees". There grew the greatest Mallorn on Middle-earth, and the king and queen resided in a great hall in that tallest of trees on the crest of a high green hill. It was walled and gated and encircled with other great trees like towers. At the very heart of the forest there was a magical hill called Cerin Amroth where once the house of an Elven-king stood. And from this place came a power and light that were like those in the Undying Lands in the Ages of the Trees.

The Galadhrim were mostly Silvan Elves, but their lords were Sindar and Noldor nobles. Their king was Celeborn, kinsman of Thingol "grey-cloak", and he was the greatest lord of the Sindar on Middle-earth. Their queen was the sister of Finrod and daughter of Finarfin, High King of the Noldor, who had remained in Eldamar after the Trees of the Valar were destroyed. By the Third Age of Sun she was highest noble of all the Elves in Mortal Lands. And though her Quenya name was Altárial, in Middle-earth she was called Galadriel, the "lady of light".

The power of the Galadhrim under such rulers was very great,
for their king and queen had lived in the first kingdom of the Sindar
in the days of Thingol and Melian the Maia and had learned much
concerning their powers. Their queen had lived in the Undying
Lands in the days of the Trees of the Valar and had visited the
Valarian Garden of Lórien, the most beautiful in all Arda. Some part

of these magical places came with these nobles to the Golden Wood of Lothlórien. A golden light was there; though it was but an ember of the glory of the Valarian Garden, the Golden Wood was brilliant and precious to the peoples of Middle-earth. This place was protected from evil powers by a force that was like the Girdle of Melian that once protected Doriath, the Sindarin kingdom. For Galadriel was bearer of the second of the three Elf Rings – Nenya, the Ring of Adamant and the Ring of Water – and her power held off the ravages of Time and made her aware of Sauron's moves and caused her people to be invisible to Sauron's eye. She commanded the Mirror of Galadriel, a silver basin that she could fill with fountain waters and by the power of her Ring could cast the image of future events on its dark, still surface.

The kingdom of the Galadhrim had been founded in a time of peace when Sauron had been taken captive by the Númenórean king before the Change of the World, in the third millenium of the Second Age of Sun. Since the first fall of Mordor, it had remained a land apart and, throughout the Third Age, the Golden Wood of Lothlórien was protected and sustained by the power of the Elf Ring Nenya. With the destruction of the One Ring, its power faded, and the queen went to the Undying Lands, the great light of Lothlórien faded as well, and Time re-found it. The Galadhrim again became a wandering folk and gradually dwindled with their Silvan brethren of the East.

GALENAS In the land of Númenor grew the broad-leafed herb Galenas, which was prized for the fragrance of its flowers. Before that land was swallowed by the Western Sea, mariners of Númenor brought it to Middle-earth, where it grew in abundance about the settlements of the Númenóreans' descendants.

However, it was not until such an unlikely people as the Hobbits discovered Galenas in their own land that the special properties of this plant were revealed. The Hobbits took the broad leaves of Galenas, dried them and shredded them and put fire to them in long-stemmed pipes. This was the herb nicotiana, which was afterwards known on Middle-earth as PIPE-WEED after the habit of the Hobbits. It was commonly smoked by Hobbits, Men and Dwarves, and they derived much comfort from it.

GALLOWS-WEED In the swamplands of Middle-earth where the evil phantoms called Mewlips lurked and the birds called Gorcrows flew, there also grew the Gallows-weed. In the lore of Hobbits this tree-hanging weed is known by name but its properties are not spoken of; for few who entered those haunted marshes ever returned.

GAURHOTH In the First Age of Sun, in the time of the Wars of Beleriand, many evil spirits in Wolf form came to Sauron the Maia. The Elves called them Gaurhoth, the "Werewolf host". From these creatures Sauron forged a mighty army that went to battle with Elves and killed many of the strongest amongst them. Sauron captured and held for a time an Elvish tower upon the River Sirion by the power of the WEREWOLVES; hence the name of that place: Tol-in-Gaurhoth, the "isle of Werewolves".

GIANTS Many beings of Giant size, both good and evil in nature, lived in Middle-earth. In the First Age of Stars there were the Ents, the Tree-herds, who measured fourteen feet in height and were of immense strength and great wisdom. Later came Giants filled with evil: those named Trolls and Olog-hai served the Dark Power and made the wild lands of the World perilous for travellers. Also, in the tales of Hobbits, there were rumours of great Giants who, in league with Orcs, guarded the High Passes in Rhovanion.

GLAMHOTH When the evil race of ORCS first entered the Grey-elven lands of Beleriand in the Ages of Starlight, the Sindar did not know what manner of being they were. Though none doubted that they were a vile and evil race, at that time they had no name. So the Grey-elves called them the Glamhoth, the "din-horde", for their cries in battle and the noise of their iron shoes and battle-gear were loud and evil.

GOBLINS Those creatures that Men now name Goblins are dwellers in darkness who were spawned for evil purposes. In earlier days they were called ORCS. Black-blooded, red-eyed and hateful in nature are these Goblin people, and though they are now reduced to beings committed to minor deeds of mischief, they were once a race bent on vast plans of terrible tyranny.

GOLODHRIM In the First Age of Sun, the NOLDOR came out of the Undying Lands and entered Beleriand. There they were greeted by the Grey-elves, who, in the Sindarin tongue, called the Noldor the Golodhrim.

GONDOR MEN Of the Dúnedain who made kingdoms upon Middle-earth, the most far-famed were the Gondor Men of the South Kingdom. Isildur and Anárion raised the white towers of Gondor in the year 3320 of the Second Age of Sun, after fleeing from the destruction of Númenor with their father Elendil, who then built the North Kingdom of Arnor.

The tale of Gondor is long and glorious. The "Annals of the Kings and Rulers" tell how, at the height of their power, the Gondor kings ruled all the lands of Middle-earth west of the Sea of Rhûn between the rivers Celebrant and Harnen. Even when the kingdom of Gondor was in decline, its rulers held all the fiefs and territories of Anórien, Ithilien, Lebennin, Lossarnach, Lamedon, Anfalas, Tolfalas, Belfalas and Calenardhon.

Within Gondor there were five cities of the first rank, two of which were great ports: ancient Pelargir, upon the delta of the Great River Anduin, and Dol Amroth, the citadel that ruled the coastal fiefs upon the Bay of Belfalas. There were three great cities in the centre of Gondor. They stood upon a vast plain between the White Mountains in the west and the Mountains of Mordor in the east. The eastern city was Minas Ithil, the "tower of the Moon", the city of the west was Minas Anor, the "tower of the Sun", and the greatest city of them all was Osgiliath, the "citadel of the Stars". Osgiliath was the capital of Gondor and was built upon both banks of the Great River Anduin; its two parts were joined by a wide stone bridge.

The kingdom of Gondor was often attacked in the Third Age and it suffered a great many troubles. In the year 1432 a long civil war began; in 1636 a Great Plague struck; and between 1851 and 1954 the Wainriders invaded. In 2002 Minas Ithil fell to the Nazgûl and the Orcs. Thereafter it was always an evil place and was renamed Minas Morgul. In 2475 the great Orcs, the Uruk-hai, came out of Mordor and in vast legions overpowered a weakened Osgiliath, setting fire to much of it and demolishing its great stone bridge over the Anduin.

In this way the realm of Gondor had been much diminished in the years before the War of the Ring. Of the three great cities at its centre, only Minas Anor remained unbroken. The Tower of the Sun stood against the gathering darkness in Mordor, Morgul, Rhûn and Harad for many centuries. It seemed that this last city of Gondor was the only power that withstood a vast conspiracy of evil, for the Dúnedain Kingdom of the North had fallen and the Elves seemed little concerned with the affairs of Middle-earth. Yet in this grim time when little hope remained, and the might of Sauron had no bounds, Gondor's Men won their greatest fame.

For within the kingdom of Gondor there stood knights who were like the great warriors of old, and in Minas Anor they still wore the high crowned helms of silver and mithril fitted with the wide white wings of seabirds. Their robes and mail were black, their armour and arms were silver; on their sable surcoats was the emblem of Gondor: a white blossoming tree under seven stars and a silver crown. In the days of the War of the Ring, though these knights were fewer than were wished for, they were of great valour, and allies came from unexpected places in the moment of need.

According to the "Red Book of Westmarch", at the time of the War of the Ring Gondor was ruled by the Steward Denethor II, for the line of kings had failed long ago. Though a strong and able Man, Denethor foolishly sought to fight Sauron with sorcerous

weapons. Therefore he sent his elder son, Boromir, in search of the One Ring, and, though Boromir was one of the Nine who went on the Quest of the Ring, he failed in his mission and perished. Denethor was afterwards without hope, the more so when his second son, Faramir, was given an apparently deadly wound by the Nazgûl. Deluded by Sauron and in despair for the kingdom of Gondor, Denethor ended his own life. Yet Faramir recovered and when the Dúnedain chieftain of the North, called Aragorn, came to Gondor Faramir recognized him as the rightful king of all the Dúnedain. So, in its time of greatest peril, the king returned, and with him came such allies that, in the Battle of Pelennor Fields, the forces of Morgul, Harad and Rhûn were crushed, and before the Black Gate of Mordor the hand of Sauron was forced in a gambit whereby his power was ended for ever.

GONNHIRRIM DWARVES were wondrous stone-masons and quarriers. Long and deep they worked within mountains to unlock treasure hoards of metals, both precious and base, and jewels of great beauty. Their vast kingdoms of Belegost, Nogrod and Khazad-dûm, which were built in Middle-earth in the Ages of Starlight, were famous, but most renowned among Elves was the Dwarves' work on the hidden Kingdom of the Grey-elves, which was named Menegroth, the Thousand Caves. Dwarf craftsmen carved a place there which was like a forest grotto of glittering beauty, with many fountains and streams and lights of crystal. For this deed Grey-elves named them Gonnhirrim, "masters of stone".

GORCROWS Ancient Hobbit folklore spoke of the swamplands where evil phantoms called Mewlips dwelt. In these haunted marshes there was also an evil breed of bird, the Gorcrow. Gorcrows were carrion birds and lived close alongside the Mewlips, the remains of whose prey they devoured.

GORGÛN The tales of Elves relate how the evil Goblin race of ORCS came into the forests of Middle-earth. These creatures were known as the Gorgûn to the ancient primitive Men called the Woses, who inhabited the Forest of Druadan, which lies in the shadow of the White Mountains.

GREEN-ELVES In Ossiriand in the lost realm of Beleriand lived the Green-elves in the last Age of Starlight and the First Age of Sun. In the High Elven tongue they were named the LAIQUENDI. These Elves wore garments of forest green so that they might be invisible to their foes in the woodland. They were not a great or powerful people, but by their knowledge of the land they survived while the mightiest Eldar fell to Melkor and his servants.

GREY-ELVES Of all the Umanyar, the Elves of the Journey who never saw the Light of the Trees, the mightiest were the SINDAR, "Grey-elves". These people were ruled by one who had seen the Light and they were protected by one who was handmaid to the Powers that made the Trees. The king of the Grey-elves was Elwë Singollo, which in the tongue of the Grey-elves was Elu Thingol, King Greymantle. Thingol was tallest of all the Elves and his hair was silver. His queen was Melian the Maia, and Ages before the coming of the Sun these two made a kingdom in the Wood of Doriath, and therein built a great city named Menegroth. So long as Melian was queen and Thingol lived, the Sindar were a prosperous and happy people. But when Thingol was drawn into the War of the Jewels and lost his life and his queen went away, the enchantment was broken, as were the people.

GWAITH-I-MÍRDAIN In the year 750 of the Second Age of Sun, many Noldor left Lindon and went to Eriador. Their lord was Celebrimbor, the greatest Elven-smith in Mortal Lands; he was the grandson of Fëanor, who made the Great Jewels, the Silmarils. In the Sindarin tongue the people of Celebrimbor were named the Gwaith-i-Mírdain, the "people of the jewel-smiths".

When the magical metal, mithril, called true silver, was discovered in the Misty Mountains Celebrimbor and his people were overcome by a desire to possess it. So they travelled to Eregion, which was named Hollin by Men, and lived at the foot of the Misty Mountains in the city of Ost-in-Edhil, near the West Door of Khazad-dûm, the mightiest city of Dwarves. The Dwarves and the Gwaith-i-Mírdain made a pact. Both races chose to put all past quarrels to rest, and in fact that peace was kept for a thousand years. For many years the trade between Dwarves and Elves brought prosperity to both races and the finest weapons, tools and jewellery that were ever wrought in Mortal Lands came out of Eregion in those days.

However, in the year 1200 one named Annatar came among them. None knew him, but his knowledge was great and he freely gave what aid he could to the Gwaith-i-Mírdain as well as gifts that he made himself. By 1500 they had come to trust him fully and planned to make many magical things with his aid. So it was that the Rings of Power were made by the Gwaith-i-Mírdain. For a full century Celebrimbor and his people laboured on this great work. However, Annatar was Sauron the Dark Lord disguised, and in that time in secret he made the One Ring, the Ruling Ring that would wield power over all the others, and with which he hoped to rule the World.

Yet once Sauron placed the Ring on his finger, the Elves knew him for the Dark Lord, and they removed their Rings and hid them

from him. The War of Sauron and the Elves followed; Eregion was destroyed and Celebrimbor was slain with the greater part of his people. In that year of 1697 of the Second Age, the few Gwaith-i-Mírdain who remained were given aid by Elrond Half-elven. At the command of Gil-galad, Elrond came out of Lindon with a guard of warriors and took the survivors to a place of refuge – a deep, narrow valley in Rhudaur – which they named Imladris but which Men called Rivendell. Thereafter this refuge of the Gwaith-i-Mírdain was the last Elf-kingdom between the Misty Mountains and the Blue Mountains.

H

HALADIN In the First Age of Sun, three hosts of Men first came to the Elf-realms of Beleriand and allied with the Noldorin Elves. The hosts were the Three Houses of Elf-friends, the Edain; of the Three Houses the Second was named Haladin. A forest-loving people, the Haladin were less numerous and smaller than those of the other Houses. Their first chieftain was Haldad, who along with many of his people was slain by Orcs. His daughter Haleth then led the Haladin to the Forest of Brethil, where they grew wiser in the ways of the woodlands. There like the wise Green-elves of Ossiriand they fought against the minions of Melkor. But, as the tide of the Wars of Beleriand turned against all the Edain, and though such a great hero as Túrin Turambar came to fight with them, the Haladin also suffered loss and dwindled before the evil onslaught.

HALFLINGS No history tells how or when the HOBBITS, the smallest of the peoples of Middle-earth, entered the World, but it is thought that perhaps it was in the First Age of Sun, as they are near relatives of Men. However in the time that Men arose, there were many wars and great deeds wherein powerful races and forces fought for supremacy, and little heed could be taken of such a weak people, who, being half the height of Men were by Men most often called Halflings.

HALF-ORCS Among the Dunlendings who, in the Third Age of Sun, came to Saruman's banner of the White Hand in Isengard, there were some whose blood, by the sorcery of Saruman, became mixed with that of the Orcs and Uruk-hai. These were large Men, lynx-eyed and evil, who were called Half-orcs. Many were counted among the strongest servants of Saruman. The Half-orcs mostly perished at the Battle of the Hornburg, either before the fortress walls or in the Huorn forest. Yet some lived beyond that day of doom and followed Saruman into exile, even to the Hobbit lands of the Shire, where they served the fallen Wizard until his last breath.

HARADRIM In the histories that were written in the days of the War of the Ring, much is told of the brown-skinned Men of the South who were named the Haradrim and how they came forth fiercely in war. Some Haradrim appeared on horseback and others on foot, and those who were named Corsairs came in dread fleets of their black ships called dromunds. But most famous were those Haradrim who rode in war towers on the broad backs of the great Mûmakil. Such Haradrim armies caused terrible destruction because Horses would not come near the Mûmakil. From their towers the Haradrim shot arrows and threw stones and spears. With tusk and trunk and great pounding feet the Mûmakil would break the shield-walls of its foes and overthrow mighty armies on Horse and foot.

In the Battle of Pelennor Fields, the Haradrim were most numerous among the servants of the Witch-king of Morgul. They were fierce and they rallied under a red banner marked with a black serpent. These warriors were clothed in scarlet cloaks and had gold rings in their ears and golden collars and great round shields, both yellow and black, studded with steel spikes. All had black eyes and long black hair in plaits braided with gold, and some as well had paint like crimson blood upon their faces. Their helmets and corselets of overlapping plates were of bronze. They were armed variously with bows, crimson-headed spears and pikes, curved daggers and scimitars. They were said to be cruel as Orcs and in battle gave no quarter and expected none.

Although most of the Haradrim in the army that came to Mordor were of brown skin, the lands of the Haradrim were vast, and part of the army came from Far Harad, where the tribesmen of the Sunlands were black. These were mighty warriors, who were compared with Trolls in strength and size.

All these people, strong though they had grown, owed their source of power to the coming of the Dark Lord Sauron. Their King of Kings was always Sauron throughout the Second and Third Ages, and allegiance to Mordor and the Dark Lord's emissaries – the Ringwraiths – was their law.

In the Second Age Sauron came among the Haradrim and gave them many gifts of power. To him they made sacrifice and gave worship. In time the might of the Haradrim increased and they ventured north against the kings of Gondor. Among them came other emissaries of the Dark Lord Sauron including a few of the Númenóreans who had turned against the Powers of Arda. In the Second Age two of these Black Númenóreans became great lords among the Haradrim and these were Herumor and Fuinur.

The "Book of the Kings" tells how the power of the Haradrim in the North was destroyed in the Second Age. As they rallied about the power of Sauron in Mordor, the Last Alliance of Elves and Men

was formed and there was a mighty battle before the Black Gate. The Gate was broken, and Haradrim, Easterlings and the Orc-hordes were crushed, and Mordor fell. And finally, after a seven-year siege, Sauron and the Ringwraiths were defeated and driven into the shadows.

This was not the end of the Haradrim, for the One Ring was not destroyed. Sauron and the Ringwraiths eventually returned in the Third Age and they again called the Haradrim to arms, promising them great wealth and making evil threats. So the Haradrim came to Mordor once again.

In the "Book of the Kings" it is told that, when the Men of Gondor sailed to Umbar and broke the power of the Black Númenóreans, the Haradrim arose in the year 1015 of the Third Age and made war on Gondor. In battle they slew Ciryandil, third in the line to the Ship-kings of Gondor, but the Haradrim could not break Gondor's hold on the port at that time. The next king of Gondor destroyed their armies in 1050 and the Haradrim had no power to come again against the Men of Gondor for nearly four hundred years, when there was a rebellion in Gondor itself. A great navy of rebels – sons of one named Castamir the Usurper – came to Umbar and made an alliance with the Haradrim against the Men of

Gondor. So for all the centuries of the Third Age, with the rebels who were named the Corsairs of Umbar and with some of the Black Númenóreans, the Haradrim raided and harassed the borderlands and shores of Gondor's realms.

In the year 1944, the histories of Gondor again speak of the land armies of the Haradrim. At that time the Haradrim and the Variags of Khand made a pact with the Easterling barbarians called the Wainriders. The purpose of their alliance was to achieve a simultaneous two-pronged attack on Gondor from the East and from the South. Thus the forces of Gondor were split, and the Wainriders succeeded and broke the army of East Gondor and slew the king, but they had not counted on the valiant general Eärnil of the southern army of Gondor. Eärnil, having swept the Haradrim and Variags from the field at the Battle of Poros Crossing, then turned to the east marches and struck down the unprepared Wainriders at the Battle of the Camp.

In the year that the War of the Ring was declared many legions of the Men of Harad went to Mordor: brown Men in crimson from Near Harad on Horse, on foot and riding the great Mûmakil in war towers; and terrible black tribesmen from Far Harad. With them came the Corsairs out of Umbar, the fierce Variags from Khand and the Easterlings from near and far: bearded axemen, footmen and cavalries. And finally there were the legions of Orcs, Uruk-hai, Olog-hai and Trolls. No greater army was amassed in that time in Middle-earth. But as is told in the "Red Book of Westmarch" their doom was sealed by power beyond strength of arms, and, though valiant in battle, they were crushed and destroyed at the Battle of Pelennor Fields and at the Black Gate of Mordor. Sauron was cast down for ever and with him all his servants. But it is told a new king who was both strong and merciful came to Gondor and he made a peace with the Haradrim that long endured into the Fourth Age of Sun.

HARADWAITH All the lands of Middle-earth that lay south of Gondor were, in the histories of the West, called Harad, meaning the "south". Its people were sometimes called Haradwaith, sometimes Southrons, and most commonly HARADRIM.

HARFOOT Most numerous and typical of the Hobbit strains were those who were named the Harfoot. They were the smallest of the Halflings and their skin and hair were nut-brown. The Harfoot were the first of the Hobbit people to leave the Vales of Anduin and cross over the Misty Mountains into Eriador. This migration was in the year 1050 of the Third Age. They were friendliest with Dwarves, for they loved hillsides and highlands, and hole-dwelling to them was a joy.

HELMINGAS In the twenty-eighth century of the Third Age of Sun, a king of great stature and strength came to the ROHIRRIM, the Horse-lords of Mark. He was ninth in the line of kings, and his people called him Helm Hammerhand. Though his rule ended in tragedy during the Long Winter and Dunlending Invasions, his legend grew strong among his foes. He was compared with a great Troll, for he hunted the Dunlendings by night and with his bare hands slew them in the snow. Even after his death the Dunlendings feared his wraith, who they claimed pursued them for many years.

So the Rohirrim often called upon the spirit of that fearful king in war, and in his honour they called his mountain stronghold Helm's Deep, and named themselves the Helmingas.

HIGH ELVES Of all the Elves, the mightiest were those of the Eldar who first reached the shores of Aman, the Undying Lands, in the days of the Trees of the Valar. These were called the High Elves, and they were those Elves who arrived in that place named "Elvenhome" and were granted great wisdom and many skills by the Valar and Maiar. In large part they dwell there still, though the Trees have been destroyed and the Undying Lands have been taken from the Circles of the World and cannot now be reached by any device of Man.

HILDOR When Arien the Sun first shone on the World, there came forth the race of MEN far to the East of Middle-earth. They were late-comers to the World, for many other races had arisen before them. Therefore the Elves named them the Hildor, for its meaning is the "followers".

HILLMEN In the Ettenmoors in Eriador there lived an evil race of Hillmen who served the Witch-king of Angmar in the Third Age of Sun. These barbarian Hillmen were fierce and numerous and they were allied with the Orkish legions. In the fourteenth and fifteenth centuries, it is told, they subdued the provinces of Rhudaur and Cardolan of the Dúnedain of the North Kingdom. After six centuries of intermittent war this alliance finally brought down Arthedain, the last of the proud Dúnedain provinces of the North in the year 1974.

But this too was the time of the Hillmen's own ruin. Hardly had the Hillmen and the Witch-king taken Fornost, the last citadel of the Dúnedain, when they were attacked by a great army led by Eärnur of the South Kingdom of Gondor, Círdan of Lindon and Glorfindel of Rivendell. In this Battle of Fornost the power of the Hillmen was broken, the Orcs exterminated and the kingdom of Angmar was destroyed. The Hillmen became a hunted people, scattered and forgotten.

HOBBITS When the bright fire of Arien the Sun came into the World and there arose the race of Men, it is claimed that in that same Age there also arose in the East the Halfling people who were called Hobbits. These were a burrowing, hole-dwelling people said to be related to Men, yet they were smaller than Dwarves, and the span of their lives was about a hundred years.

Nothing is known of the Hobbit race before 1050 of the Third Age, when it is said they lived with the Northmen in the northern Vales of the Anduin between the Misty Mountains and the Greenwood. In that century an evil force entered the Greenwood and it was soon renamed Mirkwood. It was perhaps this event which forced the Hobbit people out of the Vales. For in the centuries that followed, the Hobbits migrated westwards over the Misty Mountains into Eriador, where they discovered both Elves and Men in an open fertile land.

All Hobbits, both male and female, shared certain characteristics. All measured between two and four feet in height; they were long-fingered, possessed of a well-fed and cheerful countenance, and had curly brown hair upon their heads and peculiar shoeless, oversized feet. An unassuming, conservative people, they judged their peers by their conformity to quiet Hobbit village life. Excessive behaviour or adventurous endeavour were discouraged and considered indiscreet. The excesses of Hobbits were limited to dressing in bright colours and consuming six substantial meals a day. Their one eccentricity was the art of smoking Pipe-weed, which they claimed as their one contribution to the culture of the World.

It is said that Hobbits were of three strains. These were named the Harfoots, the Fallohides and the Stoors.

The Harfoots, the most numerous of Hobbit strains, were also the smallest. They had nut-brown skin and hair. They loved hill lands and often enjoyed the company of Dwarves. These Harfoots were the first of the Hobbit people to cross over the Misty Mountains and enter Eriador.

Nearly a century later, in the year 1150 of the Third Age, the Fallohides followed their kindred Harfoots and crossed the mountains. They entered Eriador by way of the passes north of Rivendell. The Fallohides were the least numerous of Hobbit strains. They were taller, thinner and were thought to be more adventurous than their kin. Their skin and hair were fairer, and they preferred woodlands and the company of Elves. They preferred hunting to ploughing, and of all Hobbits demonstrated the greatest traits of leadership.

The Stoors were the last of the Hobbits to enter Eriador. The most Mannish of their race, they were bulkier than the other strains and, to the amazement of their kin, some could actually grow beards. They were the most southerly of the Hobbits in the Vales of Anduin and they chose to live on flat river lands; again in a very un-Hobbit-like fashion they knew the arts of boating, fishing and swimming. They were the only Hobbits to use footwear; in muddy weather, it was claimed, they wore boots. It is said that the Stoors did not begin their western migration until the year 1300, when many passed over the Redhorn Pass; yet small settlements remained in such areas as the Gladden Fields as many as twelve centuries later.

For the most part the Hobbits of Eriador moved into the Mannish lands near the town of Bree. In the year 1601 most of the Hobbits of Bree marched westwards again to the fertile lands beyond the Brandywine River. There they founded the Shire, the land that was recognized thereafter as the homeland of Hobbits. Hobbits reckon time from this date.

By nature the Hobbits had peace-loving temperaments and by great luck they had discovered a land that was as peaceful as it was fertile. So, except for the Great Plague of 1636 which devastated all the peoples of Eriador, it was not until the year 2747 that an armed encounter took place in the Shire. This was a minor Orc raid which the Hobbits rather grandly named the Battle of Greenfields. More serious by far was the Long Winter of 2758 and the two famine years that followed. Yet, compared to the other peoples of Middle-earth, they lived in peace for a long time; other races, when they saw them, believed them to be of little worth, and in return the Hobbits had no ambitions towards the great wealth or power of others. Their limitations proved their strength, for, while greater and more powerful races fell about them, the Hobbits lived on in the Shire quietly tending their crops. Throughout the Shire lands their little townships and settlements expanded: Hobbiton, Tuckborough, Michel Delving, Oatbarton, Frogmorton and a dozen more; and after their fashion Hobbits prospered.

Of famous Hobbits little can be said before the thirtieth century of the Third Age of Sun, for before that time the entire race was almost totally unknown to the World at large. Yet, of course, the Hobbits themselves had their own sense of the famous. In the lore of the Shire the first Hobbits to be named were the Fallohide brothers Marcho and Blanco, who led the Hobbits out of Bree over the Bridge of Stonebows into the Shire. This land had been ceded by the Dúnedain of Arnor, to whose king the Hobbits paid nominal allegiance in return. In the year 1979 the last king of Arnor vanished from the North and in the Shire the office of the Thain of the Shire was set up. The first Thain was the Hobbit Bucca of the Marish from whom all the Thains descended.

A giant among Hobbits was Bandobras Took, who stood four feet and five inches tall, and, astride a horse, he had led his people valiantly against the Orcs in the Battle of Greenfields. With a club, it is claimed, he slew their chieftain Golfimbul. For his size and deeds he was called Bullroarer Took. Another Hobbit notable for his deeds within the small lands of the Shire was Isengrim Took, who was named Isengrim II, the twenty-second Thain of the Shire, architect of the Great Smials of Michel Delving and grandfather of Bandobras Took.

Yet typically among Hobbits perhaps the most honoured of heroes before the War of the Ring was a humble farmer named Tobold Hornblower of Longbottom, who in the twenty-seventh century first cultivated the plant Galenas, also called Pipe-weed. For this deed he was praised, and delighted Hobbit smokers named one superior strain "Old Toby" in his memory.

In the thirtieth century of the Third Age, however, fame in a very real sense came to the Hobbit folk. For, by chance, a great and evil power fell into Hobbit hands with which the fate of all Hobbits became entwined.

The first Hobbit to become famous in the World was Bilbo Baggins of Hobbiton, who was tempted into a leading role in the Quest of Erebor by the Wizard Gandalf and the Dwarf-king Thorin Oakenshield. This is the adventure that is told in the first part of the "Red Book of Westmarch". It is the memoir that Bilbo himself called "There and Back Again", wherein Trolls, Orcs, Wolves, Spiders and a Dragon are slain. In that adventure Bilbo Baggins achieved many deeds that those of stronger and wiser races in Middle-earth could not, and unexpected strength and bravery were revealed in the Hobbit character.

Part of that adventure tells how Bilbo Baggins acquired a magic ring, and, though this seemed of little importance at the time, it was an act that imperilled all who inhabited Middle-earth. For Bilbo Baggins, gentleman Hobbit of the Shire, had unknowingly become possessor of the One Ring.

In time the identity of the One Ring was discovered and it passed on to Bilbo's heir, Frodo Baggins. Bilbo then went to the Elven refuge of Rivendell, where he indulged his literary pursuits. For besides his memoirs in "There and Back Again" he composed a good number of original poems and a major work of scholarship, the three-volume "Translations from the Elvish".

Frodo Baggins had become the Ringbearer at the time that Sauron the Ring Lord was preparing to make war on all the World. In the year 3018 the Wizard Gandalf came to Frodo and set him on the road to Rivendell on the Quest of the Ring. If the mission was successful the One Ring would be destroyed and the World would be saved from the domination of Sauron.

In Rivendell the Fellowship of the Ring was made, wherein eight others were chosen as companions and bodyguards of the Ringbearer in his Quest. Three of that fellowship were also Hobbits destined for fame nearly as great as the Ringbearer himself. Samwise Gamgee, Frodo's man-servant, was one of these. A simple and loyal soul, Samwise more than once saved both his master and the Quest itself, and for a time was a Ringbearer.

Peregrin Took, heir to the Thain of the Shire, and Meriadoc Brandybuck, heir to the Master of Buckland, were the other two Hobbits of the Fellowship. In the course of the Quest both Pippin and Merry (as they were most often called) were made Knights of Gondor. Merry was also made the squire of King Théoden of Rohan, and, to the amazement of all, with the shield-maiden Éowyn he slew the Witch-king of Morgul at the Battle of Pelennor Fields. Pippin, as a Guard of Gondor, fought with the Captains of the West and in the last Battle before the Black Gate he slew a mighty Troll.

Merry and Pippin were the tallest of all Hobbits in the history of their race, for upon their journeys they drank Ent-draughts, the food of the giant Ents. So they towered above their people and by Mannish measure were four and a half feet tall. Further, Merry was a Hobbit scholar of note and compiled the "Herblore of the Shire", the "Reckoning of the Years", and the treatise "Old Words and Names in the Shire".

Frodo Baggins, champion of the Quest of the Ring, was also the chief historian of the War, for he wrote the greater part of the "Red Book of Westmarch". He named that history "The Downfall of the Lord of the Rings and the Return of the King". Yet though this humble and valiant Hobbit was heralded the noblest of his race, in the end it was not Frodo but another Hobbit who destroyed the One Ring in a way both unexpected and unintentional.

This was Sméagol Gollum, the only Hobbit ever to have succumbed to truly evil ways. Of all his race Sméagol Gollum's tale is the strangest. For, as is told in the histories of the One Ring, he was once a Stoorish Hobbit who in the twenty-fifth century of the Third Age lived near the Gladden Fields. There Sméagol and his cousin Déagol first discovered the lost Ring, but Sméagol murdered Déagol and took the Ring for himself. By the power of the Ring his life was lengthened, yet by it as well he was twisted beyond recognition. His form became ghoulish; he lived by foul deeds of murder, on unclean meats and the dark influence of the Ring made him shun light. He lived by dark pools and in deep caverns. His skin became hairless, black and clammy, and his body thin and gaunt. His head was like a skull, yet his eyes grew great like those of fish that flourish far beneath the seas; they bulged yet were pale and his vision was poor. His teeth grew long, like Orc fangs, and his Hobbit feet grew flat and webbed. His arms became long and his hands larger and filled with evil grasping strength.

The "Red Book of Westmarch" records that Gollum (for so he became named in this form because of the ugly guttural sound he made) resided for nearly five centuries hidden in caverns beneath the Misty Mountains, until the year 2941. Then, guided no doubt by a destiny beyond his understanding, the Hobbit Bilbo Baggins came to Gollum's cavern and took the One Ring. From Bilbo it passed to Frodo Baggins and in all the eighty years that the Ring was out of his groping hands, Gollum never ceased his searching for it. At last he came upon the Ringbearer himself. For a time Frodo Baggins almost seemed able to tame Gollum, but Gollum's soul was entirely given over to evil and he still lived by treachery. So it was that in the moment of decision, when the power of the Ring overcame the good Frodo Baggins upon Mount Doom, Gollum came upon him and fought him upon the edge of Doom. By his evil strength Gollum won the Ring, but he toppled backwards with his precious prize down into the fiery bowels of the Earth.

So by the combination of the noblest and the most evil of Middle-earth's smallest and least people the One Ring was destroyed. The World was thus saved from the horror of eternal darkness, and though Hobbits now are few, for many centuries of the Fourth Age they dwelt in honour and peace because of the deeds of their people in that mighty conflict.

HOBGOBLINS The evil beings to whom Men now give the name Goblin were in the days of Middle-earth called Orcs, and there were many kinds. Most powerful of these were the URUK-HAI: Man-sized creatures of great strength and endurance; like the smaller breeds in wickedness, but stronger and unafraid of light. Often these were the cruel leaders of the lesser Goblin folk, and they formed élite fighting units within a larger army. They are sometimes called Great Goblins, or Hobgoblins, even though they could wreak far greater evil in ancient times than now.

HOLBYTLAN The "Red Book of Westmarch" tells much of the history of the Halfling people called HOBBITS. In one part is explained how that name was derived from the name Holbytlan, which is "hole-dwellers" in the tongue of the Rohirrim.

HORSES How Horses were first made is not told in the histories of Arda, but it is known that Nahar, the steed of Oromë, the Huntsman of the Valar, was the first such being to enter the World. And though all Horses take from Nahar their form, he is the mightiest and most beautiful of the race. Golden are his hooves and his coat is white by day and silver by night. Tireless, Nahar travels over the Earth as easily as the swiftest Eagle speeds through the air.

Many Men and Elves bred Horses to their needs, but it is said that the nobler breeds were descended from Nahar, and these were the Elven Horses of Eldamar and those named the Mearas that lived in Rhovanion. These noble breeds were for the most part white or silver-grey. They were long-lived and fleet, and they understood the languages of Elves and Men.

Most famous of the High Elven Horses in the histories that have come to Men are those that the Noldor brought to Middle-earth, and best known of those Horses was one named Rochallor. This was the warhorse that Fingolfin, most valiant of the Noldor kings, rode in his great ill-fated duel with Morgoth the Enemy.

In the Third Age of Sun, the noblest Horses of Middle-earth were those wild steeds of Rhovanion that were named the Mearas. In the twenty-sixth century of the Age, Eorl, the first king of the Riders of the Mark, tamed the Mearas, and for many centuries only the king of the Mark and his sons could ride these Horses.

There were other breeds of Horses in various parts of Middle-earth, where Men, Elves and some other races – both good and evil – took them into service. Many of the people that came out of Rhûn and Harad came to war mounted on Horses or in Horse-drawn chariots. The Horses of the Ringwraiths were fearsome indeed, but more terrible still were the Horses that were taken into the domain of Sauron in Mordor. The Orcs of Mordor often came to the Horses of the Rohirrim in the night and took

them to their master, Sauron, and he twisted their noble form to evil purpose. Such a steed was the mount of the lieutenant of Barad-dûr, the Black Númenórean who was called the Mouth of Sauron. This beast was huge and black, but its tortured head was like a great skull and from its nostrils and eyes came forth red flames.

HUMMERHORNS According to a Hobbit rhyme, a race of winged insects called Hummerhorns was said to have battled a questing knight. Whether these ferocious insects were of giant size, or the knight was of some diminutive race, or whether the tale was the product of Hobbit humour cannot now be learned.

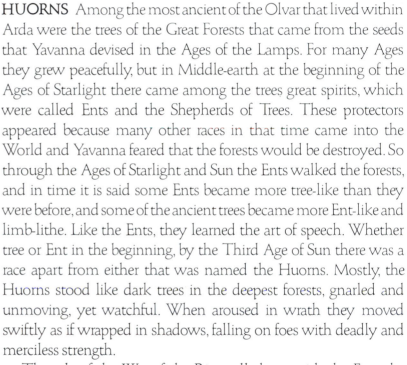

HUORNS

HUORNS Among the most ancient of the Olvar that lived within Arda were the trees of the Great Forests that came from the seeds that Yavanna devised in the Ages of the Lamps. For many Ages they grew peacefully, but in Middle-earth at the beginning of the Ages of Starlight there came among the trees great spirits, which were called Ents and the Shepherds of Trees. These protectors appeared because many other races in that time came into the World and Yavanna feared that the forests would be destroyed. So through the Ages of Starlight and Sun the Ents walked the forests, and in time it is said some Ents became more tree-like than they were before, and some of the ancient trees became more Ent-like and limb-lithe. Like the Ents, they learned the art of speech. Whether tree or Ent in the beginning, by the Third Age of Sun there was a race apart from either that was named the Huorns. Mostly, the Huorns stood like dark trees in the deepest forests, gnarled and unmoving, yet watchful. When aroused in wrath they moved swiftly as if wrapped in shadows, falling on foes with deadly and merciless strength.

The tale of the War of the Ring tells how with the Ents the Huorns, like a great forest, marched on Isengard, and how under the direction of the Ents of Fangorn they exterminated the entire Orc legion at the Battle of the Hornburg.

Yet these were wild wood spirits bent on the destruction of all who threatened the forests. They were dangerous to all who went on two legs unless the travellers were protected by the Ents.

Huorns were ancient and long-brooding, and some were black-hearted and rotten. One such sentient tree spirit inhabited the Old Forest by the banks of the Withywindle. He was the Willow Man who some called Old Man Willow. The Old Forest was but the remnant of the most ancient forest of Middle-earth, and Old Man Willow wished to prevent any further inroads into his realm. He held all the Old Forest in an enchantment by the power of his song and led all travellers to him, where with limb-lithe roots and branches he ended them.

ISTARI After a thousand years had passed in the Third Age of Sun, an Elven-ship came out of the Western Sea and sailed to the Grey Havens. Upon that ship were five aged Men with long white beards and great cloaks. Each cloak was a different colour, and each Man wore a tall pointed hat, high black traveller's boots, and carried a long staff. These were the Istari, whom Men called Wizards; their hats and staffs were their signs of office. They were an order and a brotherhood sent to Middle-earth from the Undying Lands, for it was perceived by the great Powers of Arda that a great evil was growing in Mortal Lands.

Though the Istari came secretly and in humble form, in the beginning, before their arrival in Middle-earth, they were mighty spirits. They were Maiar, spirits older than the World itself, and of that first race that came from the mind of Ilúvatar in the Timeless Halls. Yet in the diminished World of Middle-earth in the Third Age they were forbidden to come forth in power as Maiar. They were limited to the form of Men and the powers that might be found within the mortal World.

Although five Istari are said to have come to Middle-earth, only three are named in the histories that have come to Men, for the others were said to have gone to the East and they played no part in the fate of the Westlands.

First named and most praised in the Fourth Age was Gandalf the Grey, who by the Elves was called Mithrandir, by the Dwarves Tharkûn, and Incánus by the Haradrim. As a Maia in the Undying Lands he was named Olórin and was accounted wisest of his people. At that time he resided in the gardens of Lórien, the Master of Visions and Dreams, and also went often to the house of Nienna the Weeper. Tutored by the Vala Lórien in the Gardens, Olórin's wisdom for many Ages grew greater still. Also, counselled by Nienna in her house, which looks out on the Walls of the Night, to his wisdom was added pity and endurance beyond hope.

Of all the Istari Gandalf is counted the greatest, for by his wisdom the free peoples of Middle-earth were guided to victory over the Dark Lord Sauron, who wished to enslave them. In this Gandalf was aided by Narya, the Elven-ring of Fire, that Círdan, lord of the Grey Havens, gave him, for Narya had power to make Men brave and resolute. By Gandalf's instigation Smaug the Dragon was slain and the battles of Five Armies, the Hornburg and Pelennor Fields were won. By Gandalf's hand alone the Balrog of Moria was destroyed. Yet his greatest deed of all was his discovery of the One Ring and his guiding of the Ringbearer to the place of its destruction. By this action the Ring was unmade, and Sauron and all his servants and all his kingdoms were brought to utter ruin. Gandalf's task upon Middle-earth was completed by this one act and so the Third Age ended with Gandalf's departure to the Undying Lands.

Second named of the Istari is Radagast the Brown, who lived in Rhosgobel in the Vales of Anduin. Radagast played a part in the White Council, which was formed to stand against Sauron, but it seemed his greatest concern was with the Kelvar and Olvar of Middle-earth and little is told of him in the chronicles of that time. He was wiser than any Man in all things concerning herbs and beasts. It is said he spoke the many tongues of birds. Even the Beornings and Woodmen of Mirkwood and the mighty Ent guardians of the Forest of Fangorn spoke with reverence of the wisdom of Radagast the Brown, for in forest-lore he had no equal.

Last named of the Istari is Saruman the White, whom Elves called Curunír, "Man of skill". When the Istari were formed, Saruman was counted the greatest of the Order. For many centuries Saruman wandered the lands of Middle-earth and eagerly sought to destroy Sauron the Dark Lord, but after a time he grew proud and desired power for himself. In the year 2759 Saruman came to Isengard, and Beren, the Ruling Steward of Gondor, granted him the key to the tower of Orthanc, for it was thought the Istari would aid the Men of Gondor and the Rohirrim in war against the Orcs, Easterlings and Dunlendings. However Saruman made a mighty place of evil power there and summoned Orc legions and Uruk-hai, Half-orcs and Dunlendings to him. In Isengard he flew the standard of his tyranny, the black banner marked with a ghostly white hand. In his pride he grew foolish, until he was ensnared by Sauron, who commanded sorcery far greater than his own. So the greatest of the Istari who had come to destroy the Dark Lord became one of his agents. Yet Saruman's power was annihilated by the wrath of the Ents, the valour of the Rohirrim and Huorns, and the wisdom of Gandalf. Isengard was destroyed by the Ents, his army was exterminated by the Rohirrim and the Huorns, and his staff was broken and his sorcerous power was taken by Gandalf. So low did Saruman fall that in his defeat he looked for petty vengeance in the tiny realm of the Shire, where the Hobbits, the least of his enemies, resided. Here in a pathetic bid for domination Saruman was bested by the Hobbits and slain by his own servant, Gríma Wormtongue. When Saruman died, his body shrivelled to a form without flesh. It swiftly became skin, skull and bones wrapped in a ragged cloak, and from it rose a grey mist in a column. For a moment, it is said, this grey form of Saruman's Maia spirit stood over his mortal remains, but a wind came and it vanished.

K

KELVAR Before Elves and Men entered the World all things were called either Kelvar or Olvar. Kelvar were animals and living creatures that moved, and Olvar were living things that grew and were rooted to the Earth. Kelvar were granted swiftness of foot and subtlety of mind with which they might elude destruction; while the Olvar were granted powerful guardian spirits.

KHAZÂD In the mountain heart, Aulë the Smith made the race that called itself the Khazâd. These people, who Men and Elves called DWARVES, were strong and proud, but they were also a stunted and unlovely race. Yet Dwarves were the most gifted masons and carvers of stone the World had ever seen, and their great halls and delvings beneath the mountains were counted amongst the greatest wonders of Middle-earth. The most far-famed and ancient of all delvings of the Khazâd was the kingdom of Khazad-dûm, which in the Third Age of Sun was called Moria.

KINE OF ARAW Of the animals of forest and field, there were many that Oromë, the Horseman of the Valar, brought to Middle-earth. One breed of these animals was called the Kine of Araw by the Men of Gondor (Araw being the Sindarin name for Oromë). These Kine were the legendary wild white oxen that lived near the Inland Sea of Rhûn. Their long horns were much prized. In Gondor one such ox horn was made into a silver-mounted hunting horn by the first of the Ruling Stewards, Vorondil the Hunter; this was the heirloom called the Horn of the Stewards, which was destroyed in the War of the Ring.

KINGSFOIL From the lost land of the Númenóreans a herb was brought to Middle-earth that for a long while was used as a simple folk-cure for mild pains of the head and body. In the Grey-elven tongue it was named ATHELAS, but Men called it Kingsfoil, for their legends told of its magical healing properties in the hands of the Númenórean kings.

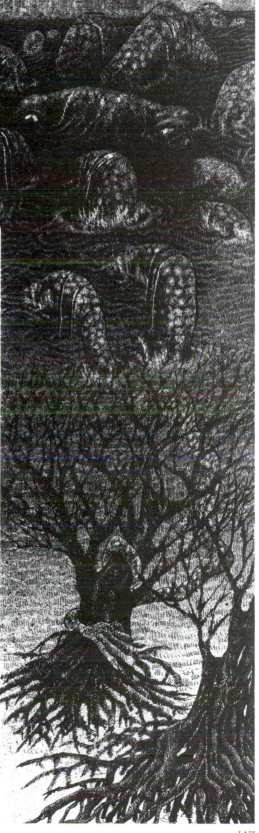

KRAKEN According to the most ancient tales, Melkor, that most evil of Powers, in his kingdom of Utumno in Middle-earth bred many terrible creatures for which there are no names in the Time of Darkness before Varda rekindled the Stars. In the following Ages these creatures were a bane on land and in dark waters to those who lived peacefully in the World.

Some of these beings of Melkor's survived below the thunders of the deep far beneath the abysmal seas in ancient, dreamless, uninvaded sleep even into the Third Age of Sun. The "Red Book of Westmarch" tells that when a fiery Balrog was loosed in the Dwarf-kingdom of Moria, another being came out from the dark waters that lay below the great mountains. This was a great Kraken, many tentacled and huge with a slimy sheen. It was luminous and green and an inky stench came from its foul bulk. Like a legion of serpents it lay in the black water beneath the mountain. Eventually it came to the clear water of the River Sirannon, which flowed from the West Gate of Moria. There it built a great wall in the river bed and made for itself a black pool, hideous and still. This being was guardian of the West Gate and none could pass without challenge. For this reason, in the "Book of Mazarbul" the Kraken was named Watcher in the Water.

KÛD-DÛKAN In each of the lands of Middle-earth the Halfling people, who were called HOBBITS by Men, bore different names according to the languages of the various peoples. In the land of Rohan the Hobbits were named Kûd-dûkan, which means "hole-dwellers". From this root word it is thought that the Hobbitish term Kuduk became commonly used both by Hobbits of the Shire and by the Men of Bree in the latter part of the Third Age of Sun.

LAIQUENDI Of the Three Kindred of Elves who chose to come out of the eastern lands of Middle-earth and search out the Land of Eternal Light in the West, there were many who, out of love for Middle-earth or in fear of the perils of the journey, forsook the quest and never came to the Undying Lands. The Nandor, one part of the Teleri, were such a people.

Denethor, son of the Nandor king Lenwë, gathered many of the Nandor to him in the Age before the Rising of the Sun and took them from the wilderness of Eriador to Beleriand, where they were welcomed by the Grey-elves of that land and given protection and many gifts of steel and gold. There they were granted a land that was called Ossiriand, "land of seven rivers", which was in the south of Beleriand. While there the Nandor were re-named the Laiquendi – "Green-elves" – because of their garments, which were green to hide them from their foes, and for their love and knowledge of all that was green and grew. They were second only to the Shepherds of Trees, the Ents, as protectors of the Olvar of the forest, and of the Kelvar as well, for the Laiquendi did not hunt the creatures of the woodlands.

For a time they were a happy people again, as no evil creatures dared to enter Beleriand in those days. The Laiquendi sang in the woodlands like the nightingales and tended the forest as if it were a great garden. Their singing was so beautiful and so constant that the Noldor, when they came to that land, renamed it Lindon, which in Quenya is "land of song". It always remained Lindon, even after all but this small part of Beleriand fell beneath the sea in the time of the Great Battle and the War of Wrath.

After the release of Melkor a great evil came to Middle-earth once again, as the "Quenta Silmarillion" relates. Melkor's armies of Orcs, Trolls and Wolves appeared and the First Battle in the Wars of Beleriand took place. Though the Grey-elves and the Laiquendi were victorious over that evil army on Amon Ereb in Ossiriand, the Laiquendi lord Denethor was slain. His people were full of great sorrow and would take no new king. They swore that they would

never again come into open battle with the Enemy but would always remain under cover of the forest, where they could ambush their foes with darts and arrows.

Ever after, the Laiquendi kept this pledge and became a tribal people, and their enemies were harassed but could not defeat them for the Laiquendi made no cities that the Enemy could find and destroy. These people were as the wind in the trees, which sometimes can be heard but never seen. And in time, after the disasters of the Fourth and Fifth Battles of Beleriand, many of the Noldor and Edain hid from the Enemy in the realm of the Laiquendi and learned much woodlore from them.

LAKE MEN Between Mirkwood and the Iron Hills lay the Long Lake and the city of Esgaroth, and it was here that the Lake Men lived in the Third Age of Sun. These were Northmen who had been traders upon the lake and the Running River. They had become wealthy trading with the Elves of the Woodland Realm in Mirkwood and with the Dwarves of Erebor, the Lonely Mountain.

Esgaroth was built upon pylons driven into the lake bottom, and a wooden bridge stood between the city and shore. It was not, however, proof against the winged Fire-drake Smaug, who in 2770 came to Erebor. In 2941 Smaug attacked Esgaroth, and, though the warrior of Dale called Bard the Bowman slew the beast, the city was ruined. Yet the Lake Men were saved from starvation, for with a part of the Dragon's hoard of jewels the town was rebuilt.

The ruler of the Lake Men, called the Master of Esgaroth, was an elected merchant. In the time of the slaying of Smaug, the Master was both cowardly and corrupt, but a new Master followed him who proved honest and wise, and the Lake Men prospered again.

LIGHT ELVES The tale of the Great Journey tells how most of the Vanyar, Noldor and Teleri reached the shores of the Undying Lands in the time of the Trees of the Valar. There they dwelt in Eldamar and were tutored by the Powers of Arda, the Valar and their people, the Maiar. The Elves grew wise and noble and learned many skills: the making of jewels and precious metals, the building of majestic cities and the finest arts of music and language. These people were called the Light Elves for they were shining in both body and spirit, and, of all peoples within the Circles of the World, they were the fairest by all accounts.

LINDAR As is told in the "Ainulindalë", all things that came into the World came out of the grand themes of the Music of the Ainur. Elves were the fairest of all beings and their singing was almost a match for the beauty of the Great Music. Among the Elves, the loveliest singers were the TELERI, who listened tirelessly to the sounds of water against river banks and on the sea shore, and their voices became fluid, subtle and strong. Because of their skill in singing they were sometimes known by the name Lindar, which means the "singers".

LITTLE FOLK The HOBBITS were known to be the smallest of the peoples of Middle-earth in the Third Age of Sun. In height they measured between two and four feet, and, though quick and nimble, they were of far less strength than Dwarves. Both Men and Elves often called them the Little Folk.

LÓMELINDI To the ears of Elves, the loveliest of the song-birds of Arda are the Lómelindi, the "dusk-singers", whom the Elves have also named TINÚVIEL and Men have called nightingales. The name of these fair creatures is woven into many tales and the voices of the most beauteous women of Elf-fame, Melian, Lúthien and Arwen, are compared to the Lómelindë's song.

LOSSOTH On the icy Cape of Forochel to the north of the Westlands there lived a people called the Lossoth in the Third Age of Sun. They were a reclusive, peaceful folk, wary of all the warlike Men of Middle-earth. In the common tongue of Men they were called the Snowmen of Forochel, and they were said to be descended from the Forodwaith of the Northern Waste.

The Lossoth were poor people of little worldly knowledge, but they were wise in the ways of their cold lands. They built their homes from snow and, in sliding carts and skates of bone, they crossed the ice lands and hunted the thick-furred animals from which they fashioned their clothes. It is claimed that the Lossoth could foretell the weather by the smell of the wind.

M

MAIAR When the World was first made, the Ainur, the "holy ones", came out of the Timeless Halls and entered this new land. The Ainur had been without shape or form in the Timeless Halls, but within the Spheres of the World they took many and various forms. These people were the Powers of Arda and the mightiest among them were the Valar, who numbered fifteen. The lesser Ainur were a multitude called the Maiar and they were the servants of the Valar. Though the Maiar were many within the Undying Lands, few are named in the histories of Men, for their concerns are seldom with mortal lands and mortal matters, but with the Valar in the Undying Lands.

Mightiest of the Maiar is Eönwë, the Herald of Manwë, the Wind Lord. Eönwë's strength in battle rivals that of even the Valar, and the blast of his trumpets is a terror to all his foes, for in the wake of its sound comes the Host of the Valar. It was he who taught the Edain great wisdom and knowledge. Ilmarë, who throws down her spears of light from the night sky, is chief of the Maiar maids. She is also handmaid to Varda, the Star Queen, who rules the Heavens.

Arien, the fire spirit who once was a Maia of Vána's golden gardens in Valinor, is most worshipped by Men. It is she who guides the flight of the Sun, for, as the "Narsilion" tells, the Sun was the last fruit of Laurelin, the Golden Tree of the Valar; it was placed in a great vessel shaped by Aulë, which was then hallowed by Manwë before being carried by Arien into the sky.

As Arien goes by day, so by night flies Tilion, the Huntsman of the silver bow. Tilion was once a Maiar of Oromë, but he now carries the vessel of the Moon, which was the last flower of Telperion, the Silver Tree of Valinor.

The Maiar Ossë and Uinen, servants of Ulmo, the Ocean Lord of the Valar, are known to all who sail on the seas. Ossë is master of the waves of Belegaer, the Western Sea, and though it is said that Ossë truly loves the Sea-elves and it was he who first brought the art of shipbuilding to the World, he is feared by all mariners. For both in joy and in wrath, he is a fearsome power. However, all mariners have a great love of Uinen, Lady of the Calms. She is the spouse of Ossë, and only she may restrain his raging tempers and his wild

spirit. Beleaguered mariners pray to her that she may lay her long hair upon the waters and calm the tumult. As Ossë loved the Sea-elves, so did Uinen love the Númenóreans; until the Downfall of Númenor and the Change of the World she always travelled before the ships of these sea folk.

Of all the tales of the Maiar, perhaps the strangest is that of Melian, who served both Vána and Estë in Valinor, but who in the Ages of Starlight came to Middle-earth. There in the forests of Beleriand she met the Eldar lord Elwë Singollo and married him. This is the only union of Elf and Maia that ever was, and, through four long Ages of Stars and one of Sun, Melian was queen of the Grey-elves and wife of Elwë, who was called Thingol and King Greymantle. In that time their realm was the fairest kingdom of Middle-earth because of the light and beauty of Melian. Yet tragically Thingol was slain near the end of the First Age of Sun. Melian wrapped herself in grief and the light of the kingdom faded. The queen rose up and returned to Valinor once again, leaving Mortal Lands for ever.

Many other good and strong spirits came to inhabit Middle-earth. These were perhaps Maiar, like Melian, yet from the histories this cannot now be learned. Chief of these, in the tales of Middle-earth, is he whom the Grey-elves named Iarwain Ben-adar, which means both "old" and "without father". By Dwarves he was named Forn, by Men Orald, and by Hobbits he was called Tom Bombadil. He was a very strange and merry spirit. He was a short, stout Man, with blue eyes, red face and brown beard. He wore a blue coat, a tall battered hat with a blue feather, and great yellow boots. Always singing or speaking in rhymes, he seemed a nonsensical and eccentric being, yet he was absolute master of the Old Forest of

Eriador where he lived, and no evil within the World was strong enough to touch him within his realm.

Other spirits, who may have been servants of the Vala Ulmo, also lived within the Old Forest. One of these was the River-woman of the Withywindle, and another was her daughter Goldberry, who was Bombadil's spouse. Goldberry was golden-haired and as beautiful as an Elf-queen. Her garments were silver and green, and her shoes were like fish-mail. In her hair and in her belt were many flowers, and her singing was like bird song.

At the end of the first millennium of the Third Age of Sun, it is told that five Maiar came to Middle-earth. They came not in grand forms but in the shape of ancient Men. Each was white-bearded and wore a traveller's cape, a peaked hat, and carried a long staff. These were the Istari, whom Men called the Wizards and much of their tale is told in the "Red Book of Westmarch". Yet only three of the five are named in the histories. Radagast the Brown was a master of birds and animals of the forest and lived near Mirkwood in

Rhosgobel. Saruman the White was in the arising of the Istari Order counted the greatest and for a time he was indeed skilful and wise, but he fell into evil ways, brought ruin down upon many and was himself completely destroyed in his efforts to make himself a great power. Gandalf the Grey was most famous of the Istari. In the beginning he was called Olórin and he served both Lórien the Master of Dreams and Nienna the Weeper; he was acknowledged the wisest of the Maiar race.

Yet not all the Maiar are good and fair spirits. Many were corrupted by the rebellious Vala, Melkor the Enemy. Foremost among these were the Balrogs, who were once bright spirits of fire, as fair as Arien who guides the Sun, but were twisted into demon forms by hatred and wrath. Cloaked in a foul darkness, the Balrogs were maned in fire and they wielded whips and blades of flame. Gothmog was their lord and the tale of the deeds of his host is long and bloody.

The spirit that took the form of a huge and fearsome Spider was named Ungoliant. She devoured light, vomited forth darkness and spun a black web of unlight that no eye could pierce. None could

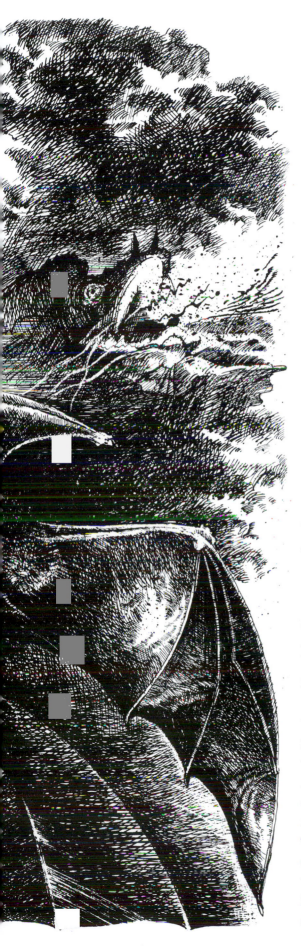

tame this spirit who perhaps was once a Maia of Melkor. Ungoliant had long since turned to serving only herself and, though she destroyed the Trees of the Valar with Melkor, she turned on Melkor at last. In the end, driven into the great deserts of the South, it is said that having no others to turn on she consumed herself.

The Vampires and Werewolves of Angband may also have been Maiar in their beginning, like the Balrogs. It is said they were malevolent spirits that took on terrible forms, yet no tale tells of their making. Of the Vampires Thuringwethil, "lady of the shadow", alone is named, and of the vast Werewolf host one named Draugluin is named both lord and sire.

One Maia is known above all others because of his great evil, as the histories of Middle-earth tell. This is, Sauron, whose name means the "abhorred". Chief servant and eventual successor to Melkor was Sauron, the Dark Lord, who was once a Maia of Aulë the Smith.

In the Ages of Darkness, while Melkor ruled in Utumno, and in the Ages of Stars, while Melkor was chained by the Valar, Sauron ruled the evil realm of Angband. On the return of his master, and through all the Wars of Beleriand until Melkor was cast into the Void, Sauron was his greatest general. He was also called Gorthaur the Cruel, and he survived longest of all the Maiar who served Melkor. Many were the wars and holocausts through the Ages of the Lamps, Trees, Stars and Sun that Sauron survived. After the terror of the First Age of Sun, it is said that Sauron reappeared in the Second Age in fair form and assumed the name Annatar "giver of gifts". Eventually, when he made himself Lord of the Rings, his evil spirit was revealed and war, like a black shadow, again covered Middle-earth.

In the Downfall of Númenor Sauron's body was destroyed. Yet his spirit fled to Mordor and by the power of the One Ring he made himself again a form, though he could no longer appear fair. Thereafter he took the shape of the Dark Lord and became a fearsome warrior with black armour on burning black skin and had terrible, raging eyes. But even this form was destroyed at the end of the Second Age when Mordor fell and the One Ring was taken from his hand. Yet so great was the power of Sauron's spirit that in the Third Age he again made himself a form. His spirit became manifest in the sorcerous power of one great lidless Eye. Like the eyes of all the great hunting cats of forest, mountain and plain made into one, and made entirely evil, was that Eye which was wreathed with deadly flame and ringed in darkness. But even this form depended on the power that was in the One Ring, and, in the war that ended the Third Age, the Ring was destroyed. Once more, and finally, Sauron's spirit was swept into the shadows and never again did this Maia arise.

MALLORN On the banks of the Silverlode, which flowed east of the Misty Mountains, was a forest land where the tallest and loveliest trees of Middle-earth grew. These were the Mallorn trees, which had barks of silver and blossoms of gold, and from autumn to spring the leaves were also golden-hued. In the Third Age of Sun, this land was called the Golden Wood and Lothlórien, "land of blossoms dreaming". This woodland of Mallorn trees was made a safe refuge from evil creatures by Elven powers, and the trees thrived and grew as they grew in no other place on Arda, except in the Undying Lands. There lived the Galadhrim, the Elves of the kingdom of King Celeborn and Queen Galadriel. And within the shelter of the Mallorn tree limbs, where the trunks forked near the crest, the Galadhrim built their dwellings, which were called telain or flets. Their king and queen lived in a great hall in the tallest Mallorn. The Galadhrim were like spirits of the woods and in that realm there was no cutting or burning of wood. It truly was a kingdom of trees, and a golden glow of Elven power shone there like none other in that Age.

MALLOS In the fields of Lebennin, near the delta of the River Anduin, there grew the flowers that Grey-elves named Mallos, the "gold snow". Their blooms were fair and never fading, and in Elven songs they were likened to golden bells calling the Elves to the Western Sea.

MEARAS All the Horses of Arda were created in the image of Nahar, the white steed of Oromë, the Valarian Horseman. The true descendants of Nahar it was believed were the Mearas, the "Horse-princes" of Rohan, for they were magical and wonderful. White and silver-grey, they were fleet as the wind, long-lived and tireless and filled with great wisdom.

The tales of the Rohirrim record how the first Mearas came to Men of Rhovanion. In the twenty-sixth century of the Third Age of Sun, the lord of the Éothéod, who was named Léod, tried to tame the most beauteous Horse his people had ever seen, but the Horse was wild and proud and threw Léod, who was killed. So the Horse was named Mansbane. However, when Léod's son, Eorl, came to the Horse it surrendered to the young lord as if in atonement. Eorl renamed him Felaróf, Father of Horses, for from him came forth the Mearas, who allowed none but the kings and princes of Eorl's Line to ride them. Though they could not speak, they understood the speech of Men, and did not need a saddle or bridle as they obeyed the spoken word of their masters, the Rohirrim of the royal house.

The Mearas were loved and honoured by their masters and the banner of the Rohirrim was always the fleet white form of Felaróf galloping upon a green field.

In the War of the Ring, the Mearas did great service. One named
Snowmane carried Théoden, the king of the Rohirrim, into the
Battles of the Hornburg and Pelennor Fields where they won great
glory for the Rohirrim, though in the end both Horse and rider
were slain by the Witch-king of Morgul. Another Meara in the War
performed greater deeds still. He was Shadowfax and, breaking the
law that none but kings and princes might ride the Mearas, he
carried the White Rider, the Istari Mithrandir, who was also named
Gandalf. Shadowfax was stout-hearted and strong-limbed, for he
stood firm with the White Rider against the terror of the Nazgûl
and outran even the loathsome Winged Beasts.

MEN The histories of Arda tell that when the Sun first shone down on the World a new measure of Time was born. With the Sun came the awakening of a race that was ordained by Ilúvatar alone. As the Elves had come forth with the Rekindling of the Stars, so Men came with the Rising of the Sun.

In the land the Elves called Hildórien "land of the followers", which was in the far East of Middle-earth, Men first opened their eyes to the new light. Unlike the Elves, Men were mortal and, even by Dwarf measure, short-lived. In strength of body and nobility of spirit Men compared poorly with Elven-folk. They were a weak race that succumbed readily to pestilence and the rough elements of the World. They were easily broken in body and spirit by all manner of things that did not touch the Elves at all. For these reasons Elves called them the Engwar, the "sickly". The Valar did not come into the East, and what skills Men could learn were taught them out of pity by the least of the Elven people, the Dark Elves who lived in the woodlands of the East. But Men were stubborn as a race, and they bred more quickly than any other people except the Orcs, and though great numbers perished they multiplied again and finally thrived in the eastern lands, and so by some were called the Usurpers.

In the Spring of Arda there was great joy, but at last Morgoth, hearing a rumour of what had taken place in the East, made his way to those lands. A shadow then came down like a great hand on the race of Men. It is said that in Men, for the most part, he found a people he could easily bend to his will.

Some fled from this evil and these were the noblest of Men. They scattered to the West and to the North, searching for the land that was rumoured to be free from Morgoth's Hand of Darkness. Eventually they reached Beleriand, where a people lived whose eyes were bright as unclouded Stars and whose spirits were fierce as the golden Sun. These were the Calaquendi, the Noldorin Elves, who recently had come out of the Undying Lands. To these Elves the Men paid homage and offered service and allegiance. Above all they wished to learn of the Light that had once been in the West and of the skills and knowledge that would bring an end to the darkness they had known in the East.

The Noldor accepted the allegiance of these Men and taught them many things of great worth. In the Noldorin language they first called Men the Atani, the "Secondborn", but later, as the greater part of the people of Beleriand spoke the Grey-elven tongue, they were more commonly named the Edain, the "second ones". They were among the noblest of Men ever to walk in Mortal Lands.

According to the "Quenta Silmarillion" the Edain were divided into three hosts: the First House of Bëor, the Second House of the Haladin, and the Third House of Hador. The deeds of the Three

COMPANY OF ADVENTURERS

In the year 2941 of the Third Age of Sun a Company of Adventurers entered the quiet lands of the Shire and disturbed the peace of that place. This Dwarf company of Thorin Oakenshield and Gandalf the Wizard were set on the Quest of the Lonely Mountain. They had come to compel the Hobbit Bilbo Baggins to join them on their Quest. Thus the Hobbits of the Shire first became enmeshed in the affairs of greater nations in the World. For though the Shire was a peaceful land, it was like an oasis in a desert of war and strife. In the land of Mordor an evil power was growing that sought to crush all the good forces of the World.

Of the affairs of the World, the Hobbits knew very little, nor did they suspect the great part they were destined to play in the histories of Middle-earth. But all had its beginning in the coming of the Adventurers to the Shire and the desire of Thorin Oakenshield to wrest the inheritance of his people from Smaug, the Dragon of the Lonely Mountain.

THE SHIRE

The green and pleasant lands of the Shire had
been the homeland of the Hobbits since the
seventeenth century of the Third Age of Sun.
Here lived Bilbo Baggins, who joined the Quest
of the Lonely Mountain and on that adventure
acquired a magic Ring. This chance discovery
drew Bilbo, his nephew Frodo Baggins and all
the Hobbits of the Shire into the greatest drama
of that Age. So it was that because of their
possession of this magic Ring the Hobbits, the
meekest and least of all peoples, came to hold
the fate of all the World in their hands.

FOREST OF MIRKWOOD

The largest forest in Middle-earth was
Greenwood the Great where Thranduil made
the Woodland Realm of the Silvan Elves. In the
year 1050 of the Third Age an evil power had
entered Greenwood. Great Spiders, Orcs, Wolves
and evil spirits had haunted the forest and,
though the Silvan Elves had not been driven
from their realm, they had not been able to halt
the spreading darkness. Thereafter Greenwood
was called Mirkwood and few dared to travel
along its dark paths.

Mirkwood was among the greatest obstacles
standing before the Dwarf company of Thorin
Oakenshield on the long road to the Lonely
Mountain. Yet, with stealth and valour, the
Hobbit Bilbo Baggins guided the company
through the many perils of the dark forest.

DEATH OF SMAUG THE GOLDEN

The tale of the Quest of the Lonely Mountain tells how the Hobbit Bilbo Baggins entered the lair of Smaug the Dragon and by quickness of wit discovered the secret of the monster's only weakness. With this knowledge, the warrior Bard the Bowman shot the Dragon through the breast. Bellowing sulphurous flame on the Lake Town of Esgaroth, Smaug fell from the sky.

BATTLE OF FIVE ARMIES

The death of Smaug, the Dragon of the Lonely Mountain, freed the treasures of the Dragon's hoard from its guardian. This attracted not only the Dwarves of Thorin Oakenshield to the Lonely Mountain but also an army of Men from the Lake Town, the army of the Elf-king of Mirkwood and an army of Dwarves from the Iron Hills. Yet another army, greater in number than the other four together, spilled into the valley under the Lonely Mountain. It was led by a vast number of evil Orcs from the Misty Mountains and they too came to claim the Dragon's wealth. Orcs by the thousand, Wolves and Wolf-riders and clouds of blood-sucking Bats fell on the gathered armies.

The Orkish legions soon had the advantage, until the huge Eagles of the North entered the fight. The battle was turned and Men, Elves, Dwarves and Eagles gained the victory. The Orcs of the Misty Mountains were destroyed and their tide of darkness was driven back. Yet this was but a brief respite, for a power in Mordor that commanded all evil grew silently stronger.

ATTACK AT THE FORD OF RIVENDELL

In 3018 of the Third Age the War of the Ring
had its true beginning. For in that year Sauron
learned that the One Ring had been found and
he sent nine Black Riders to take it.

The Hobbit Frodo Baggins, nephew of Bilbo,
was now the Ringbearer. He fled from the Black
Riders and entered Rivendell, the hidden realm
of the Elves of Elrond Half-elven who wore
the Elf Ring Vilya, the Ring of Sapphire.

At the Ford that is the border of Rivendell
Elrond commanded the river to rise up like
an army of white knights and white Horses.
Though the Black Riders attempted the
crossing this great flood overthrew them and
drove them away. The Ringbearer found refuge,
companionship and wise counsel in Elrond's
court, and it was here that the Quest of the Ring
was set, the Sword of the Dúnedain was forged
and the Fellowship of the Ring was formed.

DWARF-REALM OF MORIA

Most ancient and famous of all the Dwarf-kingdoms was that realm originally called Khazad-dûm, the ancestral home of Durin the Deathless, the first of the seven Fathers of the Dwarves. Through five Ages of Stars and three Ages of Sun the Dwarves of Khazad-dûm were prosperous and strong. In the Second Age of Sun, these were the Dwarves who had a long friendship with the Gwaith-i-Mírdain, the Elven-smiths of Eregion, who forged the Rings of Power. But in the Accursed Years of Sauron's dominion in the Second Age, the Dwarves had closed their great doors to the World. At this time, the great mansion was renamed Moria, the "dark chasm."

Yet still the Dwarves quarried and worked the forges beneath the Misty Mountains until 1980 of the Third Age of Sun. In that year the Dwarves delved too deep beneath Mount Barazinbar and an entombed Balrog was released within the halls of Moria. So terrible was the Balrog's strength and wrath that the Dwarves were either slain or driven from their kingdom.

When the Fellowship of the Ring entered Moria it was therefore a chasm of darkness that had long been abandoned by Dwarves. Its treasures had been stripped by Orkish hordes and through its barren corridors there still walked the Balrog and many bands of Orcs and Trolls.

LOTHLÓRIEN AND CERIN AMROTH

The fairest Elf-kingdom remaining on Middle-earth in the Third Age was Lothlórien where the Noldor queen Galadriel and the Sindar lord Celeborn ruled. In this wooded realm the tallest and fairest trees of Middle-earth grew, and some part of the brilliance of the Elf-kingdoms of ancient times seemed to glow in this forest.

At the very heart of Lothlórien was the hill of Cerin Amroth, where the house of the Elf-king Amroth once stood. It was said to be a fair and enchanted place where the Elf-flowers Elanor and Niphredil constantly bloomed. Here Arwen, daughter of Elrond Half-elven, and Aragorn, son of Arathorn the Dúnedain, pledged their love; and to this hill Arwen returned in the Fourth Age to seek her final place of rest.

Into the magical realm of Lothlórien came the Fellowship of the Ring, fleeing the servants of Sauron, and there among these Elves, the Galadhrim, they found shelter and rest.

The Galadhrim were wise in the ways of the forest and they lived almost invisibly on high platforms in trees. Lothlórien was also protected by the power of Galadriel and the Elf Ring Nenya, the Ring of Adamant, which she wore. By Queen Galadriel the members of the Fellowship were granted many gifts that renewed their strength and will.

BREAKING OF THE FELLOWSHIP

The Fellowship of the Ring experienced
many perils on the road through Rhovanion.
Yet, within sight of Mordor, the Fellowship
was broken by internal strife and external
disaster. One member was slain, two were taken
hostage, three went West into Rohan and the
Ringbearer and his servant fled eastwards.

He who was slain was Boromir, heir to the
Steward of Gondor, and he was placed on a
funeral boat on the River Anduin. The boat was
drawn past Tol Brandir, the tall island, and
onwards over the Falls of Rauros.

Houses of Elf-friends were renowned in the War of the Jewels against Morgoth the Enemy. Great too was the tragedy that befell the noble Edain who battled at the side of the Elven hosts. Of the tales of Men in the First Age of Sun the longest is the "Narn i Hîn Húrin", the tale of the children of Húrin, which tells of Húrin the Troll-slayer; of Túrin who slew Glaurung, the Father of Dragons; of Beren, who cut a Silmaril from Morgoth's Iron Crown; and of Eärendil the Mariner who sailed "Vingilot" and carried the Morning Star into the heavens.

In the First Age still more of the race of Men came out of the East. They were a different people whom Elves called Swarthy Men and Easterlings. They were people who had remained in the lands where the shadow of Morgoth loomed. In times of war, most of these Men proved unfaithful and, though feigning friendship with the Elves, they betrayed them to the Enemy.

When the First Age of Sun was ended and Morgoth was cast into the Void, the land of Beleriand went down beneath the Western Sea. All the enemies who inhabited Beleriand were slain, as well as most of the Elves and the Edain of that place, and so little was left to the victors.

Even the Edain who survived that Age became divided. Some fled the sinking of Beleriand and went to the East, beyond the Misty Mountains, and for a time were lost to the Elves. They lived in the Vales of Anduin with others of their kin who had never entered Beleriand in the First Age; they were known as the Northmen of Rhovanion. Others of the Edain fled Beleriand and went to the South with the Elves, where they were given a great gift by the Valar for their faithfulness and suffering. These Men were granted a land that lay in the Western Sea between Middle-earth and the Undying Lands.

The Men who went South with the Elves were named the Dúnedain, the Men of Westernesse, for their island was called Westernesse, which in the Elvish tongue was Númenórë. In the Second Age the Dúnedain were more often called the Númenóreans and they became a mighty sea power. Then too the span of the Númenóreans' lives was increased and their wisdom and strength also grew. As the "Akallabêth" relates, their history in the Second Age was glorious, but their Downfall was terrible. For the Númenóreans, corrupted by Sauron, went to war against the Valar and the Maiar, and most were destroyed. Númenórë was cast into a great abyss, the Western Sea came over it and it was no more.

Though most of the Númenóreans perished, there were those who were saved from that disaster, including some who were later known as the Black Númenóreans. They were a mighty race, but most were corrupted by their pride and by the evil influence of the Dark Lord Sauron. They lived in the land of Umbar in the South of

Middle-earth. They were a great sea power and were enemies of that other people who escaped from Númenórë.

The noblest of the Númenóreans returned to Middle-earth in nine ships; their lord was Elendil the Tall and with him were two sons, Isildur and Anárion. These Elendili, the "faithful", who were of the true line of the Dúnedain, made two mighty kingdoms in Middle-earth. The North Kingdom was started east of the Gulf of Lune by Elendil and was named Arnor, and the South Kingdom, formed by his sons, was called Gondor. The Dúnedain of Arnor and Gondor were the strongest Men of Middle-earth.

Soon however the power of Sauron in Mordor grew again, but the peoples of Middle-earth saw the threat and so they made the Last Alliance of Elves and Men, which combined all the armies of the Dúnedain and the Elves. The Men were led by Elendil and the Elves by Gil-galad, the last High King. They went to the Black Gate of Mordor and fought a terrible battle. Many Men called Haradrim from the south lands fought against them, as did others from Rhûn who were named Easterlings. Among them there were also some who came from Umbar – the Black Númenóreans; many were these races of Men who sided with the Orcs and thralls of Sauron.

But at last Mordor's Black Gate was thrown down, and those in the Alliance then laid siege to the Dark Tower, Barad-dûr, for seven years until in the end it also fell. However Gil-galad, Elendil and Anárion were killed in that war and among the rulers of the Dúnedain only Isildur remained. It was he who cut the Ring from Sauron's hand and sent his spirit to wander without form in the waste places of Middle-earth.

So began the Third Age and, though for a time it was filled with happiness, it was doomed to end in a great war. After taking the One Ring from Sauron's hand Isildur did not destroy it and in the first years of that Age tragedy befell him. The Orcs cut him down with black arrows at the Gladden Fields and for a long time the Ring was lost.

Of the Dúnedain who survived there were the sons of Isildur, who ruled the North Kingdom of Arnor, and the sons of Anárion, who ruled the South Kingdom of Gondor; and for a time their strength increased. There were also other races of Men who had arisen in the East and South, and many now appeared. The Balchoth, Wainriders and other Easterlings came of Rhûn against the Dúnedain of Gondor. From the South, the Haradrim and the Variags advanced with the Black Númenóreans. However the Men of Gondor were strong and defeated all enemies.

But in the North another power grew in the land of Angmar. A Witch-king ruled in that land, and he summoned an army of Orcs and evil creatures, as well as Hillmen of the Ettenmoors and Easterlings, to make war on the North Kingdom of Arnor, which

they laid waste. Though the evil realm of Angmar was finally destroyed by the Dúnedain of Gondor, the North Kingdom of Arnor was ended, and only a small number of that people wandered the empty lands and they were named the Rangers of the North.

In the South and from the East there came a constant flow of barbarian Men, corrupted long before by Sauron's power. The Dunlendings advanced, prepared for war, as did the Haradrim and Easterlings. The Nazgûl also came out of Mordor and from the Men of Gondor they captured the east tower of Minas Ithil, which was renamed Minas Morgul. Yet in this time Gondor gained an ally, for the horsemen known as the Rohirrim came to their aid. These were the Northmen of Rhovanion and were like the Woodmen and the Beornings of Mirkwood, or the Lake Men of Esgaroth and the Bardings of Dale, for they perpetually fought the evils made by Sauron the Dark Lord. In the scattered realms of Middle-earth a union of the Dúnedain peoples was, however, foreshadowed. For, as the "Red Book of Westmarch" relates, though the North Kingdom of Arnor was lost there always remained a true heir to the Dúnedain throne; while in the South, though the kingdom was intact, there was no longer a true heir to be named king, and the land was ruled by Stewards. The Quest of the Ring was set near the end of the Third Age, and the War of the Ring began. The One Ring was found and destroyed, and the One King came to the Dúnedain. This was Aragorn, son of Arathorn, who was named King Elessar, the true heir of Isildur. Then too came the last union of the blood of the royal lineage with that of the Elves, for Aragorn took as his wife Arwen Undómiel, daughter of Elrond Half-elven.

King Elessar proved a strong and wise ruler. For though he crushed many enemies in war, and feared nobody in battle, he made peace with the Easterlings and Haradrim, and in the Fourth Age of Sun, which was ordained the Age of the Dominion of Men, there was peace in the Westlands, and also for many years after that time, because of the wisdom of Elessar and his sons. For these were Dúnedain, who traced direct lineage to the Atanatári, the fathers of Men, who had first entered the kingdoms of the Elves, where they had learned and passed on to the race of Men much that is now thought noble and great.

MEWLIPS According to the lore of Hobbits, an evil race of cannibal spirits called the Mewlips settled in certain marshlands of Middle-earth. Hoarding phantoms very like the dreaded Barrow-wights they seemed, but they made their homes in foul and dank swamps. Travellers in their lands always walked in peril, for many were said to be waylaid and slain by these beings.

MORIQUENDI In the High Elven tongue of Quenya, all Elves who did not come to the Undying Lands in the time of the Trees of the Valar were named Moriquendi, the DARK ELVES. They were Elves of lesser power than those who witnessed the Undying Lands in the time of their greatest glory. Among the Moriquendi were: the Avari, the Silvan Elves of Lothlórien and Mirkwood, the Nandor, the Laiquendi, the Falathrim and the Sindar.

MÛMAKIL In the Third Age of Sun in the south lands of Harad, there lived beasts of vast bulk that are thought to be ancestors of the creatures Men now name elephants. Yet it is said the elephants that now inhabit the World are much smaller in size and might than their ancestors.

In the years of the War of the Ring the fierce warriors of Harad came north to the lands of Gondor at the call of Sauron, and with their armies they brought the great Mûmakil, which were used as beasts of war. The Mûmakil were harnessed with the gear of war: red banners, bands and trappings of gold and brass; on their backs they had great towers from which archers and spearmen fought. They had a natural thirst for battle, and many foes were crushed beneath their feet. With their trunks they struck down many enemies and in battle their tusks were crimsoned with the blood of

their foes. They could not be fought by mounted Men for Horses would not come near the Mûmakil; nor by foot soldiers, who would be shot from above or crushed. In war they would frequently stand as towers that could not be captured: shield-walls broke before them and armies were routed.

These thick-skinned beasts were almost invulnerable to arrow-shot. In only one place, their eyes, could the Mûmakil be blinded or even killed by arrows released with great force. When blinded they became enraged with pain, and often destroyed masters and foes alike.

NANDOR Of the Elves who undertook the Great Journey in search of the Undying Lands there were Three Kindred. The third and largest kindred were the Teleri, and because these people were so numerous their passage was slowest, and those unable or unwilling to complete the Journey were in greater numbers than the other two kindred. The first division recorded in that Journey came when the Teleri halted before the Great River Anduin and, looking beyond, saw the Misty Mountains. This mighty barrier terrified the Elves and so, rather than risk crossing the mountains, Lenwë, a lord of the Teleri, led his people away. They went southwards down the Great River and lived in places unknown to others of their kin; they were named the Nandor, "those who turn back". They were a wandering woodland folk and they had no equal in the ways of woodlore and woodcraft, or in knowledge of the Kelvar and Olvar of Middle-earth. They hunted with bows and had weapons made from certain base metals, but they did not know how to forge arms of steel with which to fight the evil creatures that, in later Ages, came out of the North.

For more than two Ages of Starlight the Nandor lived in harmony in the lands of their wanderings, in the Vales of Anduin. Some crossed over the White Mountains and came into Eriador. They grew wiser in the ways of the forests and waters, but when evil beings attacked them in the forests they were unprepared and their numbers began to dwindle. Many were slaughtered by steel-shod Orcs, Stone-trolls and ravening Wolves.

Many Nandor, practising their woodcraft, hid as best they could from the lurking terror. However Denethor, son of King Lenwë, gathered many of the Nandor to him and set off once again on the long-abandoned westward march. He sought what kindred he could to aid him, for tales had reached the Nandor of the might of the Sindar, led by one who had once been king of all the Teleri, Elwë Singollo, now named Thingol. Denethor crossed the Blue Mountains and entered Beleriand, bringing a great number of the Nandor under the sovereignty of their rightful king once again.

They were welcomed by the Sindar, who protected them, taught them some of the arts of war and granted them Ossiriand, the "land of seven rivers", as their realm. They were called Nandor no more but Laiquendi and Green-elves because of their love of green woodlands and their habit of dressing in green cloth so they might be one with the forest in the sight of an enemy. So in that Age before the coming of the Sun, they lived happily by rivers and in the forests of Ossiriand, and the sweet singing of the Laiquendi rivalled the melodies of the nightingale.

NAUGRIM During the Ages of Starlight before the kingdom of the Grey-elves had grown to its full power, a race of DWARVES who were long-bearded and armed with steel weapons came over the Blue Mountains into Beleriand. The Grey-elves thought these people deformed and unlovely, and named them the Naugrim, the "stunted people". But the Naugrim came not to fight but to trade and barter, and by this traffic both races thrived. And though the Naugrim lived in prosperous peace with the Elves, there was only an uneasy alliance and no great friendship between them.

NAZGÛL In the twenty-third century of the Second Age of Sun in Middle-earth there arose nine mighty wraiths who in the Black Speech of Orcs were named the Nazgûl, which is "Ringwraiths". And of all the evil servants and generals of Sauron the Ring Lord these Nazgûl proved to be the greatest.

It is said that the Nazgûl were once powerful kings and sorcerers among Men and they were each given a Ring of Power by Sauron. These Rings were nine of the magical nineteen Rings that Celebrimbor and the Elven-smiths of Eregion forged for Sauron. For many centuries these Men used their Rings to fulfil their own desires, yet all were ruled by the One Ring that Sauron made. Though these chosen Men lived by the power of the Rings far beyond the span of ordinary mortals, their forms faded. By the twenty-third century they were wraiths entirely, and thralls that thought only of how they might serve Sauron the Ring Lord. So they roamed the World committing terrible deeds. They wore great cloaks, black and hooded, and hauberks of mail and silver helms, yet beneath were the grey robes of the dead and their bodies were invisible. Any who looked into their faces fell back in horror, for nothing seemed to bear up helm and hood. Yet sometimes there appeared, where faces should be, the glow of two luminous and hypnotic eyes or, in rage and power, a red and hellish flame.

The weapons of the Nazgûl were numerous: they carried swords of steel and of flame, black maces and daggers with magical poisoned blades. They used spells of beckoning and spells of blasting sorcerous fire, and the curse of their Black Breath was like a plague of despair and the curse of its terror froze the hearts of their foes. The Nazgûl were untouchable to mortal Men, for arms could not harm them unless blessed by Elvish spell and any blade that struck them withered and perished.

So for a thousand years of the Second Age of Sun the Nazgûl on nine black Horses swept over the lands of Middle-earth like a nightmare of terror. And in all that time, they fared in the wars as did Sauron the Ring Lord himself. They did not perish until the realm of Sauron's Mordor fell and the seven-year Siege of Barad-dûr was broken by the Last Alliance of Elves and Men at the end of that Age. Isildur, the Dúnedain lord of Gondor, cut the One Ring from Sauron's hand, and the Nazgûl with the Ring Lord were swept away to the shadows and the waste places in the eastern lands of the World where they had no form or power.

So, the Nazgûl were both formless and powerless for thirteen centuries in the Third Age of Sun. Yet the One Ring had not been destroyed and Sauron was able to make himself a shape again. So it was in the fourteenth century he summoned again his great servants, the Nazgûl, out of the shadows. The nine Black Riders arose in the East and the greatest of these Nazgûl came to the north

of Eriador, where he made the kingdom of Angmar and built a great citadel in Carn Dûm. He called forth Orc legions and the evil Hillmen of the Ettenmoors. For more than six centuries there was continuous war in Eriador. This Nazgûl lord, who was at that time called the Witch-king of Angmar, made constant war against the Dúnedain of Arnor and out of Carn Dûm came much evil. One by one the great provinces and cities went down, until 1974, when the last – the province of Arthedain and the city of Fornost – fell to the barbarous hordes. Yet the Witch-king's possession of the Dúnedain Kingdom of the North was short-lived, for in 1975 his army was routed and destroyed by the Elf-lords Círdan and Glorfindel and by Eärnur, the king of Gondor, at the Battle of Fornost. But still the Witch-king and his master Sauron counted this as a great deed, for they were little concerned with the slaughter of Orcs and Hillmen, and the destruction of the power and the kingdom of the Dúnedain of the North in Arnor was indeed a great victory by the Dark Powers.

The Witch-king of Angmar, called the High Nazgûl, deserted the ruined lands of Eriador and returned to Mordor. And though Sauron was not yet come, but hid still in Dol Guldur in the darkness of Mirkwood, there were in Mordor the other eight Nazgûl who had come secretly three centuries before. In that time they had laboured to rebuild the evil power of that land and had gathered Orkish hordes about them. In the year 2000 the nine Nazgûl came out of Mordor to fight the Dúnedain of the South in Gondor, and two years later the eastern citadel, Minas Ithil, the "tower of the Moon", fell. The Nazgûl made this place their own and renamed it Minas Morgul, the "tower of black wraiths", and sometimes the Tower of Sorcery and the Dead City. The High Nazgûl, the Witch-king of Angmar, was now called the Morgul Lord and wore a crown of steel. It was he who slew Eärnur, the last king of Gondor, and for a thousand years he made war on the Men of Gondor with both sorcery and the might of his army, and he eroded their power and their lands.

It was not, however, until the year 2951 that Sauron the Dark Lord declared himself and came to Mordor. It is said that Sauron feared to declare himself openly before that time lest someone possessed the One Ring, which could destroy him. And it was not until later still that even the wisest among Men knew that he commanded the wraiths of Morgul, and that these wraiths were the Nazgûl of the Second Age.

In the year 3018 of the Third Age the War of the Ring had its beginning. For in that year Sauron learned where the One Ring was hidden and such was his desire that he sent all nine Nazgûl to take it. Yet they were thwarted in their errand. When they came to the borders of Rivendell the nine Black Riders were unhorsed at the

Ford of Bruinen and were driven away by the Elvish powers that commanded the river.

Yet they reappeared in still mightier forms, on steeds as dreadful as themselves. These steeds were the Winged Beasts for which Elves and Men had no name. They were ancient beings that had come into the World before the Count of Time began. Though they had beak and claw and wing, they were not birds, nor even Bats: they were serpentine beings like Dragons, yet older. They were made by Melkor, Sauron's master, in Utumno's foul pits, where serpent, Kraken and other vile creatures of hidden places had arisen. Fed on the cannibal meats of the Orcs and grown larger than all creatures of the air, the Winged Beasts carried the Nazgûl high over the lands with the speed of the winds. Despite their might and fierceness, in the War of the Ring the Nazgûl were in deadly peril, because the One Ring was in the hands of their foes. In the Battle of Pelennor Fields, the Morgul Lord, who could not be slain by the hand of Man, was brought to an end by the shield-maiden Éowyn of Rohan and the Hobbit warrior Meriadoc Brandybuck. Though eight of the Nazgûl remained they, too, were soon destroyed; as they rose to fight the enemy at the Black Gate of Morannon there was a great alarm within Mordor itself. Sauron commanded the Nazgûl to hasten to Orodruin, the Mountain of Fire, that is called Mount Doom, for there stood the Hobbit Frodo Baggins with the Ruling Ring. On their Winged Beasts the Nazgûl rushed like the north wind, yet to no purpose, because the Ring dropped into the Fire of Doom and was unmade. In that moment Sauron and all his dreadful world were destroyed. As the Black Gate collapsed, the Dark Tower of Barad-dûr toppled, and in the midst of their flight the mighty Nazgûl fell shrieking in flames that ended them for ever.

NEEKERBREEKERS In the foul Midgewater Marshes in northern Eriador there lived vast numbers of blood-sucking insects. Among them were some noisy creatures akin to crickets that were named Neekerbreekers by Hobbits. Travellers in the Midgewater Marshes were driven all but mad by the awful repetitious din of the creatures' "neek-breek, breek-neek".

NELDORETH Among the most loved of the trees growing in Middle-earth were those that Elves called Neldoreth but Men knew as beech. According to the tales of lost Beleriand, the great halls of Menegroth, the Thousand Caves, had carved pillars like the beech trees that grew within the vast Taur-na-Neldor, the Forest of Neldoreth, which was thought to be the fairest forest in Beleriand. And in the minds of Elves the Neldoreth was loved the more because in part it was like the Golden Tree of the Valar, called Laurelin, which once lit the Blessed Realm with Golden light.

The triple-trunked beech of Doriath that was named Hírilorn was mightiest of the Neldoreth that ever grew in Middle-earth, and in it was built the guarded house of Lúthien – as the Quest of the Silmaril relates.

NIMBRETHIL In lost Beleriand there grew many fair white birch trees, which were called Nimbrethil in the tongue of the Grey-elves. "Vingilot", the mighty ship that Eärendil the Mariner sailed over Belegaer, the Western Sea, to the Undying Lands, was built with timber from these huge trees.

NIPHREDIL At the end of the First Age of the Chaining of Melkor, when Stars lit the Earth, the fairest child that ever entered the World was born to Melian the Maia and Thingol, king of the Sindar. She was born in the woodlands of Neldoreth in Beleriand and was named Lúthien. To the woodland at that time came the white flower Niphredil to greet fair Lúthien. This flower was said to be a Star of the Earth, as was this only daughter born of Eldar and Maia union. Though many Ages of Stars and Sun passed, and Lúthien with her lover Beren had long ago gone from the Spheres of the World, the Star flower Niphredil remained as a memory to the fairest daughter of the Earth.

In the Third Age of Sun, the white flower grew still in the Golden Wood of Lothlórien, where, mixed with the gold flower Elanor, it thrived. In the Fourth Age of Sun the fairest Elf-maid of that Age came to the forest. This was Arwen Undómiel, and she, like Lúthien, shared the same fate of tragic love for a mortal, and in that forest Arwen plighted her troth to Aragorn, the Dúnedain. Years later in that same forest she chose to die on a bed of these white and gold flowers.

NOEGYTH NIBIN   The ancient tales of lost realm of Beleriand tell of a race whom the Grey-elves called Noegyth Nibin. They were small people – smaller even than Dwarves, from whom they descended. Men called them PETTY-DWARVES, and in the First Age of Sun Mîm, the last of this dwindled race, was bloodily slain by Húrin.

NOLDOR   Mightiest of Elves who inhabited Middle-earth were the Noldor, and most far-famed in the songs and tales that have come to the ears of Men. For these were the Elves who wrought the Great Jewels called the Silmarils, as well as the Rings of Power. The mightiest wars that were ever known to Elves and Men were fought over these great works.

Of the Eldar who came to the Undying Lands, the Noldor were the Second Kindred. The name Noldor means "knowledge", which, above all the Elves, they strove hardest to possess. In the years of the Trees of the Valar their king was Finwë, and at that time great was their joy in learning from their tutors, the Valar and the Maiar. In that golden and silver light everlasting the Noldor grew strong and noble. Their city of Tirion on the green hill Túna, which looked over the starlit sea, was mighty and beautiful. For the city was built in the Pass of Light named Calacirya, the only passage through the vast Pelóri Mountains, which enclosed the lands of Eldamar and Valinor. Through this gap flowed the Light of the Trees and it fell on the west of the city. To the east, in the shadow of Túna, the Elves looked on the Stars that shone over the Shadowy Seas.

So it was that the Noldor became wise people, but they especially excelled in the crafts of Aulë, Maker of Mountains. They cut the great towers of Eldamar from rock and carved many things of beauty out of radiant white stone. They were first to bring forth the gems that lay in the mountain heart. They gave the stones freely, and the mansions of the Elves and the Valar glinted with the gems of the Noldor, and the very beaches and pools of Eldamar, it is said, shone with the scattered light of gems.

To the king of the Noldor and his queen, Míriel, was born a son named Curufinwë, who was called Fëanor, which is "spirit of fire". Of all craftsmen who learned the skills of Aulë, Fëanor was mightiest. Even among the Maiar there were none to surpass him. For he was first to make those magical Elven-gems that were brighter and more magical than the Earth stones. They were pale in the making, but when set under Stars they were compared to the eyes of the Elves, for they took on the light of the Stars and shone blue and bright. Fëanor also made other crystals called Palantíri, the "seeing stones", which were the magical stones that, many Ages later, the Elves of Avallónë gave to the Dúnedain. But greatest of the deeds of Fëanor was the making of those three fabulous gems that captured the mingled Light of the Trees of the Valar within their crystals. These were the most beautiful jewels that the World has ever seen, for they shone with a living light. Yet, as is told in the "Quenta Silmarillion" and the "Noldolantë", the high ambitions of Fëanor, coupled with the evil deeds of Melkor, led to the greatest bane that was ever known to the Elven peoples. For Melkor came forth and with the Spider Ungoliant destroyed the Trees of the Valar, slew Finwë and stole the Silmarils. Fëanor swore an oath of vengeance that was a curse on his people for ever more. In anger he followed Melkor, whom he named Morgoth the "dark enemy of the World", to Middle-earth. So began the War of the Jewels and the Wars of Beleriand, which were fought through all the days of the First Age of Sun.

During this Age of war the Noldor also brought great gifts to Middle-earth. And for a time there arose the Noldor kingdoms in Hithlum, Dor-lómin, Nevrast, Mithrim, Dorthonion, Himlad, Thargelion and East Beleriand. Fairest of the Noldor realms were the two hidden kingdoms: Gondolin, which was ruled by Turgon; and Nargothrond, which was held by Finrod Felagund.

In the War of the Jewels Fëanor was slain, as were all his seven sons: Amras, Amrod, Caranthir, Celegorm, Curufin, Maedhros and Maglor. His brother Fingolfin and Fingolfin's children, Fingon, Turgon and Aredhel, were also killed by Morgoth. And though Finarfin, the other brother (and third son of Finwë), had remained in the Undying Lands where he ruled the remnant of the Noldor in Tirion, all his children went to Middle-earth and his four sons, Aegnor, Angrod, Finrod Felagund and Orodreth, were killed. So of all the Noldor lords and their children only Finarfin's daughter Galadriel survived on Middle-earth.

Through the years of the First Age Morgoth and his servants destroyed all the Noldorin kingdoms. At that time there were in Beleriand many other people whose doom in part was tied to that of the Noldor. Because of these wars, the realms of the Grey-elves who were also called the Sindar were destroyed, as were the Dwarf-realms of Nogrod and Belegost and most of the kingdoms of the Three Houses of the Edain.

But finally the Valar and the Maiar came forth out of the Undying Lands against Morgoth. Thus occurred the Great Battle and the War of Wrath. Before this mighty force Angband fell and Morgoth was cast into the Eternal Void for ever. Yet the struggle was so great that Beleriand was broken and most of the land was swallowed up beneath the sea.

Of all the royal lines of the Noldor few who survived the War of the Jewels could claim direct descent. So it was that Gil-galad, son of Fingon, son of Fingolfin, set up the last Noldor high kingdom in Mortal Lands. This was in Lindon, the last part of Beleriand to remain after the Great Battle. With Gil-galad lived Celebrimbor, son of Curufin, only prince of the House of Fëanor to live into the Second Age. Galadriel, daughter of Finarfin, Elrond and Elros the Half-elven and many Sindar lords also came, as well as Círdan of the Falathrim, the Laiquendi and the Edain – the Men who were loyal to the Elves during the Wars.

At that time many of the Elves took ships from the Grey Havens and sailed to Tol Eressëa in the Bay of Eldamar in the Undying Lands and built there the city of Avallónë. The Edain were also given a fair island in the Western Sea, called Númenórë, and they too left the lands of Middle-earth.

Yet all those of royal Noldorin line remained. Gil-galad ruled Lindon and Círdan held the Grey Havens. But in the year 750 of the Second Age, it is said Celebrimbor came out of Lindon and made a kingdom at the foot of the Misty Mountains in the land of Eregion, near the Dwarf-realm of Khazad-dûm. These Elves were named the Gwaith-i-Mírdain, the "people of the jewel-smiths", and the Elven-smiths, in the legends of later times. It was here through subtle persuasions of Sauron that the Rings of Power were forged. These were made by Celebrimbor, grandson of Fëanor, who created the Silmarils; and so was wrought the second great work of the Noldor over which another cycle of bitter wars was fought. For Sauron at that time made the One Ring that would rule all the other works of the Noldor. In anger and fear the Elves arose, and the War of Sauron and the Elves was fought. Celebrimbor and most of the Gwaith-i-Mírdain were slain; Eregion was laid waste, and,

though Elrond Half-elven came with an army, all he could do was rescue those few who remained and take refuge in Imladris, which Men called Rivendell. There the only Noldor stronghold between the Blue and the Misty Mountains was made.

In this time, Lindon itself was in peril, but descendants of the Edain, the Númenóreans, brought their immense fleets and drove Sauron into the East. Later still they returned and captured the Dark Lord, but they did not destroy him. They held him prisoner, and in this way came their Downfall. For he turned them against the Valar and they were swallowed into the sea for their folly.

So Sauron returned to Middle-earth where only the Noldorin realms of Lindon and Rivendell stood, though the kingdoms of Greenwood the Great and Lothlórien had been built with Noldorin and Sindarin nobles and Silvan subjects. But with Sauron's return there was war again. The Last Alliance of Elves and Men was made and in that war, which ended the Second Age, Gil-galad and the king of the Dúnedain were slain by Sauron, but Sauron himself was destroyed with all the realm of Mordor.

Thereafter there was no High King of the Noldorin Elves in Middle-earth, yet the kingdoms remained. The lordship of Lindon and the Grey Havens fell to Círdan, while Elrond still ruled in Rivendell. During the Third Age the most beautiful kingdom was Lothlórien, where Queen Galadriel reigned, the noblest Noldor still to live in Middle-earth. Though few Noldor lived among those named the Galadhrim in the Golden Wood, it was the brightest and most like the Noldorin realms of old.

As is told in the "Red Book of Westmarch", when at the end of the Third Age the One Ring was unmade and Sauron was destroyed, Elrond was summoned out of Rivendell and Galadriel came out of Lothlórien to the white ships that would take them into the Undying Lands. With the queen gone, Lothlórien faded, and the Noldorin kingdoms of Middle-earth dwindled in the years of the Fourth Age. And it is said that Círdan the Shipwright took the last of the Noldor to the Undying Lands. There dwell now the remnant of the Noldorin people who suffered most grievously, inflicted the greatest sorrow, did the greatest deeds, and won the most fame of all the Elves in the tales that have come down through the Ages. What their deeds have been since the sailing of the last ship, only the Great Music at the End shall make known to those who live in Mortal Lands.

NÓMIN When Men entered the lands of Beleriand in the First Age of Sun, they saw for the first time the Elves of Finrod Felagund, lord of the NOLDOR. These Men were amazed at the beauty and knowledge of these Elves, whom they named the Nómin, which means the "wise".

NORTHMEN In the Third Age of Sun many Men who were descended from the Edain of the First Age inhabited the northern Vales of Anduin. These Men were of many tribes and kingdoms and they were called the Northmen of Rhovanion. Though no single lord governed these Northmen, they were constant enemies of Sauron and all his servants. For through all Rhovanion these proud Men often fought the Orcs, Easterlings and Wolves of the Dark Lord, and at times they even dared to join battle with the great and ancient Dragons that came out of the Northern Waste.

These Northmen remained in Rhovanion for many centuries and did not succumb to the evil power of Sauron. In the histories that concern the last centuries of the Third Age of Sun, the names of some of these strong and noble people are recorded: the Beornings and the Woodmen of Mirkwood; the Lake Men of Esgaroth; the Bardings of Dale; and, perhaps the most powerful and far-famed, the Éothéod, from whom the Rohirrim, the Riders of the Mark, were descended. These were all strong and noble Men, and, in the War of the Ring, they proved to be true allies of the Dúnedain, attacking minions of the Dark Lord Sauron on the battle-field, in woodland and in mountain pass.

From the eleventh century of the Third Age the Northmen were allies of the Gondor Men against the Easterling invaders. Many entered the army of Gondor and their fortunes from that time followed the doom of the Gondor kings.

NÚMENÓREANS When the First Age of Sun was ended and the power of Morgoth was broken, there remained but a remnant of the race of Men called the Edain, who were the allies of the Elves in the terrible Wars of Beleriand.

After the Great Battle, the Valar took pity on the Edain who had suffered so grievously and whose lands had been lost, and the Valar created a great island for them in the Western Sea between Middle-earth and the Undying Lands. With this land they were given a gift of long life and greater powers of mind and body and many skills and much knowledge that had previously only been granted to Elves. These people were much changed and were now called the Númenóreans for their land was Númenor or Westernesse. But it was also named Andar "land of gift" and Elenna "land of the Star" and Mar-nu-Falmar or Atalantë.

The deeds of the Númenóreans in the Second Age of Sun were outstanding, for the Númenóreans were greatly strengthened by the gifts of the Valar and the Eldar. First of the kings of Númenor was Elros Half-elven, the brother of Elrond who later ruled in Rivendell. Elros chose to become mortal, yet his rule lasted 400 years; and in that land he was named Tar-Minyatur. All over the World the Númenóreans sailed, even as far as the Gates of Morning in the East. However they could never sail westwards for a ban had been made that could not be broken: no mortal might tread the shore of the Undying Lands of Eldamar and Valinor.

In Númenor the fortunes of Men increased, while darkness rose in Middle-earth once again. For though Morgoth was gone from the World, his great servant, the Dark Lord Sauron, had returned

and the Men in the southern and eastern lands of Middle-earth worshipped his dark shadow.

The tale of the Rings of Power tells how, at this time, Sauron made a sorcerous Ring with which he hoped to rule all Mortal Lands, and he made war on the Elves and slew them terribly and drove them back into the Blue Mountains. But the power of the Númenóreans had also grown, and they came to the aid of the Elves and made war on Sauron, and he was driven out of the western land. For a time there was peace and the Númenóreans again increased, building the ports of Umbar in the South and Pelargir in the North of Middle-earth. But they grew proud and wished to declare themselves lords of Middle-earth as well as lords of the seas. So in the year 3262 of the Second Age of Sun they came to the Dark Land of Mordor with such a mighty host of arms and Men that Sauron could not withstand them. Sauron came out of Mordor without daring to give battle. He was made prisoner and was taken in chains to the tower of the king of Númenor.

In that place Sauron achieved the greatest evil that was ever committed against the race of Men: he corrupted the great king of Númenor, Ar-Pharazôn. In Númenor great temples were built to Morgoth the Lord of Darkness and human sacrifice was made on his altar. Then Sauron advised the Númenóreans to make war on the Valar and Eldar who lived in the Undying Lands. The greatest fleet that ever sailed the World was then assembled and it sailed into the West towards the land that was forbidden to Men. Passing through the Enchanted Isles and the Shadowy Seas, the fleet came to the Undying Lands. As the vast navy reached the Undying Lands the "Akallabêth" tells how a great doom fell on the World. Though the king came to conquer, his first step brought the Pelóri Mountains down on him and all his vast armada. To a man the Númenóreans were lost, but this was not all, for a greater disaster followed. The waters rose up in wrath and Meneltarma – the mountain that was the centre of Númenor – erupted and great flames leapt up and all of Númenor sank in an immense whirlpool into Belegaer, the Great Sea.

Thus came what was called the Change of the World. For in that year, 3319 of the Second Age of Sun, the Undying Lands were taken from the Circles of the World and moved beyond the reach of all but the Chosen, who travelled in Elven-ships along the Straight Road through the Spheres of both Worlds.

Yet a part of the Númenórean race lived on. For some had fled the sinking of Númenor and had sailed in nine ships to Middle-earth. These were the Elendili, the "faithful", and they made two mighty kingdoms in Arnor and Gondor. Others, too, survived the Downfall of Númenor and were in later times named the Black Númenóreans and they settled in the land of Umbar.

OLIPHAUNTS Into the Hobbit lands of the Shire crept many legends about the mysterious hot lands that lay far in the South of Middle-earth. Most fascinating to the Hobbits were the tales of the giant Oliphaunts: tusked war beasts with huge pounding feet. It was rumoured that the savage Men of Harad placed battle towers on the backs of these creatures when they rode into battle. Sensible Hobbits in fact never believed these tales were anything but the workings of fanciful minds, even though some of their own people claimed to have sighted these creatures, which the Men of Gondor commonly called MÛMAKIL.

OLOG-HAI In the Third Age of Sun, it is said that the Ring Lord Sauron who ruled in Mordor took some of the ancient Trolls that Melkor bred in Angband and from them made another race that was known as the Olog-hai in Black Speech. The creatures of this race were true Trolls in size and strength but Sauron made them cunning and unafraid of the light that was deadly to most of the Troll race. The Olog-hai were terrible in battle for they had been bred to be like ravening beasts that hungered for the flesh of their foes. They were armoured with stone-hard scale and were easily twice the height and bulk of Men. They carried round shields, blank and black, and were armed with huge hammers, clutching claws and great fangs. Before their onslaught few warriors of any race could hold firm a shield wall of defence and blades unblessed by Elvish spell could not pierce their strong hides to release their foul black blood.

Yet strong as they were, the Olog-hai were wholly destroyed at the end of the Third Age. For these creatures were animated and directed solely by the will of the Dark Lord Sauron. So when the One Ring was destroyed and Sauron perished, they were suddenly without senses and purpose; they reeled and wandered aimlessly. Masterless, they lifted no hand to fight and so were slain or lost. Therefore the histories of the Fourth Age do not speak of the Olog-hai for they had already passed from the World for ever.

OLVAR In the Music of the Ainur were many prophecies. One was that before Elves and Men entered the World there would come spirits who would be guardians of all Olvar: living things that grow and are rooted in the Earth. For the Olvar, from the great forest trees to the smallest lichen, could not flee their enemies, and so Yavanna brought forth their guardians called the Ents.

ONODRIM In the forests of Middle-earth in the time of the Rekindling of the Stars there came forth a giant people. These were the great Tree-herds, who were more often known as the ENTS but the Sindarin Elves called them the Onodrim. These fourteen-foot giants were secret protectors of the forest, and in form they were likened to both tree and Man. For the most part the Ents were gentle and slow to act. They were indifferent to the wars of other peoples, unless those disputes greatly diminished their forest realms. Yet once their anger was aroused, their wrath and power were beyond measure, and they annihilated their foes. During the War of the Ring the rebel Wizard Saruman learned the cost of incurring such anger, for the Onodrim destroyed both his army and his fortress of Isengard.

ORCS Within the deepest Pits of Utumno, in the First Age of Stars, it is said Melkor committed his greatest blasphemy. For in that time he captured many of the newly risen race of Elves and took them to his dungeons, and with hideous acts of torture he made ruined and terrible forms of life. From these he bred a Goblin race of slaves who were as loathsome as Elves were fair.

These were the Orcs, a multitude brought forth in shapes twisted by pain and hate. The only joy of these creatures was in the pain of others, for the blood that flowed within Orcs was both black and cold. Their stunted form was hideous: bent, bow-legged and squat. Their arms were long and strong as the apes of the South, and their skin was black as wood that has been charred by flame. The jagged fangs in their wide mouths were yellow, their tongues red and thick, and their nostrils and faces were broad and flat. Their eyes were crimson gashes, like narrow slits in black iron grates behind which hot coals burn.

These Orcs were fierce warriors, for they feared more greatly their master than any enemy; and perhaps death was preferable to the torment of Orkish life. They were cannibals, ruthless and terrible, and often their rending claws and slavering fangs were gored with the bitter flesh and the foul black blood of their own kind. Orcs were spawned as thralls of the Master of Darkness; therefore they were fearful of light, for it weakened and burned them. Their eyes were night seeing, and they were dwellers of foul pits and tunnels. In Melkor's Utumno and in every foul dwelling in

Middle-earth they multiplied. More quickly than any other beings of Arda their progeny came forth from the spawning pits. At the end of the First Age of Stars was the War of the Powers in which the Valar came to Utumno and broke it open. They bound Melkor with a great chain, and destroyed Melkor's servants in Utumno and with them most of the Orcs. Those who survived were masterless and went wandering.

In the Ages that followed were the great migrations of the Elves, and, though Orcs lived in the dark places of Middle-earth, they did not appear openly, and the Elven histories speak not of Orcs until the Fourth Age of Stars. By this time the Orcs had grown troublesome. Out of Angband they came in armour of steel-plate and linked chains, and helmets of iron hoops and black leather, beaked like hawk or vulture with steel. They carried scimitars, poisoned daggers, arrows and broad-headed swords. This brigand race with Wolves and Werewolves dared in the Fourth Age of Stars to enter the realm of Beleriand where the Sindarin kingdom of Melian and Thingol stood. The Grey-elves knew not what manner of being the Orcs were, though they did not doubt they were evil. As these Elves did not use steel weapons at that time, they came to the Dwarf-smiths of Nogrod and Belegost and bartered for weapons of tempered steel. Then they slaughtered the Orcs and drove them away.

Yet when Melkor returned to Beleriand in the last Age of Stars, out of the Pits of Angband the Orcs came, rank upon rank, legion upon legion, in open war, and this was the beginning of the Wars of Beleriand. For in the valley of the River Gelion they were met by Thingol's Grey-elves and Denethor's Green-elves. In this First Battle the Orcs were decimated and driven shrieking in flight to the Blue Mountains, where they found no refuge but only the axes of the Dwarves. None of that army escaped. Yet Melkor had sent forth three grand armies. The second army overran the western lands of Beleriand and besieged the Falas, but the cities of the Falathrim did not fall. So the second army of Orcs joined the third army and marched north to Mithrim, where they thought they might entrap and slay the newly arrived Noldorin Elves. But the Orcs were little prepared for these Elves. In strength of body the Noldor were far beyond the darkest dreams of the Orcs. The eyes of these Elves alone seared the flesh of the Orcs, and the fierce light of Elven swords drove them mad with pain and fear. So the second Battle of Beleriand was fought against the Noldor whom Fëanor led, and this battle was called the Battle under Stars, the Dagor-nuin-Giliath. And though the Noldor king Fëanor was slain, the second and third armies of Melkor were entirely destroyed.

A second Noldor army led by the lord Fingolfin came out of the West and the great light of the Sun mounted the Ramparts of the

Sky as if with a great shout that brought fear to every servant of Melkor. So the First Age of Sun began and for a time the Orcs were checked by the new light of the Sun. However, soon under cover of darkness Orcs came in yet another grand army, more numerous than the other three and more heavily armed, hoping to catch the Noldor unaware. In the Glorious Battle, the Orc legions were slaughtered again. At this time the Siege of Angband was begun and, though Orcs at times sallied forth in bands, for the most part they were held within Angband's walls. Yet Melkor's might grew, for by dark sorcery he bred more of the Orc race and also the race of Dragons, and about him were Balrogs, Trolls, Werewolves and monsters many and great. When he deemed himself ready the mighty host came into the Battle of the Sudden Flame, and this broke the Siege of Angband and the Elven-lords were defeated. From this mighty battle is counted the reign of terror that the Orcs remember as the Great Years.

At that time Tol Sirion fell and the kingdoms of Hithlum, Mithrim, Dor-lómin and Dorthonion were overrun. The Battle of Unnumbered Tears was also fought: this was the Fifth Battle in the Wars of Beleriand and the Elves and Edain were completely defeated. The evil Orc legions of Angband then marched into Beleriand. The Falas fell to the Orcs, as did both the cities of Brithombar and Eglarest. The Battle of Tumhalad was fought and Nargothrond was sacked; because of disputes with Dwarves and the Noldor, Menegroth was twice overrun and the Grey-elf lands were ruined. Finally Gondolin, the Hidden Kingdom, fell. So Melkor's victory was all but complete; his Orc legions went wherever they wished in Beleriand. All the Elven kingdoms were ruined; no great city stood; and the lords and the greatest part of the Elves and Edain were slain. Such is the tale of days that are joyful to the black hearts of the Orcs.

Yet the terror of that Age finally came to an end. For the Valar, the Maiar, the Vanyar and the Noldor of Tirion, all came out of the Undying Lands and the Great Battle was joined. In it Angband was destroyed and all the mountains of the North were broken. Beleriand with Angband fell into the boiling sea; Melkor was cast out into the Void for ever more and his servants the Orcs were exterminated in the North.

Still the Orcs survived, for in the East and the South part of the race lay hidden in foul dens beneath dark mountains and hills. There they bred and multiplied. Eventually they came to Melkor's general, Sauron, offering their services, and he became their new master. In the Second Age of Sun they served Sauron well in the War of Sauron and the Elves and in all his battles until the War of the Last Alliance, when the Age ended with the fall of Mordor and with most of the Orkish race again being exterminated.

Yet in the Third Age of Sun, as in the Second, those Orcs hidden in dark and evil places lived on. Masterless, the Orcs raided and ambushed for many centuries, but made no grand schemes of conquest until more than a thousand years of the Age had passed, when, as a great and evil Eye, Sauron re-appeared in the dark realm of Dol Guldur in southern Mirkwood. As in the Second Age, the dark destinies of Sauron and the Orcs were again made one, and for two thousand years of the Third Age Orkish power increased with that of their Dark Lord.

Their power first grew in Mirkwood near Dol Guldur; then in the Misty Mountains. In 1300 the Nazgûl re-appeared in Mordor and the realm of Angmar in northern Eriador and the Orcs flocked to them. After six hundred years of terror, Angmar fell but the evil realm of Minas Morgul arose in Gondor, and there again the Orcs increased with those of Mirkwood, the Misty Mountains and Mordor for the next thousand years.

Yet it was said that Sauron was not fully pleased with his Orkish soldiery and he wished to increase their strength. And though no tale tells of it, it was believed that Sauron through terrible sorcery made a new breed of greater Orcs. For, in the year 2475, those creatures called the Uruk-hai came out of Mordor and sacked Osgiliath, the greatest city of Gondor. These Uruk-hai were Orcs grown to the height of Men, yet straight-limbed and strong. Though they were truly Orcs – black-skinned, black-blooded, lynx-eyed, fanged and claw-handed – Uruk-hai did not languish in sunlight and did not fear it at all. So the Uruk-hai could go where their evil brethren could not, and, being larger and stronger, they were also bolder and fiercer in battle. Clad in black armour, often carrying straight swords and long yew bows as well as many of the evil and poisoned Orc weapons, the Uruk-hai were made élite men-at-arms and most often were the high commanders and captains of the lesser Orcs.

In the centuries that followed, the Uruk-hai and the lesser Orcs grew still greater in power and made alliances that they might ruin all the kingdoms of Men and Elves that were in the Westlands. Therefore the Orcs made treaties with the Dunlendings, the Balchoth, the Wainriders, the Haradrim, the Easterlings of Rhûn and the Corsairs of Umbar to achieve their aim. The Orcs came even to the realms of the Dwarves. In the year 1980 Moria was taken by a mighty Balrog demon. With him were the Orcs of the Misty Mountains, who had come out of their capital of Gundabad in great numbers to inhabit the ancient Dwarvish city, heaping great contempt on the Dwarf people and slaying whosoever came near this most ancient realm.

Yet in the North this was to be the undoing of the Orcs, for the Dwarves were so enraged that they cared not at what cost they would have revenge. So it was that from 2793 to 2799 there was waged a seven years' war of extermination called the War of the Dwarves and Orcs. In this war, though dearly it cost the Dwarves, almost all the Orcs of the Misty Mountains were hunted out and slain, and at the East Gate of Moria the terrible Battle of Azanulbizar was fought. The Orcs were destroyed and the head of their Orc general, Azog, was impaled on a stake. So it was that for a century the Misty Mountains were cleansed of this vile race, yet in time they returned to Gundabad and Moria.

In the year 2941 a second great disaster befell the Orcs in the North. After the death of the Dragon Smaug, all the Orc warriors of Gundabad came to the Dwarf-realm of Erebor and the Battle of Five Armies was fought beneath the Lonely Mountain. The Orcs were led by Bolg of the North, son of Azog, and he wished to have vengeance on the Dwarves, but all he achieved was his own death and that of all his warriors.

In the War of the Ring, the last great conflict of the Third Age of Sun, the Orkish legions were everywhere, as the "Red Book of Westmarch" relates. From the Misty Mountains and the shadows of Mirkwood the Orcs came to war under banners both black and red. Fearless Uruk-hai with shields and helmets carrying the emblem of the White Hand came out of Isengard, where the rebel Wizard Saruman ruled. In Morgul both greater and lesser Orcs were marked with a white moon like a great skull; and under Sauron's command were the countless Orcs of Mordor of whatever breed, who were marked with the symbol of the Red Eye. All of these prepared for war and many others as well. They fought numerous skirmishes and ambushes, as well as the Battles of the Fords of Isen, the Battle of the Hornburg, the Battle of Pelennor Fields, the Battle under the Trees and the Battles of Dale. In these assaults thousands on both sides fell, and, though in many of these battles the Orcs were utterly vanquished, it is told that Sauron held back the greatest part of his force within Mordor until the enemy came to the northern gateway of his realm.

All was to be resolved in this one last battle before Morannon, the Black Gate. All the dreadful forces of Mordor were gathered there and at Sauron's command they fell on the army of the Captains of the West. However at that very moment, in the volcanic fires of Mount Doom, the One Ring of Power which held all Sauron's dark world in sway was destroyed. The Black Gate and the Black Tower burst asunder. The mightiest servants of Sauron were consumed in fire, the Dark Lord became black smoke dispelled by a west wind, and the Orcs perished like straw before flames. Though no doubt some Orcs survived, they never again rose in great numbers, but dwindled and became a minor Goblin folk possessed of but a rumour of their ancient evil power.

PERIANNATH In the histories of the War of the Ring it is told how the smallest and most timid of races, the HOBBITS, were the means by which the War was won. And so the Periannath, as the Hobbits were known in the Grey-elven tongue, became famed in the songs of Elves and Men and were praised for their valour.

PETTY-DWARVES The tales of Elves in the First Age of Sun tell of a remnant of an exiled people of the Dwarves who, lived in the land of Beleriand long before the Elves came. These were the Petty-dwarves and they inhabited the forest land of the River Narog and delved the halls of Amon Rûdh and Nulukkizdîn (which later became the Elven kingdom of Nargothrond). But when the Sindarin Elves came into the nearby land of Doriath, not knowing what manner of being these people were, they hunted them for sport. In time they learned they were but a diminished Dwarvish people who had become estranged from other Dwarves by some evil deed done long before in the land east of the Blue Mountains. So the Sindar ceased their persecution of this unhappy race, whom they called the Noegyth Nibin.

Yet in Beleriand these people dwindled. Having no allies in a land of strife, they enter the histories of Elves in the tales of Túrin. By that time the Petty-dwarves numbered only three: their lord, who was named Mîm, and his two sons, Ibun and Khîm. The "Tale of Grief" relates how Mîm led Túrin Turambar and his followers into the ancient Dwarf-delvings of Amon Rûdh, where they found shelter. But, later, Mîm was captured by Orcs and saved his own life by betraying Túrin and his band. So the Orcs made a surprise attack and slaughtered these Outlaws. Mîm won his freedom to no purpose, for both his sons perished, and, though he lived to gather a great Dragon hoard that Glaurung left behind in ruined Nargothrond, it happened that Túrin's father, the warrior called Húrin, came to Mîm's door. With a single blow Húrin slew Mîm in vengeance and so ended the life of the Petty-dwarf, the last to live within the Circles of the World.

PHANTOMS OF THE DEAD MARSHES Between the vast falls of the Great River Anduin and the dark mountains of Mordor there was an immense dreary fenland called the Dead Marshes. These Marshes were terrible and perilous, and in the Third Age of Sun they were an evil and haunted place. For it is told that at the end of the Second Age there was a mighty war before the Black Gate on the plain of Dagorlad. Innumerable warriors among the Last Alliance of Elves and Men died on that plain, and countless Orcs fell also. And so Elves, Men, Orcs and many other servants of Sauron were all buried on Dagorlad.

But in the Third Age the Marshlands spread eastwards and the graveyards of the warriors were swallowed by the fens. Great black pools appeared and they were crawling with evil beings. There were serpents and creeping life in these marshes, but no bird would visit the foul waters. From the evil stench and slime of these pools, where so many warriors rotted, haunting lights were seen. And these lights were said to be like candles lit, and in this light could be seen the faces of the dead: faces fair and evil; faces grim and decayed with death; evil Orkish faces and those of strong Men and bright Elves. Whether they were spirits or mirages of the dead is not known. These Phantoms of the Dead Marshes appeared in the pools but could not be reached. Their light beckoned travellers like a distant dream, and if travellers fell under their spell they would come to the dark water and disappear into the hideous pools. Such was the fate of those who travelled that way to the East. Such was the fate of those Easterlings called Wainriders, who in the twentieth century of that Age were driven far into the Dead Marshes after the Battle of the Camp.

PIPE-WEED Before the days of the War of the Ring the Hobbits were a quiet folk who could claim little influence on the World beyond the Shire. But of one thing, however, they did boast to be the makers and masters, and that was the smoking of the herb nicotiana, which was named Galenas in Elvish. When originally brought from the land of Númenórë by Men, it was prized only for the scent of its flower.

It was the Hobbits of Bree who grew it specially for the purpose of smoking in long-stemmed pipes. Knowing not the Elvish name for the plant, or caring little if they did, they renamed it Pipe-weed after its most common use. Hobbits derived great enjoyment from this pastime, and, in the way of Hobbits towards things of pleasure, smoking Pipe-weed was rated as a high art.

The Hobbits were also connoisseurs of fine Pipe-weeds, rating those of Bree and Southfarthing highest; then Longbottom Leaf, Old Toby, Southern Star and Southlinch. So from the centre of Bree, this most famous Hobbit habit spread over Middle-earth and was widely practised by Men and Dwarves.

PONIES On Middle-earth Ponies proved excellent servants of Hobbits and Dwarves, who, owing to their stature, could not ride on the backs of Horses. As beasts of burden, the Ponies also hauled the ore and trade ware of Dwarves and the field crops of Hobbits and Men.

In the annals of the Hobbits mention is given to those Ponies that aided the nine who went on the Quest of the Ring. By Tom Bombadil these were named: Sharp-ears, Swish-tail, Wise-nose, White-socks and Bumpkin. Bombadil's own Pony was called Fatty Lumpkin. The faithful beast that Samwise Gamgee befriended was just plain Bill.

PÚKEL-MEN On the great citadel of Dunharrow was set an ancient maze of walls and entrances that would break the advance of any army before it reached the Hold of Dunharrow. At each gate in the road huge stone guardians stood. These guardians were called Púkel-men by the Rohirrim who came to Dunharrow centuries after the race that had built this maze had vanished.

The Púkel-men statues were of crouched, pot-bellied Man-like beings with almost comic, grimacing faces. They have been compared to the Wild Men called the Woses of Druadan. Indeed it is likely that the Púkel-men were ancestors of the Woses, but of their relationship with the builders of Dunharrow no tale tells.

The builders of the vast fortifications were themselves only known as the Men of the White Mountains. They were thought to be the ancestors of the Dunlendings and in the early years of the Second Age they thrived for a time in the White Mountains.

QUENDI As the "Ainulindalë" tells, all things that came forth in the World were formed in the grand themes of the Music of the Ainur. And it was Ilúvatar alone who conceived of the themes that brought forth the race of ELVES. So when the Elves came to the World, awakening to the sight of Stars and the sound of water, it was as if the Music of the Spheres had been born within them. Of all beings in the World they were the first to speak. The voices of the Elves were beautiful and subtle as water, and they were curious of all things and went about the World naming all that they saw. They were teachers to all the races and creatures on Earth who would learn the arts of speech and song.

So it was that the Elves named themselves the Quendi, which is the "Speakers", after their greatest art, and they named their language Quenya, which is simply the "speech". All tongues of the World came from this one source, which is the root and which is most fair to the ears of all who love forms of beauty. The giant Ents were the first race to learn speech from the Quendi, but soon the skill spread until even Men and the evil Orcs and Trolls learned of its use.

And though Quenya was the first tongue of the Quendi, it was not their only tongue. For the Avari and the Silvan Elves spoke dialects that changed through the Ages of Stars and Sun as the lands of Middle-earth changed. Because of the Teleri's long exile upon Tol Eressëa the tongue of this Third Kindred who inhabited Alqualondë was also a dialect of the ancient speech. Only among the Vanyar and the Noldor in the Undying Lands did Quenya remain close to the language that was spoken at the time of the Awakening.

Because the Sindar Elves for many Ages ruled the western lands and because they were more numerous than the Noldor exiles, all the Eldar in Middle-earth commonly used the Sindarin tongue. Indeed, by the Third Age of Sun, only the Eldar, the Ents and the Dúnedain lords still knew Quenya, and even to these it was the language not of daily use but that of high ceremony, ancient songs and tales and Elvish histories.

RANGERS OF ITHILIEN At the end of the twenty-ninth century of the Third Age of Sun, Túrin II, the Ruling Steward of Gondor, decreed that a brotherhood of knights be formed in North Ithilien, for Gondor's power in that land was threatened by enemies from Mordor and Morgul. So the band called the Rangers of Ithilien was formed. These knights were dressed in foresters' green, and they fought with bows, spears and swords. In the years before the War of the Ring, their captain was Faramir, second son of Denethor, Gondor's Ruling Steward. Greatest of their dwellings was that refuge of caves and tunnels behind a great waterfall that looked far over the Vales of Anduin. This place was called Henneth Annûn, the "window of the sunset".

RANGERS OF THE NORTH Through many centuries of the Third Age of Sun in the lands of Eriador, there roamed grim-faced Men clothed in cloaks of forest-green or grey, with clasps like silver Stars on their left shoulders. They were grey-eyed, armed with sword and spear, and they wore long leather boots. By the common folk of Eriador they were called Rangers, and they were thought to be a strange, unfriendly people. For though they wandered over all the lands of Eriador on foot or on strange shaggy Horses, they did so silently. Indeed few knew who these tough weather-worn Rangers were, or from where they had come. But, as the "Red Book of Westmarch" reveals, the Rangers were in fact the last nobles and knights of that once great Dúnedain realm of Arnor, and their chieftain was the High Dúnedain king. In the years before and after the War of the Ring this was Aragorn, son of Arathorn, who as a Ranger was called Strider. At that time one named Halbarad, who was slain on Pelennor Fields, was Aragorn's chief lieutenant among the Rangers, while the famous sons of Elrond Half-elven, Elladan and Elrohir, also rode in that company.

At the War's end Aragorn was crowned King Elessar, lord of the twin Dúnedain realms of Arnor and Gondor, and the Rangers were honoured among the greatest Men of that re-united kingdom.

RAVENS Many races of birds lived on Middle-earth. Among those named in the tales were the Eagles, which were noblest of all birds, and the Ravens, which were strong and long-living.

Part of the tale of the slaying of Smaug, the Dragon of Erebor, tells of the Ravens of Erebor, which in the Third Age of Sun served the Dwarves of Durin's Line. These Ravens were wise counsellors and swift messengers of the Dwarves, and they were skilled in many tongues. At that time Roäc, son of Carc, was lord of the Ravens. He was ancient, his life having spanned more than one hundred and fifty years. By his will and wisdom he ruled the Ravens. And in the common tongue of Westron Roäc spoke to his Dwarvish friends and brought them news and aid.

REGION Among the trees of Middle-earth was one that Elves called Region, and Men called holly. Part of the realm of Sindar was named after that tree. This was the dense forest area of East Beleriand, which lay within the guarded realm of Doriath.

Holly was widespread in Middle-earth, but in few places did it grow luxuriantly. One of the areas where it was most widely known was Eregion, which means "land of the holly". The Elven-smiths lived there in the Second Age of Sun, and it was there that the mighty Rings of Power were forged.

RINGWRAITHS Nine was the number of the mighty wraiths that Sauron released in Middle-earth after the forging of the Rings of Power. In Black Speech they were named the NAZGÛL, which in the common tongue is "Ringwraiths"; and they were the chief servants and generals of Sauron.

The tale of the evil deeds of the Ringwraiths is long, and the phantom shadows of these Black Riders brought terror to the hearts of even the bravest peoples of Middle-earth.

RIVER-WOMEN In the histories and writings of Middle-earth, mention is made of the River-women. Whether, like Ossë and Uinen, these were Maiar of Ulmo, Lord of the Waters, or whether they were spirits who came into the World like Ents, is not told; but it is certain they were chiefly concerned with the Kelvar and Olvar of the World.

The "Red Book of Westmarch" tells how the River-woman of the Withywindle had a daughter named Goldberry, who was the wife of Tom Bombadil. This River-daughter was golden-haired and bright as an Elf-maiden. Her garments were often silver and green, and flowers continuously blossomed in the spring of her light and laughter.

ROHIRRIM In the year 2510 of the Third Age of Sun a host of golden-haired horsemen came to the Battle of the Field of Celebrant to rescue the routed army of Gondor from the Balchoth and Orc hordes. These were the Éothéod whom the Men of Gondor later named the Rohirrim, the "Horse-lords". They were Northmen who inhabited the Vales of Anduin, and they were renowned as warriors and Horse-masters.

King Eorl the Young was most praised of their people, for he first tamed the Mearas, the noblest and fairest Horses of Middle-earth, which were said to be descended from Nahar, Oromë the Vala's steed. And, as is told in the "Book of Kings", it was Eorl the Young who had brought his warriors to the Battle of the Field of Celebrant. At the desire of the Men of Gondor, Eorl made a kingdom in the province of Calenardhon, which was renamed Rohan and the Mark. And he was made the first of the kings of Rohan who for five centuries of the Third Age ruled the Mark.

Yet the Rohirrim were often called to war, to defend both Gondor and Rohan, for they were bordered by many enemies. The Rohirrim were constantly prepared for battle and always wore silver corselets and bright mail. They were armed with spears and with long swords that were set with green gems. Their hair was braided in long golden plaits, and they wore silver helmets with flowing horsetail manes. They carried green shields emblazoned with a golden Sun and green banners adorned with a white Horse.

So armed, and mounted on steeds white and grey, the blue-eyed Rohirrim advanced against Easterlings, Dunlendings, Haradrim, Uruk-hai and Orcs.

On the rolling hills near the White Mountains were built the royal courts of Edoras in which was Meduseld, the feast hall of Rohan's kings, which was roofed with gold. The histories of the nine kings of the Mark are chronicled in the "Annals of the Kings and Rulers". After Eorl the Young, the king of the greatest fame was Helm Hammerhand, the last of the First Line of kings. For though in his time Rohan suffered disaster by Dunlending Invasions, famine and the bitter cold that came in the Long Winter of the year 2759, this king's valour and strength was so great that his name alone brought terror to his enemies. For it is said Helm walked through blizzards of snow without weapons, and with his hands alone slew his foes. And though he died before the Long Winter ended, the Dunlendings claimed his wraith remained to haunt them for many years after.

The tale of the War of the Ring tells how Théoden, the last of the Second Line of kings, fell under the power of the Wizard Saruman. But with the aid of Gandalf Théoden threw off that enchantment and led his warriors to victory at the Battles of the Hornburg and of Pelennor Fields against the Dark Powers. And though he was an old Man, it is told how he slew a king of Harad

211

on the Pelennor Fields and was granted a warrior's death there also, for he in turn was slain by the Witch-king of Morgul.

So the lordship of the Rohirrim passed to Théoden's sister's son, who was named Éomer. He was counted among the greatest kings of the Mark, for with the Men of Gondor he made firm the old alliance. After the War of the Ring he often subdued the peoples of the East and South, and the Rohirrim had victory and their children lived in peace in the Fourth Age of Sun.

Yet in the War of the Ring there was one other of the Rohirrim who won the greatest fame. This was Éowyn, the fair sister of Éomer. For though she was slender and tall she was filled with strength and was wise in the use of weapons of war. As a warrior of Rohan she came to the Battle of Pelennor Fields, and over Théoden, the fallen king, she stood against the Witch-king of Morgul. She then achieved a deed that in four thousand years of terror the mightiest warriors of all Middle-earth could not, for it had been foretold that the Witch-king could not be slain by the hand of Man. So Éowyn revealed that she was not a Man but a shield-maiden, and with her sword she first slew the Winged Beast that was the wraith's steed and then with the aid of the Hobbit, Meriadoc Brandybuck, she slew the Witch-king himself.

212

SEA-ELVES Of all the Elves, the Third Kindred, the TELERI, most loved the seas of Ulmo the Ocean Lord and lived longest on the shores of Belegaer, the Sea of the West. They were wisest in its lore and so were named the Sea-elves. They were the first people to build ships, for they were taught by Ossë, a Maia of the turbulent waves. His spouse was Uinen, Lady of the Calms, and together they taught the Sea-elves about the life in the sea: its fishes and its grottoes and gardens, and the wealth of its stones and pearls.

And so the Sea-elves sailed on the sea in the fairest ships, which were white and shaped like the great Swans of Ulmo that once drew them to the shores of Eldamar. And in the Undying Lands they sail and sing with voices like the rippling waves, for they know the language of the sea, which is subtle beyond the reckoning of the wisest of the races of Men.

SECONDBORN Before the World was made, in that dimension before Time began, it had been foretold that Ilúvatar alone would call forth two great peoples out of the World to Be. The Firstborn of Ilúvatar was the immortal race of Elves, who arose with the Rekindling of the Stars. Those named the Secondborn, the mortal race of MEN, came into being when Arien the Sun first shone on Middle-earth. In the Quenya tongue Secondborn translates as "Atani", and in Sindarin as "Edain"; and these were the names by which the first Men of Beleriand were known.

SHADOW HOST In the War of the Ring there was a great battle before the ancient port of Pelargir when the ships of the Corsairs of Umbar were conquered by phantom warriors. These warriors were the DEAD MEN OF DUNHARROW, ghosts who through the long years of the Third Age had lingered on Earth because of a broken oath. To fulfil that oath and become released from limbo, this Shadow Host led by Aragorn, son of Arathorn, came to battle against the Corsairs, enemy of the Dúnedain. Once victory was assured the vast phantom army vanished from Earth for ever.

SILVAN ELVES In the Ages that followed the Rising of the Sun and the Moon, many of the gentle Wood-elves of the East drifted westwards. They were descended from the Avari, who refused the summons of the Valar and did not go on the Great Journey in the years of Starlight. In the years of Sun these were named Silvan Elves, for most of them lived in forests; they were a tribal people who built no cities and had no kings.

In the years that followed the First Age of Sun, however, the numbers and lands of these Noldorin and Sindarin Elves had dwindled and to swell their kingdoms these High Elves took Silvan Elves as their subjects. In this way the Silvan Elves learned much of the High Elven language and culture, and many of the skills that had come from the Undying Lands. For a time the Silvan Elves grew strong and prosperous under these lords. The greatest power and beauty were to be found in the Silvan Elves whom Celeborn and Galadriel ruled in the Golden Wood of Lothlórien. For Celeborn, kinsman of Thingol, was counted among the greatest lords of the Sindar, and Galadriel was the daughter of the High King of the Noldor, who had remained in the Undying Lands; thus she was noblest of Elves who remained in Middle-earth. The power of Celeborn and Galadriel over the Golden Wood held evil powers at bay, and the Silvan Elves remained prosperous through the troubles of the Third Age though thrice attacked. These Elves were the Galadhrim, "tree-people", and not until Queen Galadriel finally went to the Undying Lands did the light and glory of the Golden Wood fade.

It is also told in the Elvish writings how in Greenwood the Great (which was later named Mirkwood) through the Second, Third and Fourth Ages of Sun there was the Woodland Kingdom of the Sindar lord Thranduil. The concealed city of the Silvan Elves of Thranduil was beautiful and magical, for it was the diminished image of the ancient Sindar realm of Menegroth – once the fairest city of Middle-earth. But a part of its beauty had lived on and withstood the dark invasions of the Third Age, even the Battle under the Trees during the War of the Ring. It is told that in the Fourth Age, the son of the king took part of the Silvan Elves of this realm to the woodlands of Ithilien in Gondor. This prince was named Legolas and he became lord of the Elves in Ithilien. For a time these people also prospered, for this was the Elf who had won fame in the War of the Ring and who with his great friend Gimli the Dwarf had fought in the battles of the Hornburg, Pelargir and Pelennor Fields. Indeed, as one of the Fellowship of the Ring, his bright Elvish eyes, his forester's knowledge and his keen archery were much needed in the Quest. And though Legolas ruled his new realm for many years in the Fourth Age, after a time, with Gimli, he took an Elven-ship to the Undying Lands.

SIMBELMYNË Near Edoras, the Golden Hall of the kings of the Mark, there lay the great barrow graves of the kings who for the last five hundred years of the Third Age of Sun had ruled Rohan. By the end of the Third Age the graves were laid in two rows: one of nine for those of the First Line; the other of eight for those of the Second Line. And on these graves, like glittering snow, grew the white flowers called Simbelmynë, which in common speech of Men is "Evermind". They blossomed in all seasons, like the bright eyes of Elves, glinting always with starlight.

Simbelmynë grew whitest and thickest on the grave of Helm Hammerhand, the ninth king of the First Line, who during the Siege of the Hornburg went alone among his foes, the Dunlendings. And Simbelmynë reminds these foes of him who was the fiercest king of the Mark. Through the famine of the Fell Winter Helm Hammerhand had sounded his mighty horn and like a snow-troll hunted his foes and slew them. And though he perished at that time, his wraith was said still to walk the land and his horn could be heard in the Helm's Deep.

SINDAR How the Grey-elves, who are called the Sindar, came to be a separate race is told in the tale of the Journey of the Elves. In the beginning they were of the Third Kindred, the Teleri, and their king was the High King of all the Teleri. In those first years he was named Elwë Singollo and he was the tallest of Elves. His hair was silver and he alone of the Teleri (with the Noldor lord Finwë and the Vanyar lord Ingwë) was taken by Oromë, the Horseman of the Valar, to the Undying Lands to experience the Light of the Trees of the Valar. When Elwë Singollo was brought back to his people to tell them what awaited the Elves in the Undying Lands no one was more eager to reach the Light than he. The Teleri were largest of the hosts that went to the West but because they were so numerous they were always farthest behind on the long road. Many of the Teleri were lost on that Journey, but Elwë always urged them on, until they came at last to Beleriand beyond the Blue Mountains.

In Beleriand for a time they made a camp near the River Gelion in a wood. In this place, according to Elven-lore, Elwë Singollo entered the Wood of Nan Elmoth and fell under a timeless spell. His people searched for him, but as years passed many gave up hope and gave the kingship to Olwë, his brother, and they resumed their Journey to the West. But many others would have no other king and would not leave that place. So these people remained in Beleriand and called themselves the Eglath, the "forsaken", and thereafter they were divided from the Teleri.

In time, the Eglath had their reward, for Elwë Singollo returned from the Wood of Nan Elmoth but the great change that had occurred in him amazed his people. With him came the source of

216

his enchantment: Melian the Maia, Elwë's queen and wife. The light of her face was brilliant and lovely, and the Eglath worshipped her and wept in joy at the return of their king.

The king was changed in other ways, for he wished no longer to go to the West but to stay in the Forest of Beleriand and draw about him his people and make a kingdom there. The light on the face of Melian was to him more fair than that of the Trees. So a new kingdom was made; its people were no longer called the Eglath but the Sindar, the "Grey-elves", and the Elves of the Twilight.

In the Ages of Stars the Sindar became the greatest of the Elvish people in Mortal Lands and all the lands of Beleriand belonged to them. They found a remnant of the Teleri, called the Falathrim, living by the sea and these people, under their lord Círdan, welcomed the returned king and swore allegiance to him. So it was too with a remnant of the Nandor who had come to Beleriand (and were later named the Green-elves and Laiquendi); these people also accepted Elwë as their king. In time, a new Elvish tongue arose among the Sindar and in that Sindarin language their king was no longer Elwë Singollo, but Elu Thingol "King Greymantle".

In the Ages of Starlight, it is told, a strange people who called themselves Khazâd came out of the Blue Mountains; the Elves called them Naugrim, the "stunted people". They were Dwarves, who came in peace to trade with the Elves of Beleriand. There was great prosperity between the two peoples and they learned many crafts from each other. With the help of the Dwarves the greatest Elven city of Middle-earth was built, called Menegroth the "thousand caves". Though it was a city within a mountain, it was described as a beech forest in which gold lanterns shone, birds sang, beasts wandered and silver fountains ran. It was always light there and throughout the forests around Menegroth, for this Sindarin kingdom was all-powerful, being ruled by a combination of Elf and Maia. From the union of Elu Thingol and Melian came forth a daughter who was called Lúthien, and the tales say she was the fairest creature ever to enter the World.

But the Ages of peace beneath the Stars drew to an end; war broke out in Valinor and the Trees of the Valar were destroyed. Melian, however, was a wise queen, gifted with foreknowledge, and she chose to take the Sindar away from the evil that was to befall the land about them. She cast a powerful spell and wove an enchantment in the Great Forest of Doriath around Menegroth, so that the Sindarin realm became a hidden kingdom. This enchantment was stronger than any citadel's high walls and was named the Girdle of Melian, and no evil could break that spell from without, and all evil was lost before it could enter.

So, though the Noldor, pursuing Morgoth, came out of the Undying Lands and in Beleriand the War of the Jewels raged, for the

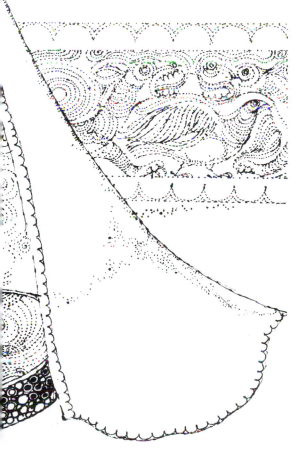

most part the Sindar were not at risk. Nor did they choose to deal with or aid these Kinslayers, for they had heard of the Noldorin deeds in the Undying Lands and how the Noldor had slain their kindred the Teleri of Alqualondë.

But as is told in the tale of Lúthien and Beren, great evil came in unexpected ways from within the kingdom. For of the race of Men, one named Beren came to Thingol and asked for the hand of Lúthien. Thingol, looking on mortals with disdain, was tempted to put him to death, but rather than slay him he set him an impossible task. As a bride-price Beren was to cut a Silmaril from Morgoth's Iron Crown and bring it to Thingol. This was the Quest of the Silmaril, which brought so much evil to the Sindar. This Quest drew the Sindar into the Doom of the Noldor and the curse that lay on the Silmarils.

In a deed beyond belief, Beren with the help of Lúthien and the Wolfhound Huan completed his task, but he incurred not only the wrath of Morgoth but also that of the Dwarves and the Noldor. For, desiring the Silmaril, the Dwarf workmen who lived within the Hidden Realm and had laboured for Thingol now murdered him and stole the jewel, though they could not escape and were themselves killed. On the death of Thingol, Melian veiled her power and, weeping, left Middle-earth for ever. In that moment the ring of enchantment fell from the Hidden Realm.

Now that a barrier no longer guarded it, the Dwarves of Belegost and the Noldor sons of Fëanor came to the citadel of Menegroth and laid it waste. So the great kingdom was gone for ever, though a few of its lords survived.

In the Second Age of Sun some of these Sindar lords with many of the Noldor took ships to Tol Eressëa and built the city and haven of Avallónë. But there were other Sindar lords who remained in the remnant of Beleriand called Lindon. As the years passed some sons of the Sindar lords left Lindon for the lands beyond the Misty Mountains, where they made new kingdoms among the Silvan Elves. Two of the most famous were Thranduil, who went to Greenwood the Great and there made the Woodland Realm, and Celeborn, the kinsman of Thingol, who with the Noldor princess Galadriel made the kingdom of Lothlórien, the Golden Wood. Then too some Sindar lords settled in Rivendell with Elrond and in the Grey Havens with Círdan the Shipwright. In the War of the Ring the most famous Elf was Legolas, the son of Thranduil. Legolas was one of the nine heroes of the Fellowship of the Ring, and after the War of the Ring he founded one last woodland Elf-colony in the fair forests of Ithilien in Gondor.

Finally, in the Fourth Age of Sun, all the Eldar powers were fading from the World, and with the other Elves the last of the Sindar sailed from the Grey Havens to the Undying Lands.

SNAGA Among those evil beings that in the histories of Middle-earth are named Orcs, there were many breeds, each it seemed being made to suit some particular evil. The most common breed was that which in Black Speech was called Snaga, meaning "slaves". Orcs, being creatures filled with hatred, were also self-contemptuous, for they were indeed a race of slaves and were thralls to the Dark Powers who directed them.

SNOWMEN In the northern land of Forochel, in the Third Age of Sun, there lived a primitive people who were descendants of the ancient Forodwaith. In Sindarin these were the LOSSOTH, but in the common western tongue they were called the Snowmen of Forochel. They were not a strong people and they chose to live on the shore of a great icy bay so that they might be beyond the reach of the more warlike folk of the South. They were a wary people, but wise in the ways of ice and snow and able to withstand the harshness of the wastes. They hunted where other folk could find no game; they built warm homes of snow where others would perish of terrible cold; and they travelled swiftly over ice with skates of bone and sledges where others would flounder and make no passage at all. Indeed they were undisputed masters of this frozen land of their choice.

SOUTHRONS A part of the histories of the Westlands is given to the fierce people who, in the Second and Third Age of Sun, came from the hot deserts and forests of the Sunlands, which lay in the South of Middle-earth. These people were ruled by many kings and lords, until in time Sauron the Maia corrupted them and called them to war. The Dúnedain named them Southrons, though more often they were called the HARADRIM.

The Southrons were brown- and black-skinned Men who came forth fiercely in war, ornamented with much gold. Their banner was a black serpent on a scarlet ground. Their armour was of bronze, their robes crimson, and they carried spears and scimitars. They came on foot, by sea, on Horses and on the backs of the mighty war beasts that are named Mûmakil.

SPEAKERS The ELVES were conceived in the Music of the Ainur and were the first race to give voice to the music and make song. They were also the first race to use speech in Arda, and it is said that their speech was as bright and subtle as starlight on running water. For their language was not just the first but also the fairest tongue that ever was conceived. The Elves therefore called themselves the Speakers, which in that first Elven tongue was the "Quendi". All living beings who could learn such skills were taught the arts of language from these first Elves.

SPIDERS Among the foulest beings that ever inhabited Arda were the Great Spiders. They were dark and filled with envy, greed and the poison of malice. Greatest of the giant beings that took Spider form was Ungoliant, a mighty and evil spirit that entered the World before the Trees of the Valar were made. In the waste land of Avathar, between the Pelóri Mountains and the dull cold sea of the South, Ungoliant lived alone for a long while. She was dreadful and vile, and possessed of a web of darkness called the Unlight of Ungoliant that even the eyes of Manwë could not penetrate.

The Great Spider Ungoliant was the most infamous creature, for she came with Melkor to Valinor and destroyed the Trees of the Valar. And, as she devoured the Light of the Trees, Ungoliant tried to take even Melkor as her prey. Had not the demons of fire called Balrogs come and lashed her with their whips of flame, she might have devoured the Lord of Darkness himself.

But come the Balrogs did, and they drove Ungoliant from the North. And so this heart of darkness came into Beleriand and she entered that place called Nan Dungortheb, the "valley of dreadful death", where other monsters of her race lived. Though not so vast nor so powerful as Ungoliant, these Spiders were none the less immensely strong, for Melkor had bred them long ago among the evil monsters that came forth before the Light of the Trees was made. Ungoliant now bred with them, and few Elves or Men ever dared to enter that valley.

Yet, perhaps Ungoliant was too vast an evil for the World to hold. In time she travelled beyond Beleriand to the south lands, pursuing whatever she could consume, for her gluttony was a fearful thing, and it is said that in her ravening hunger she finally consumed herself in the deserts of the South. In Nan Dungortheb her many daughters lived all the years of the First Age of Sun, but, when the land was broken in the War of Wrath, it is said few could save themselves from the rushing waters.

But, among the few, one great daughter called Shelob and some of the lesser Spiders crossed the Blue Mountains and found shelter in the Shadowy Mountains, which walled the realm of Mordor. In the mountain passes of this evil place the Spiders grew strong again, and in the Third Age of Sun they came into the forest of Greenwood the Great. This they made evil with the ambush of their webs and so Greenwood went dark and was re-named Mirkwood. Though the Spiders of Mirkwood were but small forms compared to their great ancestors, they were large in number and wise in their evil craft of entrapment. They spoke both Black Speech and the common tongue of Men, but in the Orkish fashion, full of evil words and slurring rage.

After the First Age of Sun only Shelob the Great approached the majesty of Ungoliant; she inhabited the place called Cirith Ungol,

the "Spider's pass", in the Shadowy Mountains. For two Ages she lived in this pass, and, though many a Dúnedain and Elvish warrior came to her realm, none could stand before her and she devoured them all. Like her great mother she spun black webs and vomited darkness from her belly. She was armed with venom from her great beak and horns, and she had a long claw of iron on each of her many gnarled and jointed legs. Her bloated body was black and thick-skinned. There was no vulnerable place on the beast except the great, globed cluster of her eyes. Her vast form was black and stained, with hair-like spikes of steel and an underbelly paled with streaks of green slime and luminous with her septic poisons. Vast and strong as she was, Shelob's long life ended before the Third Age was gone. She met her end at the unexpected hand of the Hobbit Samwise Gamgee, the least of all her challengers. For the Hobbit put out one of Shelob's great eyes, and by her own act Shelob impaled herself upon his Elven-blade. Before the end of the Third Age, the greater part of the Great Spiders had also disappeared from the World, for after the mortal wounding of Shelob, Mordor and Dol Guldur were destroyed and the Spiders of the Shadowy Mountains and the Spiders of Mirkwood perished.

STOORS Alone of the three Hobbit strains, those named Stoors knew the arts of boating, fishing and swimming. They were lovers of flat river lands and were most friendly with Men. The Harfoots thought the Stoors a queer folk. Last of the Hobbits to settle in the Shire, the Stoors had attained a Mannish appearance in the eyes of the Harfoots, for they were heavier and broader than the other strains and, unlike other Hobbits, they were able to grow beards.

SWANS It is told in the tale of the Great Journey of the Elves how the Teleri were brought at last to Eldamar by the Swans of Ulmo after long exile on Tol Eressëa, the Lonely Isle.

Ossë the Maia had come to the Teleri and taught them how to build a great fleet that could carry all their Kindred. Once the ships were made, the Swans of Ulmo, Lord of the Waters, came out of the West. These brilliant creatures were foam white and they circled in great broken rings round the ships of the Elves. The feathered glory of these birds was nearly equal to the size and strength of the Eagles

of Manwë. By many long ropes, the Swans drew the great fleet of Elven-ships to Eldamar. Then, vast and stately, as if unaware of their mission and hearing some wild call, they departed. But before those indifferent beaks let drop the towing lines, that white rush engendered in the hearts of Elves a knowledge of the winds that play on the seas and a mastery of their white ships that sail on them. It is said that when these Elves listen to the sea on the Shore they hear those great wings beating still.

After that time the Teleri were named Sea-elves because of the wisdom that they gained from the great Swans. In that place to which the Swans of Ulmo had brought them the Teleri made a city named Alqualondë, the "haven of Swans". There they made the finest ships of Arda, even more cunningly fashioned than those first ones, and they built them in the forms of the Swans of Ulmo, with vast, white wings and beaks of jet and gold.

SWARTHY MEN In the First Age of Sun those Men who came after the Edain to Beleriand were named EASTERLINGS. However, some called them Swarthy Men, for they were shorter, broader and darker of hair and eye than the Edain. Mostly they were a less worthy people, and they betrayed the Elves.

But, in the Third Age, Swarthy Men was a name given to the tall, brown-skinned HARADRIM, who many times made war on the Men of Gondor. They were fierce Men dressed in crimson and gold. On foot, on Horse and on the mighty Mûmakil they went into battle with scimitar, bow and spear.

SWERTINGS In the last centuries of the Third Age of Sun rumours and tales reached the peaceful Hobbit lands of the Shire about the wars between the Men of Gondor and the fierce warrior people far to the south who were named the HARADRIM. In the dialect of the Shire the Haradrim were called Swertings.

TARELDAR Those of the Elven people who heeded the summons of the Valar, departed to the West and looked on the Blessed Realm in the days of the Light of the Trees were in the Quenya tongue called Tareldar and HIGH ELVES. They were a great people who thrived and built Elven cities and kingdoms the like of which had never been seen in Middle-earth, and never will be again, for the Tareldar were clear-sighted and keen-eyed beyond imagining. To compare them to the Moriquendi is to compare diamonds to coal.

TARKS In the Westron dialect there were many words taken from Elvish that were twisted in Orkish use. One of these was the Quenya word "tarkil", meaning the Dúnedain. In the Orc usage this became Tark, a word of contempt for the GONDOR MEN.

TASARION Among the most ancient of trees were those that the first Elves called the Tasarion. With many other kinds of tree they had come into the World in the Ages of the Lamps at the wish of Yavanna, Queen of the Earth. The Tasarion were strong and long-lived, and in the Ages of Starlight the greatest forest of these trees on Middle-earth was in the Nan-tasarion, the "valley of the Tasarion", in Beleriand. And though this forest was destroyed when Beleriand sank beneath the sea, the species of Tasarion survived all the changes of the World, and even the great invasions by the race of Men. For the Tasarion are the trees Men call the WILLOW.

TELCONTARI At the end of the War of the Ring a new line of kings was established to rule over the dual realms of Arnor and Gondor. The first of this line was Aragorn, son of Arathorn, who became King Elessar. He chose Telcontar as the name of his House, for this was the Quenya form of Strider, the name by which he went in his years of exile. His descendants and successors preserved the name of the House that Aragorn had founded, calling themselves the Telcontari.

GOLDEN HALL OF THE ROHIRRIM

The greatest allies of the Dúnedain in the Third Age were the Rohirrim. These were the finest horsemen of Middle-earth and from Meduseld, the Golden Hall, their kings had ruled Rohan for five hundred years. At the outbreak of the War of the Ring, however, the Rohirrim withheld their aid from the Dúnedain because their king was under the evil influence of the rebel Wizard Saruman. But Gandalf and three others of the Fellowship of the Ring came to the Golden Hall, and because of these emissaries the knights of Rohan cast off their fear. Honouring their old alliance with the Dúnedain of Gondor, the Rohirrim bravely entered the War of the Ring.

FALL OF ISENGARD

In the War of the Ring, it seemed that the evil allies of Sauron the Ring Lord arose everywhere out of the dark lands. One such mighty ally was the rebel Wizard Saruman who held the tower and citadel of Isengard. Once thought to be a friend of the Men of Gondor and Rohan and therefore granted the keys to Isengard, Saruman later became seduced by the Ring Lord and was drawn into league with him. Thereafter Saruman surrounded himself with Orcs, Uruk-hai, Dunlendings and Half-orcs.

Other beings unexpectedly came into the War because they had been harmed by the servants of Saruman who had burned and laid waste the forests about Isengard. The mighty giants called Ents came against Saruman. Half-Men, half-trees, these ancient guardians of the forests were the tallest and strongest race on Middle-earth. While Saruman's great armies marched out to fight the Rohirrim, rank upon rank of these fearsome giants attacked Isengard. Their strength was so great that with their bare hands alone the Ents tore down the very walls of the fortress. They imprisoned the Wizard within his own tower and made a fair garden of that evil place.

BATTLE OF THE HORNBURG

Before the Rohirrim could support their allies, the Men of Gondor, in the War of the Ring against the Dark Lord of Mordor, they discovered they must first deal with an enemy that had arisen within their own lands. For the army of the rebel Wizard Saruman, which comprised a multitude of Uruk-hai, Orcs, Half-orcs and fierce Dunlendings, had advanced out of Isengard and had come wrathfully on the Horsemen of Rohan. At great cost, the army of Isengard drove the Rohirrim before them, until the Horsemen were forced to seek refuge in the ancient citadel in Helm's Deep called the Hornburg. Here three of the Ring Fellowship – Aragorn, the Dwarf Gimli and the Elf-prince Legolas – joined the Rohirrim.

A great battle was then fought and, though the Enemy stormed the earthwork defences and broke the very gates of the fortress, they were driven from the high walls by the Rohirrim cavalry. Then on the battle-ground of Deeping-coomb the Enemy was trapped by a second army of Rohirrim brought by Gandalf, supported by an even mightier army of Huorns that the Ents commanded. So the army of Isengard was utterly crushed and the threat to the lands of Rohan was removed.

229

THE DEAD MARSHES

Between the Fal ls of Rauros on the River Anduin and the mountains of Mordor was the vast fenland called the Dead Marshes. On this foul, trackless wasteland few ever dared to travel, for not only were the Marshes pathless and the waters stagnant and poisoned but they were also haunted by the phantoms of dead Men, Elves and Orcs. Yet, to achieve his Quest, Frodo the Ringbearer and his companion had to cross the Marshes, so they forced the creature called Gollum to guide them through this evil land.

THE WITCH-KING OF MORGUL

The mightiest servant of Sauron was the Nazgûl lord called the Witch-king. This wraith served Sauron through the Accursed Years of the Second Age of Sun, but with the fall of the Ring Lord at the end of that Age he faded from the World. In the year 1300 of the Third Age this wraith was resurrected by Sauron and went to Angmar, where he became known as the Witch-king of Angmar. Through many centuries of war he destroyed the Dúnedain of Arnor, though Angmar was destroyed soon after. He then rose again in the South and took command of the tower of Minas Morgul in Gondor.

In the War of the Ring the Witch-king was the most immediate and most deadly foe of the Men of Gondor. To him came the Orc legions, Uruk-hai, Olog-hai and Trolls out of Mordor. To him also came the Easterlings, the Variags and the Haradrim allies. As the Ringbearer passed into Mordor he watched the Witch-king and his mighty army pour out of the dark citadel of Minas Morgul and march to war against the Men of the White Tower of Gondor.

232

WOUNDING OF SHELOB THE GREAT

In the mountains of Mordor there was one little-used pass called Cirith Ungol. Few ever attempted to enter Mordor by this way, for the guardian of the pass was Shelob the Great, last ancient daughter of Ungoliant, the Great Spider that devoured the Trees of the Valar.

Yet dangerous as this pass was, the Ringbearer and his companion penetrated it, for this was their only chance of entry into Mordor. By the treachery of Gollum and the strength of Shelob, the Ringbearer was struck down and brought near to death until his servant, Samwise Gamgee, valiantly leapt to his defence. With the Elf-blade Sting, Sam wounded the Great Spider, and with the light of the Phial of Galadriel he poured deadly pain into her open wounds. Mortally hurt, Shelob dragged her evil form away from the fight and, tortured by the light of the Phial, she died miserably in her foul den in that high pass of Cirith Ungol.

BATTLE OF PELENNOR FIELDS

The greatest battle of the War of the Ring was fought on Pelennor Fields before the White Tower of Gondor, which was besieged by the army of the Witch-king of Morgul. Haradrim cavalry and infantry in scarlet and gold marched into battle with elephantine Mûmakil, Variags of Khand and axe-bearing Easterlings. Orcs, Uruk-hai, Olog-hai, Trolls and Half-orcs out of Mordor joined this vast host. Ranged against them were the Captains of the Outlands from Dol Amroth, Lossarnach, Anfalas, Morthond, Ethir and Pinnath Gelin. This army of Gondor was driven back from Osgiliath and Rammas Echor to seek shelter within the citadel of Minas Tirith. For two days and two nights the battle raged. Siege towers, catapults and great rams battered the walls and rained fire and stones on the Men of Gondor: All seemed lost: darkness covered the land, the Morgul hordes swarmed over the Field and the Witch-king shattered the great gates of the city. Then, unexpectedly, the Rohirrim allies of Gondor rode into the Field. Before them the Haradrim were routed and the siege machines destroyed. Though the soldiers of Gondor rushed in to support the Rohirrim, this charge would not have won the day had not the Dúnedain lord Aragorn arrived with the Rangers of the North and the Men of Lebennin and Lamedon in the ships they had captured from the Corsairs. Caught between these three forces, the army of Morgul was overthrown and the Witch-king slain. To a Man – by steel, fire or water – all enemies on the battle-ground were put to death.

DESTRUCTION OF MORDOR

With the power of the Witch-king of Morgul broken, the victors of Pelennor Fields came to the Black Gate of Mordor to challenge the Dark Lord Sauron. Yet this was a deception for, in the moment of the attack on the Black Gate of Mordor, the Ringbearer achieved his Quest. On their Winged Beasts the Nazgûl rushed like the north wind to hinder his purpose, yet to no avail, for the One Ring was dropped into the fires of Mount Doom. With the end of the Ring, Sauron and all his world were destroyed: the Black Gate collapsed, the Dark Tower of Barad-dûr toppled and the Earth was rent open. In the midst of their flight, the Nazgûl and the Winged Beasts burst into flames and fell shrieking from the sky.

DEPARTURE OF THE RINGBEARERS

When the War of the Ring ended there was peace and prosperity in Middle-earth once again. At that time it was also ordained that the great Elvish powers should pass from Mortal Lands. So it was that Elrond, Galadriel and Gandalf, the keepers of the Three Elf Rings, and Bilbo and Frodo Baggins, two bearers of the Ruling Ring, came to the Grey Havens. There in an Elven-ship they sailed westwards to the Undying Lands.

TELERI There were Three Kindred of Elves who in the years of Stars undertook the Great Journey from the East of Middle-earth to the Undying Lands. The first two were named the Vanyar and the Noldor, and they were the first of the Elvenhost to reach the Undying Lands beyond the Great Sea. The people of the Third Kindred were the Teleri; their destiny differed from the first two Kindred, for they were the largest in number of the Elven people and so their passage was slowest across the lands of Middle-earth. In the course of the Great Journey the Teleri became a scattered and divided people.

At the Marchlands of the West of Middle-earth the Teleri tarried and stood back in fear of crossing the Great River Anduin and the Misty Mountains. Some Elves broke away from the main host and went South into the Vales of Anduin, where they lived for many centuries. These people were named the Nandor, and they took one called Lenwë as their lord.

But the main host of the Teleri continued westwards, over the Misty Mountains and the Blue Mountains, to the land that was later named Beleriand. Then the greatest division of the Teleri occurred. The Teleri were encamped in a great forest beyond the River Gelion, when they lost their king, Elwë Singollo, who alone among them had seen the Trees of the Valar in the Undying Lands. Elwë walked into the Forest of Nan Elmoth and there, enchanted, fell under a spell of love for Melian the Maia. In that spell he was held, though years passed and his people searched for him. A part who called themselves the Eglath, the "forsaken", would go no further without him. They remained faithful to him until, at last, he returned with Melian his bride. The Eglath were renamed the Sindar, the "Grey-elves", and under this union of Elf and Maia they built the most powerful kingdom of Elves on Middle-earth in the years of Starlight.

But long before King Elwë returned, the larger part of the Teleri had taken his brother Olwë as king and had gone west again to the Great Sea. There they awaited some sign from the Valar that would bring them to the Undying Lands. The Teleri waited a long time on the shores of Middle-earth and grew to love the sea under the Stars. While on the shores they sang songs sad and brave. Of all Elves they were the loveliest of singers, and of all Elves they loved the sea the most. By some they were called the Lindar, the "singers", and by others the Falmari, the Sea-elves. Hearing the Elven-songs Ossë, the Maia of the waves, came to them and sang to the Teleri of the waves and the sea. They learned much from Ossë of the ways of the sea and their love for the sight and sounds of those turbulent shores of Middle-earth increased.

So it was that, when Ulmo the Ocean Lord came to the Teleri with that rootless island that was his ship, once again some of the

kindred forsook the Journey. These were named Falathrim, the "Elves of the Falas", who for the love of the shores of Middle-earth remained. They chose Círdan as their lord, and they settled in the havens of Brithombar and Eglarest. In later years they were the first shipbuilders of Middle-earth.

The greatest part of the Teleri went West with Ulmo, though Ossë pursued them and sang to them and would not let them forget the blessings of the seas. Ulmo, seeing how they so loved the waves, was loath to take them beyond the reach of the sea. So when he came within sight of the Undying Lands he did not take them ashore but anchored the island in the Bay of Eldamar within sight of the Light and the land of their kindred, though it was beyond their reach. Once again the Journey of the Teleri was stayed, and for an Age they again lived apart from their kindred. Their language changed with their stay on Tol Eressëa, the "lonely isle"; the sounds of the sea were always on their tongue, and their language was no longer that of the Vanyar and Noldor.

The Valar were, however, displeased with their brother Ulmo, for they wished to bring the Third Kindred to the actual shore of their realm. At their bidding Ulmo relented, and he sent Ossë to them once more. Reluctantly, Ossë taught them the art of building ships and, when the ships were built, Ulmo sent to them vast winged Swans, which drew the Teleri finally to Eldamar.

The Teleri were grateful to reach their journey's end at last and great indeed was the welcome they were given. The Noldor and Vanyar came from the city Tirion upon Túna with many gifts of gemstones and gold. And in time the Teleri came to know the Light of the Trees and the wisdom of the Valarian people.

Under their king Olwë, the Teleri built beautiful mansions of pearl and ships, like the Swans of Ulmo, with eyes and beaks of jet and gold. They named their city Alqualondë, which is the "haven of Swans". Remaining close to the waves they had learned to love, they walked the shores or sailed on the Bay of Eldamar. The Teleri were a happy people and so they remain; their ships constantly sail out through the arching sea-carved stone gate of their haven and city. They know little of war and strife; their concerns are with the sea, with ships and with singing. These are their chief joys.

War came to them twice, and each time it was unlooked for and unexpected. The first time, according to the "Aldudénië" – the tale of the Darkening of Valinor – Fëanor, lord of the Noldor, came to the Teleri of Alqualondë, desiring their ships to go to Middle-earth so that he could avenge his father's death and regain the Silmarils from Morgoth. King Olwë denied him his wish, however, and so the fierce Noldor slew many of the Teleri and took their ships. This was the first slaying of Elf by Elf known in Arda. It has always been counted a great evil and has been held against the sons of Fëanor ever since.

Only once more did the Teleri of Alqualondë in any way test themselves in war. This was the War of Wrath when the Valar, the Maiar and the Eldar went to the Great Battle at the end of the First Age of Sun and defeated the rebel Vala, Melkor, whom the Elves named Morgoth. But even then the Teleri did not fight but only used their ships to carry the Vanyar and Noldor warriors from the Undying Lands to Middle-earth. Though they would help the Noldor, they would not die on their behalf on the battle-field for they well remembered the First Kinslaying.

The "Akallabêth" tells that, when Númenor tore open the belly of the World with its Downfall, the Spheres of mortal and immortal lands fell apart. Thereafter only the ships of the Teleri could ever cross the gap between the Spheres. The fair, white Swan ships of the Teleri are a wonder and a miracle and the mortal World has never since seen their like, though they still sail in the Bay of Eldamar and will do so until the Unmaking of Eä.

THRUSHES The "Red Book of Westmarch" tells that in the Third Age of Sun there were many bird races such as Crows and Ravens that possessed languages that Elves, Dwarves or Men might know. But the ancient breed of Thrush that lived in Erebor had for a time an alliance with the Men and Dwarves of that place. The Men of Dale and some of the Lake Men of Esgaroth knew the Thrush language and used these birds as messengers. Thrushes would also come to Dwarves in friendship, and, though the Dwarves did not understand the quick Thrushes' speech, the Thrushes understood Westron, the common daily speech of Dwarves and Men.

These birds were especially long-lived. Legend relates how one very old Thrush of Erebor came to the Dwarves of Thorin Oakenshield and bore a message to Lake Town to the heir of Dale named Bard the Bowman. Men, Elves and Dwarves had reason indeed to be grateful to this Thrush, for on the strength of its message Bard the Bowman learned of the weakness of the Dragon of Erebor, and with that knowledge slew the beast.

TINDÓMEREL Fairest of the song-birds of Arda was the Tindómerel, the "twilight-daughter", which common Men called the nightingale. Elves loved this night-singer, which they named TINÚVIEL "maiden of twilight" and told many tales in which nightingales play a part.

TINÚVIEL Among the songs and tales of Elves much is made of the night-singing bird that men call the nightingale. Of all birds its song is most loved, for like the Elves themselves it sings by the light of the Stars. This bird has many names: Dúlin "night-singer", Tindómerel "twilight-daughter", Lómelindë "dusk-singer" and Tinúviel "twilight-maiden".

The greatest legends of this bird came from Doriath. For always about the Queen of the Grey-elves, Melian the Maia, were the sweet voices of nightingales. In time a daughter was born to Melian and King Thingol – the only child born of Elf and Maia in the Circles of the World. She was the most beautiful of Elves, the fairest singer of all her race, and so she was named Lúthien Tinúviel. The "Lay of Leithian" tells how by the magic of her song she wielded immense power in Arda. But like the short-lived night bird she faded from the World, for she took the mortal Beren, son of Barahir, as her husband, and she herself was made mortal. So the fairest being in Arda was gone long before the First Age of Sun was ended.

Many songs recall Lúthien's beauty, and in the "Tale of Aragorn and Arwen" it is said that in the Third Age of Sun the dark beauty of Lúthien again found form in Arwen, daughter of Elrond Half-elven. Arwen was also called Tinúviel. Her song was beautiful and, like Lúthien, she married a mortal and chose a mortal life.

TOROGS During the Wars of Beleriand there came forth in the service of Morgoth, the Dark Enemy, a race of Man-eating Giants of great strength. Elves named these creatures Torogs, from which Men later invented the name TROLLS. The lore of Middle-earth was filled with tales of this evil but stupid race of Giants who often beset the lone unwary traveller.

TREES OF THE VALAR From the seeds devised by Yavanna, Queen of the Earth, there grew in the Ages of the Lamps the trees of the Great Forests of Arda. Many of these were the same as trees we now know, yet taller in those days and of greater girth. There were trees of oak, alder, rowan, fir, beech (which was called Neldoreth), birch (called Brethil), and holly (named Region). But there were others that have now vanished from the World: the red-gold Culumalda of Ithilien and the golden Mallorn, the tallest tree of Middle-earth, which stood in Lothlórien.

Yet the most amazing and beautiful of all the trees that ever grew were the two Trees of the Valar, which appeared after the Ages of the Lamps. After Melkor had destroyed the Lamps of the Valar, which had lighted all the World, the Valar left Middle-earth and came to the Undying Lands. There they made a second kingdom, which they named Valinor, and Yavanna, Giver of Fruits, sat on the green mound Ezellohar near the western golden gate of Valimar and sang, while the Valar sat on their thrones in the Ring of Doom and Nienna the Weeper silently watered the Earth with her tears. First, it is told, there came forth a Tree of silver and then a Tree of gold; glowing with brilliant Light, they grew as tall as the mountains of Aulë. Telperion was the elder of these Trees and had leaves of dark green and bright silver. On his boughs were multitudes of silver flowers from which fell silver dew. In praise Telperion was also called Ninquelótë and Silpion. Laurelin, the younger of the Trees of the Valar, was the "song of gold". Her leaves were edged with gold yet were pale green; her flowers were like trumpets and golden flames, and from her limbs fell a rain of gold Light. In praise Laurelin was also named Culúrien and Malinalda, the "golden tree."

So it was that these two Trees stood in the Undying Lands, and lit the lands with silver and gold. From the rhythm of the Light of the Trees of the Valar came the Count of Time, for Time had not before been measured, and so began the days and years of the Trees, which were many long Ages – longer far than the years of the Stars or the Sun. The Light of the twin Trees in the Undying Lands was eternal, and those who lived in it were ennobled and filled with immense wisdom.

In their Light the Valar lived in bliss, while Middle-earth was plunged in darkness and Melkor strengthened the power of his

kingdom of Utumno and his armoury of Angband. Yet after a time Varda, who made wells beneath the Trees in which the dews of Light fell, took the silver Light of Telperion and climbed the vault of the skies and rekindled the faint Stars. She made them more brilliant, and the evil servants of Melkor on Middle-earth quailed in fear. For the starlight was now like spears to them, or like daggers of ice, that cut them deep. In this Light of the Stars the Elves came forth. Joyfully were they awakened by that Light.

Though the life of the Trees of the Valar was long, their end was tragic and disastrous. For, it is told, Melkor made a pact with Ungoliant the Great Spider, and they came invisibly in the Unlight of the Spider, and the Trees were blasted with sorcerous flame, and the sap of their lives was drawn out. Their Light was extinguished and they were left but shattered trunks and roots blackened and poisoned. The wells of Light were drained and consumed by the Spider Ungoliant, and a terrible darkness fell on Valinor. So in all the World the Light of the Trees was gone, except in the three jewels called the Silmarils that the Elves of Eldamar had made, in which a little of the Light from the Trees was preserved. But Melkor took these gems too though he did not destroy them, and it was for these Silmarils that the long disastrous War of the Jewels of all the next Age was fought.

Mournfully, the Valar came again to the Trees, and again they sent for Yavanna and Nienna. Over the dead Trees Yavanna sang her green song and Nienna wept tears of endurance beyond hope, and from the charred ruins came a single golden fruit and a single silver flower. These were named Anar the Fire Golden and Isil the Sheen. The "Narsilion" tells how Aulë the Smith made great lanterns

about these radiant lights that they might not fade. Manwë hallowed them, and Varda lifted them into the heavens and set them on a course over all the lands of Arda. In this way these small fragments of the living Light of the Trees of the Valar were brought to the whole World and they were called the Sun and the Moon. Arien the Maia fire spirit carries the Sun, Anar, which is also named Vása, the "heart of fire"; and Tilion the Maia hunter carries the Moon, Isil the silver flower, which is also called Rána.

It was not in their Light alone that the Trees remained in the World, for Yavanna made the tree Galathilion in the image of Telperion though it did not radiate Light. She gave this tree to the Elves of Tirion, who knew it as the White Tree of the Eldar. Many of its seedlings grew and still grow in Eldamar. One of these was Celeborn, which bloomed on Tol Eressëa and brought forth the seedling that Elves gave to the Men of Númenor. This seedling became the tree named Nimloth the Fair, the White Tree of Númenor, which grew in the royal court until King Ar-Pharazôn destroyed it. With that act the Isle of Númenor was doomed. Yet a sapling had already been taken from Nimloth by the princes of Andúnië, and before the Downfall of Númenor one prince named Elendil the Tall took this sapling to Middle-earth. His son first planted the fruit of Nimloth in Minas Ithil in Gondor, and until the Fourth Age of Sun the White Trees of Gondor bloomed. Though three times a White Tree perished in plague or war, a sapling was always found and the line never died out. These White Trees were a living link with the most ancient past of the Undying Lands, and they were a sign of the nobility, the wisdom and the goodness of the Valar come to mortal Men.

248

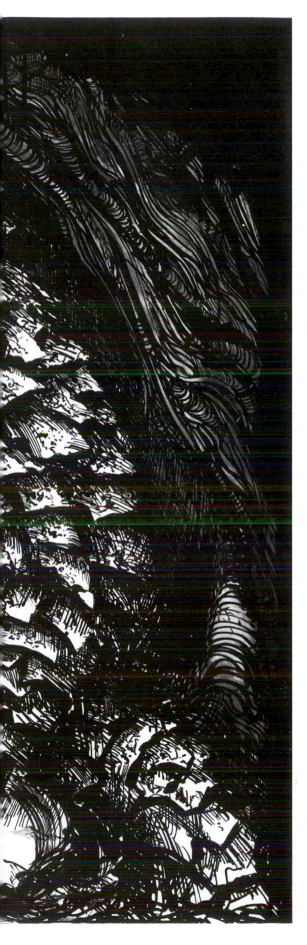

TROLLS It is thought that in the First Age of Starlight, in the deep Pits of Angband, Melkor the Enemy bred a race of giant cannibals who were fierce and strong but without intelligence. These black-blooded giants were called Trolls, and for five Ages of Starlight and four Ages of Sun they committed deeds as evil as their dull wits allowed.

Trolls, it is said, were bred by Melkor because he desired a race as powerful as the giant Ents, the Tree-herds. Trolls were twice the height and bulk of the greatest Men, and they had a skin of green scales like armour. As Ents were to the substance of wood, so Trolls were to stone; though not so strong as Ents who could crush stone, Trolls were rock hard and powerful. Yet in the sorcery of their making there was a fatal flaw: they feared light. The spell of their creation had been cast in darkness and if light did fall on them it was as if that spell were broken and the armour of their skin grew inwards. Their evil soulless beings were crushed as they became lifeless stone.

The stupidity of Trolls was so great that many could not be taught speech at all, while others learned the barest rudiments of the Black Speech of Orcs. Though their power was often brought to naught by the quick-witted, in mountain caverns and dark woods Trolls were rightly feared. They desired most a diet of raw flesh. They killed for pleasure, and without reason – save an undirected avarice – hoarded what treasures they took from their victims.

In the Ages of Starlight they wandered Middle-earth freely and with Orcs made travel a great peril. They often went to war alongside Wolves and Orcs and other evil servants of Melkor at this time. But in the First Age of Sun they were far more wary, for the great light of the Sun was death to them and only in darkness did they go forth in the Wars of Beleriand. It is told in the "Quenta Silmarillion" that in the Battle of Unnumbered Tears Trolls in great numbers were the body guard of Gothmog, Lord of the Balrogs, and, though they fought neither with craft nor skill, they fought fiercely and knew nothing of fear. Seventy of their number were slain by that one great Edain warrior called Húrin, yet other Trolls came on and at last took him captive.

After the War of Wrath and the First Age of Sun, many of the Troll race remained on Middle-earth and hid themselves deeply under stone. When Sauron the Maia arose in the Second Age, he took to himself these old servants of his master, Melkor. Sauron also gave the Trolls craftiness of mind born of wickedness, and they became more dangerous than before. Freely they wandered in dark places of the World.

So in the Third Age of Sun when Sauron for a second time arose in Mordor, there were still many evil and slow-witted Trolls who haunted Mortal Lands. Some of these were called Stone-trolls;

others were Cave-trolls, Hill-trolls, Mountain-trolls and Snow-trolls. Many tales of the Third Age tell of their evil. In the Coldfells north of Rivendell they slew the Dúnedain chieftain Arador. In the Trollshaws of Eriador for centuries three Trolls fed on village folk of that land. By Troll standards these three Trolls were mental giants, for they spoke and understood the Westron tongue of Men and had an elementary if faulty knowledge of arithmetic. None the less by quickness of wit the Wizard Gandalf craftily turned them to stone. In Moria the Balrog commanded many huge Cave-trolls.

Yet it is said Sauron was not yet pleased with the evil of these servants and sought to put their great strength to better use. So it was that, towards the end of the Third Age, Sauron bred Trolls of great cunning and agility who could endure the Sun as long as Sauron's will was with them. These he called the Olog-hai, and they were great beasts with the reasoning intelligence of evil Men. Armed with fangs and rending claws and stone-scaled as others of the Troll race, they also carried black shields, round and huge, and swung mighty hammers that crushed the helmets of foes. So, in the Mountains of Mordor and the forests about Dol Guldur in Mirkwood where the Olog-hai were sent to war by Sauron, a great evil was loosed upon Sauron's foes. In the War of the Ring on Pelennor Fields and before the Black Gate of Mordor the terror of these savage beings caused terrible destruction. Yet they were held by a mighty spell, and, when the Ring was unmade and Sauron went into the shadows, the spell was broken. The Olog-hai drifted as if their senses were taken from them; they were like mute cattle wandering dark fields and for all their great strength they were scattered and slain.

TURTLE-FISH In the lore of Hobbits there is the tale of a great Turtle-fish that is called the FASTITOCALON. Whether the tale grew from the sighting of a leviathan upon the sea or was the product of Hobbit fancy cannot now be discovered, for no other race upon Arda speaks of this mighty creature.

ÚLAIRI The long histories of the Rings of Power tell how after the War of Sauron and the Elves there arose nine wraiths in the lands of Middle-earth. These were the Úlairi, who were called the NAZGÛL in Black Speech and whom Men knew as the Ringwraiths. Once great lords among Men, the Úlairi succumbed to the temptation of the sorcerous Rings and in time became slaves of the Dark Lord Sauron. The tale of their destruction of the realms of Elves and Men is long and terrible.

U

ÚMANYAR Of all those newly arisen Elven people who in the years of Starlight chose to heed the summons of the Valar and leave Middle-earth to come to the Undying Lands, only a part completed the Great Journey. Those who reached the Undying Lands, the continent of Aman, were named Amanyar, while those who were lost on the way, and broke away from the main hosts, were named the Úmanyar "those not of Aman". The main races of the Úmanyar were called Nandor, Laiquendi, Falathrim and Sindar, but there were also many smaller tribes and families amongst those lost on that long road of many perils.

URUK-HAI In the year 2475 of the Third Age a new breed of Orkish soldiery came out of Mordor. These were called the Uruk-hai. They were black-skinned, black-blooded and lynx-eyed, nearly as tall as Men and unafraid of light. The Uruk-hai were of greater strength and endurance than the lesser Orcs, and more formidable in battle. They wore black armour and black mail; they wielded long swords and spears and carried shields emblazoned with the Red Eye of Mordor.

As the spawning of lesser Orcs was counted among the greatest evils of Melkor, so was the breeding of Uruk-hai numbered among Sauron's most terrible deeds. By what method Sauron bred these beings is not known, but they proved to be well suited to his evil purpose. Their numbers multiplied and they went among all the lesser Orcs and often became their captains or formed legions of

their own, for the Uruk-hai were proud of their fighting prowess and disdainful of the lesser servants of Sauron.

When the Uruk-hai multitude came unexpectedly on the Men of Gondor with spear and sword, they drove the Men before them and stormed Osgiliath, set torches to it, and broke its stone bridge. Thus the Uruk-hai laid waste the greatest city of Gondor.

This, however, was but the beginning of the work of the Uruk-hai, for these great Orcs were valued by the Dark Powers and they fell to evil deeds with a passion. Throughout the War of the Ring, the Uruk-hai were among the forces that came from Morgul and Mordor. And under the banner of the White Hand of Saruman they came in vast numbers out of Isengard into the Battle of the Hornburg. Yet with the end of the War and the fall of Mordor the Uruk-hai were as straw before fire, for with Sauron gone the Uruk-hai, with the lesser Orcs and other evil beasts, wandered masterless and were slain or driven into hiding where they might only feed on one another, or die.

URUKS In the Third Age of Sun there came out of Mordor a terrible race of giant Orcs. In Black Speech they were named the URUK-HAI, but they were commonly called Uruks. They were as tall as Men with all the evil traits of Orcs, yet they were stronger and unafraid of light.

URULÓKI The Urulóki Fire-drakes that came forth in the First Age of Sun from the Pits of Angband were part of the great race of Dragons. Of all creatures they were the most feared. These Urulóki "hot serpents" were fanged and taloned, dreadful in mind and deed, and filled with breath of flame and sulphur. The first of their kind was Glaurung, Father of Dragons, but he had many offspring, who in turn produced many broods. Of all creatures they were the greatest despair of Men and Elves, and the bane of Dwarves.

VALAR When Eä, the "World that Is", was given substance there came into it a part of the first race, the Ainur, the "holy ones". In the Timeless Halls they had been beings of pure spirit, who the "Valaquenta" records entered the World and taking earthly form became divided into two peoples. The people that were less powerful were numerous and their tale is recounted in the name of the Maiar; the greater powers were fifteen in number and they are here accounted as the Valar, the Powers of Arda.

It is told in the ancient books that, when the Valar and Maiar came and first shaped the rough form of the World, they strove to make the perfect beauty that they had perceived in the Vision. Yet in this there was strife among the Valar and war marred their work. But at last the first kingdom of the Valar called Almaren was made on an isle in the middle of the vast lake in Middle-earth, and all the World was lit by two brilliant Lamps that stood to the North and South. Thus began the Ages of the Lamps. Yet one of the Valar revolted and broke the Great Lamps of the Valar and destroyed Almaren and its fair gardens.

So the Valar left Middle-earth and went West to the Continent of Aman where they placed the Pelóri Mountains about them and made their second kingdom of gardens and mansions more fair than the first. This kingdom was called Valinor, and its city of domes, bells and great halls was named Valimar. At this time, the Trees of the Valar, which gave Eternal Light, golden and silver, were made and all of Aman was lit within the borders of the Pelóri Mountains; the kingdom was a miracle of beauty.

First of the Valar is Manwë, who lives on Taniquetil, the highest mountain of Arda. He is the Wind Lord and the First King. All of Arda is his domain, but his chief love is the element of the air, and so he is also called Súlimo "lord of the breath of Arda". He sits on a burnished throne clothed in azure robes, the Sceptre of Sapphire in his hand. Like sapphire too are Manwë's eyes, but even more bright, and as fearsome as lightning. Manwë sees all the World beneath the skies. The turbulence of the air is his mind's workings; his wrath is

the thunder-storm that rocks the Earth and breaks even the mountain towers. All the birds of the air are his, the Eagles above all others. His is the Breath of the Earth and the Breath of the peoples of Arda. Speech and sound itself are thus parts of his element, and the arts he loves above all others are poetry and song.

Within the domed halls of Ilmarin, the "mansion of the high airs" which Manwë made on Taniquetil, there also resides the queen of the Valar. She is Varda, the Lady of the Stars, fairest of all the Valar for the light of Ilúvatar is still on her. She is a spirit of light that is like a fountain of diamonds. It was Varda who made the Stars, and so Elves call her Elentári and Elbereth, the "Star queen"

Her name is a talisman to all those who would have light dispel darkness. It was Varda who filled the Lamps Illuin and Ormal with the Light that lit all the World, and later too she took the dew of the Trees of the Valar and made the Stars brighter still. She made the forms of the Stars that are called the constellations: the Butterfly Wilwarin, the Swordsman Menelmacar, the Sickle Valacirca, the Eagle Soronúmë and many others. In these forms may be read the fate of all the peoples of the World.

It is said that Elves worship Varda above all others, for it was her Stars that called them into the World and part of her early light is for ever held in their eyes. For this deed they named her Tintallë and Gilthoniel, the "kindler", and for ever they sing to her by starlight and call her the Exalted and the Lofty.

Next of the Valar is Ulmo, whose element is Water. He is the Ocean Lord, whom all mariners know and Dwarves and Orcs fear. Most often he is vast and formless in his deep watery World, but his arising is like a high tidal wave come to shore; his helmet is wave-crested and his mail is emerald and brilliant silver. He raises Ulumúri, the great white horns of shell, to his lips and blows deep and long. When he speaks his voice too is deep as the sounding depth of the sea. Yet his form is not always fearful, nor indeed does he always appear as the Ocean Lord. For his is water in all its forms, from the spring rains and the fountains, to the rush of brooks and

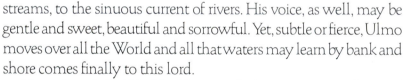

streams, to the sinuous current of rivers. His voice, as well, may be gentle and sweet, beautiful and sorrowful. Yet, subtle or fierce, Ulmo moves over all the World and all that waters may learn by bank and shore comes finally to this lord.

Nourisher of the World is Yavanna, for her name means "giver of fruits"; she is also Kementári, "queen of the Earth". She takes many forms, but often stands as tall as the most elegant cypress, green-robed and lit with a golden dew. All those who love the fruits of the Earth love Yavanna and worship her. She is the force that through the green fuse drives the flowers, and the first seeds of all the Olvar were devised and planted by her. She is the protectress of all the fleet-footed Kelvar of woodland and field. It was Yavanna who brought forth the mighty forests of Arda, and she who, during the Ages of Darkness, protected life in the lands of Middle-earth with the Sleep of Yavanna – a great enchantment cast over Mortal Lands. The greatest of her works was the making of the Trees of the Valar, and, after their destruction, it was she who coaxed from their charred stalks a single flower and a single fruit, from which the Moon and Sun were made.

Spouse of Yavanna, with whom she shares the element of Earth, yet more deeply, is Aulë the Smith, Maker of Mountains, master of all crafts, deviser of metals and gemstones. He is named Mahal the "maker" by Dwarves, for he is the power that fashioned these people from earth and stone. Imperfect though they were, the Dwarves were strong and stubborn as the stones themselves and loved all things that concerned their lord. Aulë was also friend and tutor of the Noldorin Elves, who first cut out the gemstones and excelled in building towers and cities of bright stone. They came often to his mansions, cut deep in the mountain roots of Valinor, and learned many of his skills. The greatest of his deeds was the vast work that he undertook in the earliest Ages, when he shaped the forms of the Earth itself.

Deeper still than Aulë's mansions are the Halls of Mandos, which are on the western shore where the waves of Ekkaia, the Encircling Sea, wash the Undying Lands. This is the House of the Dead where the Vala Námo lives, who by all, after his mansion, is called Mandos, the Speaker of Doom. A master of spirits is the Doomsman and, of the Valar, most aware of the Will of Ilúvatar. He is unbending and unmoved by pity, for he knows all the fates that were declared in the Music. In the lore of Elves, the spirits of slain Elves are called to the Lord of the Dead and they inhabit his mansion in the place called the Halls of Awaiting.

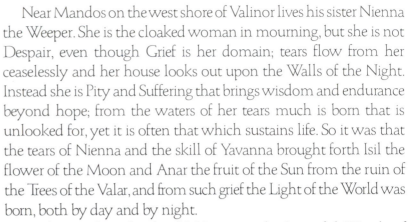

Near Mandos on the west shore of Valinor lives his sister Nienna the Weeper. She is the cloaked woman in mourning, but she is not Despair, even though Grief is her domain; tears flow from her ceaselessly and her house looks out upon the Walls of the Night. Instead she is Pity and Suffering that brings wisdom and endurance beyond hope; from the waters of her tears much is born that is unlooked for, yet it is often that which sustains life. So it was that the tears of Nienna and the skill of Yavanna brought forth Isil the flower of the Moon and Anar the fruit of the Sun from the ruin of the Trees of the Valar, and from such grief the Light of the World was born, both by day and by night.

In the southern lands of Valinor are the beautiful Woods of Oromë, where Oromë, Tamer of Beasts and the Huntsman, resides. All nations of horsemen love him as well as those who live by hunting and those who are herdsmen and foresters. Oromë is fearsome when hunting and his wrath in battle is dreadful. With spear and bow, the Huntsman rides out on his steed Nahar, a beast white and silver with hooves of gold that shake the Earth. When Oromë blows his great hunting horn Valaróma, all evil creatures flee before him, the mountains and woods echo with sound and in his train come hunting hounds and Maiar and Eldar huntsmen on furious Horses. Most often this Huntsman is called Oromë the "horn-blower", which is Araw to the Men of Gondor and Béma in Westron; to Elves he is Aldaron in Quenya and Tauron in Sindarin, which mean "forest lord".

Now these are the eight Valar who are called the Aratar, the mightiest of the powers who dwelt in the Spheres of the World. Yet there are six more Valar, and one more after them who fell into evil ways and thus is counted last.

Those who desire eternal youth worship Vána, wife of Oromë and younger sister of Yavanna. Vána the Ever-young is her name; she has gardens of golden flowers and her chief delights are bird song and flower blossom.

Nessa the Dancer is named next; she is Oromë's sister. She loves the fleet woodland creatures and they come to her, for she is herself a wild spirit who dances unceasingly on the green and never-fading grasses of Valinor.

The husband of Nessa is Tulkas the Strong, who entered Arda last of all the Valar. He is called the Wrestler and also Astaldo the "valiant". He is the strongest of all the Valar, quick and tireless, gold-haired and gold-bearded; even in war he carries no weapon for his naked strength and great heart overwhelm all enemies.

Brother to Mandos is Lórien, the Dream Master. Like Mandos, Lórien is named after the place of his dwelling, for Lórien is the fairest garden within Arda. His true name is Irmo, but to all he is Lórien, King of Dream and Vision.

Within the fair gardens of Lórien is the Lake Lórellin in which there is an island filled with tall trees and gentle mists. Here Estë the Healer, the gentle one, lives. Her mantle is grey, and rest is what she grants. She is praised by all, but her gifts are most desired by those whose suffering is great.

The Vala named Vairë is the wife of Mandos, and she is called the Weaver. Within her husband's halls she tirelessly weaves on a loom the tapestries of history and fate long before those events are come in the course of Time.

Last of the Valar is he who in the beginning was mightiest of the Ainur. He was named Melkor, "He who arises in Might". He owned in part the powers of all the Valar, but chiefly his realm was Darkness and Cold. He moved over Arda like a black cloud that was dreadful to behold, like the World's nightmare come into daylight. All evil that was and is in the World had its beginning in Melkor, for he revolted against Ilúvatar in the Timeless Halls and came to Arda in anger, wishing to make his own kingdom. He brought corruption into the World, and with him came a part of the Maiar twisted by his malice. He made his fortress, Utumno, and his armoury, Angband, deep under the mountain roots of

Middle-earth. In Arda he waged five great wars against the Valar and put out the fairest lights of the World by destroying both the Great Lamps and the Trees of the Valar.

In the beginning Melkor appeared in forms both fair and evil: his wiles were many and even Manwë the First King was deceived. Yet after the Darkening of Valinor, he always assumed his evil form and the Elves called him Morgoth, the "dark enemy of the World". This warrior king was like a great tower, iron-crowned, with black armour and a shield black, vast and blank. His countenance was evil for the fire of malice was in his eyes, his face was twisted with rage and scarred by the claws of Thorondor the Eagle lord and the knife of Beren the Edain. He bore eight other wounds and his hands were burned from the fire of the Silmarils, so he was perpetually in pain. Grond the mace, called the Hammer of the Underworld, was his chief weapon and it sounded like thunder and split the Earth with its force. Yet, in the War of Wrath all this power was destroyed, though Melkor summoned Dragons, Balrogs, Orcs, Trolls and every other evil being to his aid. This war was the end of him, and, though much of his evil and some of his servants remained, he alone of the Valar was driven from the Spheres of the World and now dwells for ever in the Void.

VALARAUKAR Of the Maiar, the servants of the Valar, there were many who were of the element of fire. Melkor came among these fire spirits in the earliest days and corrupted many of them, turning them against Ilúvatar and the Valar. From brilliant beings they were transformed to demons that burned with hate: they were hulking monsters robed in darkness and they carried whips of flames. Feared by all, these corrupted Maiar were named Valaraukar "scourges of fire", but more commonly in Middle-earth they were known as the BALROGS, the "demons of might", and under that name the history is told of their evil deeds in Mortal Lands.

VAMPIRES Whether it was from bird or beast that Melkor bred the evil bloodsucking Bat of Middle-earth, no tale tells, but in the First Age of Sun in the Wars of Beleriand it is told how, in this winged form made large and armed with talons and steel, Vampire spirits came into the service of Melkor the Dark Enemy.

In the Quest of the Silmaril, Thuringwethil, the "woman of secret shadow", was a mighty Vampire and was the chief messenger to travel between Angband and Tol-in-Gaurhoth, where Sauron ruled the Werewolf legions. When Tol-in-Gaurhoth fell, Sauron himself took on Vampire shape and fled. Once the sorcerous power of Sauron was broken many evil enchantments were also shattered. The shaping cloak that gave Thuringwethil the power to take Bat-shape fell from her, and the Vampire's dread spirit fled.

VANYAR Of the Three Kindred of Elves who undertook the Great Journey from Middle-earth to the Undying Lands, least is told in the histories that have come to Men of that Kindred which is counted first and whose king, Ingwë, is named High Lord over all the Elven peoples. This race is the Vanyar, who are also known as the Fair Elves. They seem golden, for their hair is blondest of all peoples. They are most in accord with the Valar and are much loved by them; the counsel of the Lord of the Valar, Manwë, and Varda his queen is always theirs.

The Vanyar have had little to do with Men. Only once have they returned to Middle-earth and then it was to fight against Morgoth the Enemy in the War of Wrath, which ended the First Age of Sun. None of the Vanyar stayed on in Middle-earth; all returned to the Undying Lands.

What is known of the Vanyar has come to the ears of Men from the Exiles – the Noldor who returned to Middle-earth at the time of the Arising of Men. Though they are the least numerous of the Three Kindred the Vanyar are the most wise and valiant.

With the Noldor in their first days in the Undying Lands they built the city of Tirion on the green hill of Túna. This was a great city with white walls and towers, and tallest of the towers of all the Elves was Mindon Eldaliéva, the Tower of Ingwë. From it shone a silver lamp over the Shadowy Seas and in the court of the Tower of Ingwë stood a seedling named Galathilion from the tree Telperion, which flourished with the Elven people.

But after a time, the Vanyar came to love the Light of the Trees still more, for it inspired them to compose songs and poetry which are their chief loves. So it was that they wished to settle where their full power might be seen. Thus Ingwë led his people out of Tirion to the foot of Taniquetil, the Mountain of Manwë, the High Lord of the Valar. Here the Vanyar pledged to stay, and there they have remained though the Trees have faded long ago.

VARIAGS In the land of Khand, south of Mordor, there lived a fierce folk called the Variags during the Third Age of Sun. They were allied to the evil Easterlings and Haradrim and were servants of the Dark Lord Sauron. The histories of the West tell how twice the Variags came forth at the bidding of Sauron against Gondor. In the year 1944, with the Men of Near Harad, the Variags fought the army of Eärnil of Gondor and were defeated at Poros Crossing. More than a thousand years later the Variags with the Haradrim and Easterlings came to the aid of Sauron's armies from Morgul and Mordor in the War of the Ring. But this was the last time they fought Gondor, for an end came to Sauron's power and so to the alliance between Sauron and the Variags, who remained within their own lands for many years of the Fourth Age.

WAINRIDERS An Easterling people out of the lands of Rhûn in the nineteenth century of the Third Age of Sun came to make war on the Men of Gondor. They were a numerous well-armed folk with great Horse-drawn wains and war chariots. By the western Men they were named Wainriders and for a hundred years they made war on the Gondor Men. In 1856 the first battle was fought, in which the Wainriders defeated Gondor and her allies, the Northmen. They killed King Narmacil II, took the lands of Rhovanion and enslaved the Northmen who lived there.

The Wainriders ruled Rhovanion until the last year of that century, when the Northmen revolted and Calimehtar, the new king of Gondor, brought his army north. In battle at Dagorlad, the Wainriders were driven east to Rhûn by this new king. But still the Wainriders fomented trouble on the borderlands of Gondor and, with the aid of the Ringwraiths and the Haradrim, in 1944 they made yet another war on Gondor. And so, from both the East and the South, the Men of Gondor were forced to divide their armies. Gondor's King Ondoher went to the East, where his army was broken by the Wainriders and he and his two sons were slain. But the southern army of Gondor defeated the Haradrim army and then marched East. It surprised the victorious Wainriders and annihilated them with an avenging wrath. Their encampment was set alight, and those not slain in the Battle of the Camp were driven into the Dead Marshes where they perished. Thereafter the name of the Wainriders vanished from the annals of the West and they were not named again in any of the histories of Elves or Men.

WARGS In the Third Age of Sun in Rhovanion, there lived an evil breed of Wolves that made an alliance with the mountain Orcs. These Wolves were named Wargs and often when they set off for war they went with the Orcs called Wolf-riders, who mounted the Wargs like Horses. In the battles of the War of the Ring, the Wargs were devastated along with most of the Orc hordes, and after that time the histories of Middle-earth speak no more of these creatures.

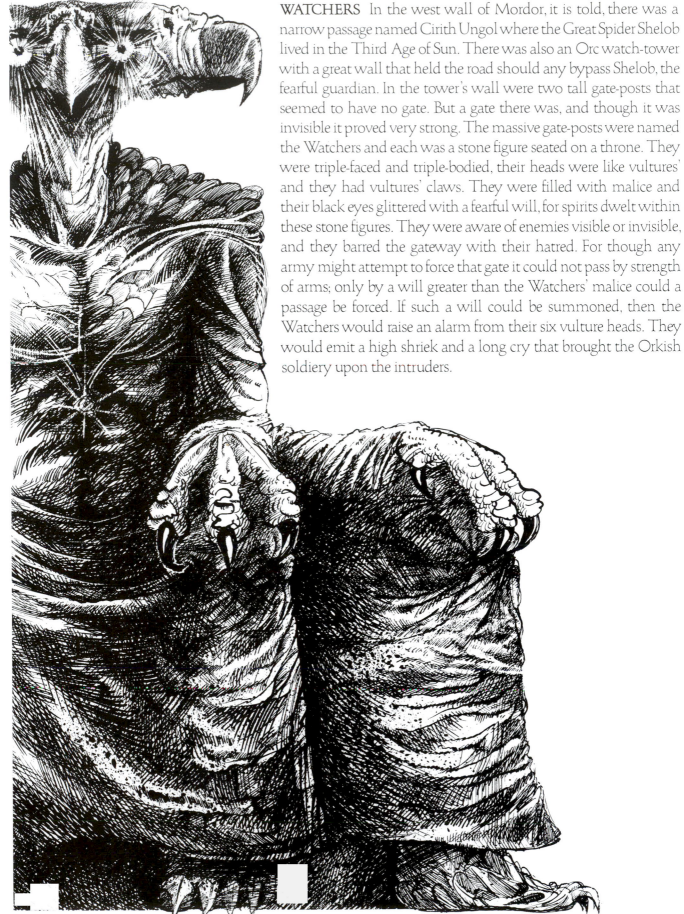

WATCHERS In the west wall of Mordor, it is told, there was a narrow passage named Cirith Ungol where the Great Spider Shelob lived in the Third Age of Sun. There was also an Orc watch-tower with a great wall that held the road should any bypass Shelob, the fearful guardian. In the tower's wall were two tall gate-posts that seemed to have no gate. But a gate there was, and though it was invisible it proved very strong. The massive gate-posts were named the Watchers and each was a stone figure seated on a throne. They were triple-faced and triple-bodied, their heads were like vultures' and they had vultures' claws. They were filled with malice and their black eyes glittered with a fearful will, for spirits dwelt within these stone figures. They were aware of enemies visible or invisible, and they barred the gateway with their hatred. For though any army might attempt to force that gate it could not pass by strength of arms; only by a will greater than the Watchers' malice could a passage be forced. If such a will could be summoned, then the Watchers would raise an alarm from their six vulture heads. They would emit a high shriek and a long cry that brought the Orkish soldiery upon the intruders.

WEREWOLVES In the First Age of Sun there came to Beleriand a race of tortured spirits who were thralls of Melkor. Whether they were Maiar spirits who once served Melkor in Utumno and were shorn by the Valar of their earthly forms, or whether they were evil beings of another kind, is not known. Yet it is certain that these evil spirits entered the forms of Wolves by sorcery. They were a fearsome race and their eyes glowed with dreadful wrath. They spoke and understood both the Black Speech of the Orcs and the fair speech of the Elves.

In the long Wars of Beleriand the greatest number of these Werewolves came, under the banner of Sauron, to the Noldor tower on the River Sirion, and it fell before them. The tower was re-named Tol-in-Gaurhoth, the "isle of Werewolves", and Sauron ruled there. Beneath Tol-in-Gaurhoth there were deep dungeons, and on the battlements the Werewolves stalked.

In the Quest of the Silmaril Huan, the Wolfhound of the Valar, came to Tol-in-Gaurhoth and slew many Werewolves. At last one named Draugluin, sire and lord of the Werewolf race, came to fight Huan. There was a great battle, but in the end Draugluin fled to the tower to the throne of Sauron, his captain. Before Sauron Draugluin spoke the name of Huan, whose coming had been foretold, then he died. Sauron, the shape-shifter, then became a Werewolf himself. In size and strength he was greater than Draugluin, but even so Huan held the bridge and took Sauron by the throat, and by no act of sorcery or strength of limb could Sauron free himself. He therefore surrendered the tower to Beren and Lúthien whom the Wolfhound served. The evil enchantment fell from Tol-in-Gaurhoth and the Wolf forms of the dread spirits fell from the Werewolves. Sauron fled in the form of a great Vampire Bat, and the power that held the realm of the Werewolves was broken in Beleriand for ever.

WEREWORMS In the tales of the Hobbit folk there lived in the Last Desert, in the East of Middle-earth, a race that was named the Wereworms. Though no tale of the Third Age of Sun tells of these beings, the Wereworms were likened to Dragons and serpents. To Hobbits they were perhaps but memories of those creatures that stalked the Earth during the Wars of Beleriand in the First Age.

WEST ELVES In the age of the Awakening of the Elves a great Messenger came out of the West. He was the Vala Oromë, and he beckoned the Elves to a land of Eternal Light. Some chose to make the Journey to the West and were called West Elves or ELDAR. Those who chose to remain were named East Elves or Avari, the "unwilling". The East Elves dwindled and became lesser spirits, while the West Elves grew mighty and famous.

WESTMANSWEED In Middle-earth a herb came into use that the Hobbits discovered gave great pleasure if slowly burned and the smoke inhaled. This was the herb nicotiana, which in the Westron tongue was named Westmansweed, but most commonly was simply called PIPE-WEED. Its use spread from the Shire lands of the Hobbits widely over Middle-earth and was enjoyed, for better or worse, by Men and Dwarves.

WILD MEN Long before the coming of the kings of Gondor, a primitive race of woodland hunters dwelt in the Druadan Forest. They were the WOSES, whom others called the Wild Men, and they were a tribal people armed with bows and blow-pipes. They were wiser in the ways of the forest than any race of Men in Arda.

WILLOWS In the Ages of the Lamps when the Great Forests of Arda were made, ancient Willow trees appeared within the forests. The Willow spirits were strong and loved swamp-lands and slow river courses. They lived quietly for a long time and cared neither for the new-come race of Men, nor for the older races of Dwarves and Orcs who hewed and burned wood. Some among the Willows grew sentient and limb-lithe; and they were numbered among those named Huorns and their will was bent on destroying all enemies of the forests.

Among Willows, the mightiest recorded in the tales of Middle-earth is Old Man Willow, who in the Third Age of Sun lived on the banks of the Withywindle in the Old Forest. He was black-hearted, limb-lithe and filled with a great enchanting power of song. All the land of the Old Forest was held in sway by his will. His great song bent all paths to his feet. Travellers were held in his hypnotic spell; a great song of water and wind on leaves brought them to a deep sleep by his ancient trunk. And with gnarled root or the gaping cavern of his trunk he would capture them, then crush or drown them in the river. His power made the Old Forest rightly feared by travellers, and, but for the power of Tom Bombadil, few could have passed safely through his domain.

WILWARIN During the Spring of Arda, which was in the years of the Lamps, the Valar brought forth forests and many creatures that had no voice, yet were beautiful to behold. Among them was the Wilwarin, which in later times Men called the Butterfly. So content were the Valar with this lovely creature that, when Varda took the silver dew of Telperion to make brilliant the light of the Stars, she also placed the shape of the Wilwarin as a constellation among the wide-wheeling Stars of the heavens.

WINGED BEASTS In the time of the War of the Ring it is told how those undead spirits called the Nazgûl were carried aloft by Winged Beasts. Swifter than the wind were these creatures that had beak and claw of bird, neck of serpent and wing of Bat. It is said they were fed on Orkish meats and grew beyond the size of any other winged creature of the Third Age. Yet black and evil as the Winged Beasts were, they were not undead beings and wraiths like their masters; rather they were living creatures like Dragons, but more ancient still. They had been bred by Melkor in lurking shadows in the Ages of the Lamps, when Kraken and serpent came from the Pits of Utumno.

Yet ancient as they were, and though strong and fearsome in their service to Sauron in the War of the Ring, their time on Middle-earth was brought to an end. One Winged Beast was slain by the Elf Legolas, and a second was killed by the sword-maiden Éowyn; those that remained were destroyed in the holocaust that consumed Mordor in the last year of the Third Age.

268

WITCHES In Middle-earth there were beings of many races who wielded sorcerous powers. Among the late-come race of Men, those who gave themselves over to sorcerous powers were known as Witches. The most powerful Witches were the Ringwraiths, who were named Nazgûl in Black Speech. For these were the Men who were given Nine Rings of Power by Sauron and who brought so much terror into the World.

Of the nine Witches, one emerged whose power was supreme. In the Third Age of Sun, he arose in the north of Eriador and made himself an evil realm in Angmar. For many centuries Men spoke fearfully of this Witch-king of Angmar who laid waste the North Kingdom of the Dúnedain. Later the same Witch-king arose again in the South against the realm of Gondor and took from Gondor a tower that afterwards was named Minas Morgul. There the Witch-king ruled until the days of the War of the Ring, when he was destroyed, and he and the other Witches vanished for ever from the face of Arda.

WIZARDS Those whom common Men named Wizards were, as ancient tales reveal, chosen spirits from the Maiar of Valinor. Elves called them the ISTARI, and under that name the greater part of their deeds in Middle-earth is recorded.

These Wizards came from the West to redress the imbalance that was made by the Dark Lord Sauron in Middle-earth. They came in secret in the form of Men, for it was doomed they could not come forth in the full force of their immortal Maiar spirits but were to be limited to the powers that they might acquire in Mortal Lands. They appeared as old Men dressed in long robes and, filled with the wisdom of the lands, they travelled. They were far-famed as clever conjurers. It is said there were five who in the Third Age of Sun wandered the lands of Middle-earth, but the histories of the Westlands speak of three only: Saruman the White, Gandalf the Grey and Radagast the Brown.

WOLFHOUNDS From the realms of Melkor the Dark Enemy in the Ages of Stars many evil beasts came to torment the people of Middle-earth. Chief among these creatures were the Wolves and Werewolves of Melkor. In defence the Elves bred hunting hounds with which they might destroy these evil beings.

In the histories of Middle-earth, the greatest of these Wolfhounds was one named Huan, who was not born in Mortal Lands. He was bred by Oromë, Huntsman of the Valar, who had given him to the Noldor prince Celegorm in the Undying Lands. The Valarian Wolfhound was an ageless beast that never tired or slept. He was immortal in the manner of Elves and of massive size. By decree of the Valar Huan spoke only three times with words, though he could always understand the speech of Elves and Men. He could not be slain by sorcery nor could spells bewitch him.

Brought to Middle-earth by the exiled Noldor princes, a great doom fell on Huan. In the Quest of the Silmaril he played a large part: for love of Lúthien Tinúviel he went to the Sauron's tower on the Isle of Werewolves. There he killed many evil beasts on the bridge of the Isle and finally slew Draugluin, lord and sire of Werewolves and chief of Sauron's servants in that realm. Then Sauron himself came forth in Werewolf form and there was a terrible struggle on the bridge of Tol-in-Gaurhoth between Huan and Sauron. Sauron was a mighty terror in that form, but Huan's power was even greater. He took the greatest of the Maiar by the throat and with crushing strength held him, bringing him near to death. And so Sauron gave over the tower to Huan and Lúthien and surrendered the hero Beren who was imprisoned in that place. All the powers of enchantment dropped away from Tol-in-Gaurhoth, the servants of Sauron fled, and Sauron, in the shape of a great Vampire, in fear and wrath flew across the sky.

Yet still another battle lay before Huan, the Wolfhound. This was with the Wolf Carcharoth, the Red Maw, who was the evil guardian of the Gates of Angband. This was the greatest Wolf that ever entered the World and he was raised by Morgoth's hand. By chance the Wolf had swallowed the Silmaril that Beren had taken from Morgoth's crown. The jewel burned within the Wolf and he went mad with the torment. None could stand before Carcharoth's fury, even the warrior Beren fell before his power. And as was foretold Huan came and there was the greatest battle of beast against beast that ever was fought. All the goodness of the Valar was with Huan and all the evil of Morgoth with Carcharoth. The hills sounded with their battle but at last Huan slew Carcharoth though he himself was mortally hurt by the evil beast, for in the fangs of the Wolf was a dread poison. Knowing death was upon him he came to Beren who was also dying and spoke for the last time with words, saying only "farewell".

WOLF-RIDERS The "Red Book of Westmarch" records how some among the Orcs of Rhovanion came into the Battle of Five Armies mounted on the backs of the Wolves that were called Wargs. These Orcs were named Wolf-riders by Elves and Men and they formed the cavalry of the Orc legions.

But this alliance of Orc and Wolf was not newly formed in that Age, for both Wolves and Orcs were bred by the evil hand of Melkor the Enemy in the Ages of Stars. Their pact of evil began before the race of Men awoke and the light of the Sun flooded the World. The histories of Beleriand in the last Ages of Stars tell how the Sindarin Elves of Beleriand fought the Wolf-riders many times.

WOLVES Before the Sun shone, in the Pits of Utumno in Middle-earth many evil beasts were bred that stalked the World with the evil Orcs. Chief of the beasts that allied with the Orcs were the Wolves, which first came into the Westlands in the years of Stars. Some of great size served as mounts for Melkor's servants and they were a source of great terror.

In the first Age of the Sun the Werewolf race was bred. The mightiest was Draugluin, their sire and lord. These were not, however, true Wolves but tortured spirits held within the Wolf-form. Their power was great for they were favourites of Sauron the Maia. They came to him in legions and hunted in the lands of Beleriand. From the Noldor they took the tower of Tol Sirion, which was later named Tol-in-Gaurhoth, the "isle of Werewolves", and there they made a kingdom of evil.

Though by the Third Age of Sun Wolves were lesser beings than those of the early Ages, they remained a dreaded race. The "Chronicle of the Westlands" tells of a race of White Wolves that came out of the Northern Waste during the Fell Winter of 2911 and stained the snows of Eriador with the blood of Men. The "Red Book of Westmarch" tells much of the Wargs, a breed of Wolf that in Rhovanion made a pact with the Orcs of the Misty Mountains and carried that breed of Orcs called the Wolf-riders into battle on their backs. And though indeed the Wargs alone were much feared, this alliance with Orcs was a greater evil yet. Indeed in the famous Battle of Five Armies, the strongest element of the Orkish forces was its cavalry, mounted on great Wargs.

The greatest Wolf legend is about Carcharoth, the Red Maw, who in the First Age of Sun was reared by Morgoth on living flesh and filled with great powers. So Carcharoth, who was also named Anfauglir, the "jaws of thirst", grew to a huge size and his strength seemed without comparison. His eyes were like red coals and his teeth were like the poisoned spears of an Orc legion. Carcharoth was guardian of the Gates of Angband and none could pass him by strength of body alone. The walls of Angband were sheer and dread; chasms of serpents lay on either side of the road and Carcharoth lay unsleeping before the Gate.

In the Quest of the Silmaril, Carcharoth bit off Beren's hand at Angband's Gate and swallowed the Silmaril, which burned him with a fierce fire. In his torment Carcharoth slew Elves and Men as his accursed flesh was consumed by the fire; yet his power became greater still. For Carcharoth's wrath was like the self-destroying unquenchable flame of a shooting Star. But at last he met the one he was long doomed to battle: Huan, the Wolfhound of the Valar. And, though he bit Huan with venomous teeth and thereby ensured that Huan's death would soon follow, Carcharoth was slain by the Wolfhound near the sweet waters of Esgalduin.

WOOD-ELVES In most of the woodlands of Middle-earth east of the Misty Mountains that had not been wholly consumed by the evils of Morgoth and Sauron lived the remnant of the Avari, the people who had refused the Great Journey to the West. These people, who were called Wood-elves or more often SILVAN ELVES, had dwindled with the rising of Morgoth's power in the East. To survive, they became wise in the ways of the sheltering forests and hid themselves from their enemies. They were wise in wood-lore, and their eyes were bright as all Elves' with starlight. They were not a powerful people like their High Eldar kindred, but they were greater than Men or any race that followed them.

Although the histories of Arda tell little of the fate of the Wood-elves and are mostly concerned with the Eldar, many tales are told of two realms of these lesser Elves. In the Second Age of Sun the Sindar lord Thranduil came out of Lindon and crossed over the Misty Mountains. He discovered many Wood-elves in the forest of Greenwood the Great (which was later named Mirkwood). There Thranduil was made king of the Woodland Realm of these Elves. Similarly Galadriel the Noldor noblewoman and Celeborn the Sindar lord came to the Wood-elves of Lothlórien, who made them king and queen of the Golden Wood.

WOODMEN In the Third Age of Sun there lived in Mirkwood a people who were called the Woodmen of Mirkwood and who were descended from the Northmen. In alliance with the Beornings and the Elves of the Woodland Realm, they fought the evil that had come in that Age to Dol Guldur in the south of Mirkwood. From that place came Orcs, Spiders and Wolves in legion, and the battle to cleanse that great forest was long and dreadful. In the War of the Ring this struggle was named the Battle under the Trees. Through the north ran the Elves, Woodmen and Beornings, destroying the evil minions of Dol Guldur as fire through straw. The Elves of Lothlórien took Dol Guldur, and broke its walls and destroyed its dungeons. So, at the end of the Age, the forest was cleansed and renamed the Wood of Greenleaves, and the lands between the north realm of the Wood-elves and the south woods called East Lórien were given to the Woodmen and the Beornings to keep as their reward and their proper right.

WORMS The most powerful creatures that Morgoth ever bred in Arda were the Great Worms that came out of the Pits of Angband in the First Age of Sun. Morgoth armed these creatures with scales of iron, mighty teeth and claws, and great powers of flame and sorcery. Men and Elves called these ancient Worms of Morgoth DRAGONS and they were among the most fearful of beings in all the histories of Middle-earth.

WOSES In the War of the Ring a strange primitive folk named the Woses came to aid the Rohirrim and Dúnedain in breaking the Siege of Gondor. These wild woodland people lived in the ancient Forest of Druadan, which was in Anórien below the White Mountains. They knew wood-craft better than any Man, for they had lived as naked animals invisibly among the trees for many Ages and cared not for the company of other peoples. They were weather-worn, short-legged, thick-armed and stumpy-bodied. The Men of Gondor called the Woses the Wildmen of Druadan and believed that they were descended from the even more ancient Púkel-men.

By the end of the Third Age, Orcs, Wolves and other malevolent creatures often came into Druadan. Though the Woses drove them away, often with poison arrows and darts, the evil beings always returned. So it was that, though the Woses desired no part in the affairs of Men beyond their forest, their chieftain, who was named Ghân-buri-Ghân, offered to help the Rohirrim reach the Battle of Pelennor Fields. For in a victory for the Rohirrim and the Dúnedain in Gondor the Woses saw some release from this continual woodland warfare.

When victory did indeed come and the Orc legions were destroyed, the new king of Gondor and Arnor granted that the Druadan Forest would for ever be the inalienable country of the Woses to govern and to rule as they saw fit.

XYZ

YRCH Near the end of that time known as the Peace of Arda, the Sindarin Elves of King Thingol and Queen Melian found in the East an evil they had not known before. The woodlands and mountains on their borders began to stir with evil beings for which they had no name. These beings were the terrible Goblin people, who were destined always to be the chief servants and harbingers of evil powers. In the Sindarin tongue they were named Yrch in imitation of their own word for themselves: Uruks. In later Ages they became ORCS in the common language of Westron.

The Nandor and Laiquendi fled before these dark creatures, who were armed with weapons of steel. But King Thingol with warriors in bright Dwarf-mail and tall helms went to war against the Yrch and slaughtered them until the battle grounds were covered with their black blood. The Yrch fled from Beleriand and never crossed the Blue Mountains again until the time of the return of Morgoth, their creator and master, out of the Halls of Mandos.

A GENEALOGY OF THE RACES OF ELVES

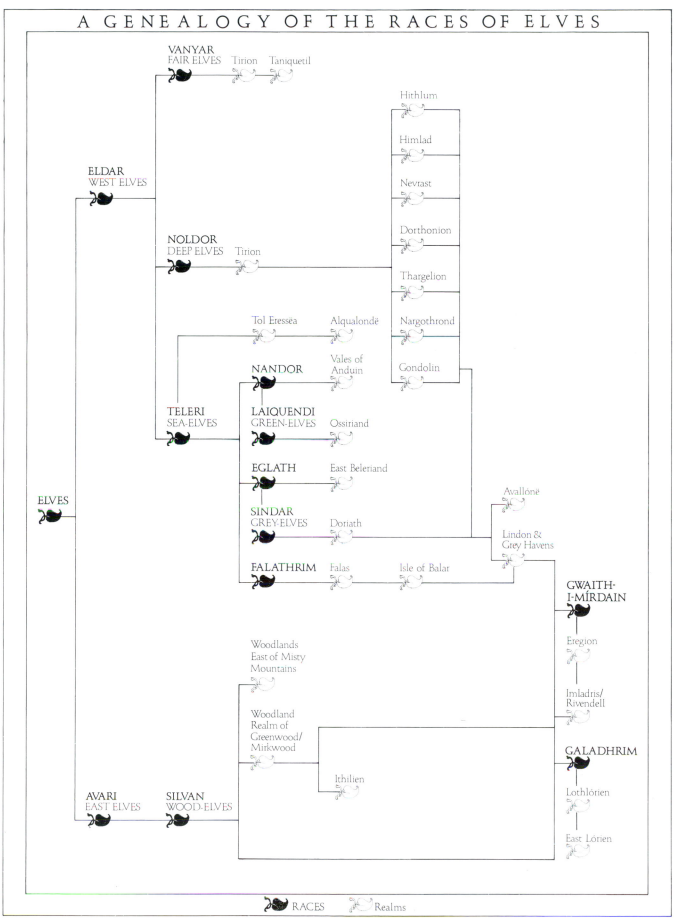

VANYAR
FAIR ELVES · Tirion · Taniquetil

ELDAR
WEST ELVES

NOLDOR
DEEP ELVES · Tirion

Hithlum

Himlad

Nevrast

Dorthonion

Thargelion

Nargothrond

Gondolin

Tol Eressëa · Alqualondë

NANDOR · Vales of Anduin

TELERI
SEA-ELVES

LAIQUENDI
GREEN-ELVES · Ossiriand

EGLATH · East Beleriand

SINDAR
GREY-ELVES · Doriath

ELVES

Avallónë

Lindon &
Grey Havens

FALATHRIM · Falas · Isle of Balar

GWAITH-
I-MÍRDAIN

Eregion

Imladris/
Rivendell

Woodlands
East of Misty
Mountains

Woodland
Realm of
Greenwood/
Mirkwood

Ithilien

GALADHRIM

AVARI
EAST ELVES

SILVAN
WOOD-ELVES

Lothlórien

East Lórien

RACES · Realms

A GENEALOGY OF THE RACES OF MEN

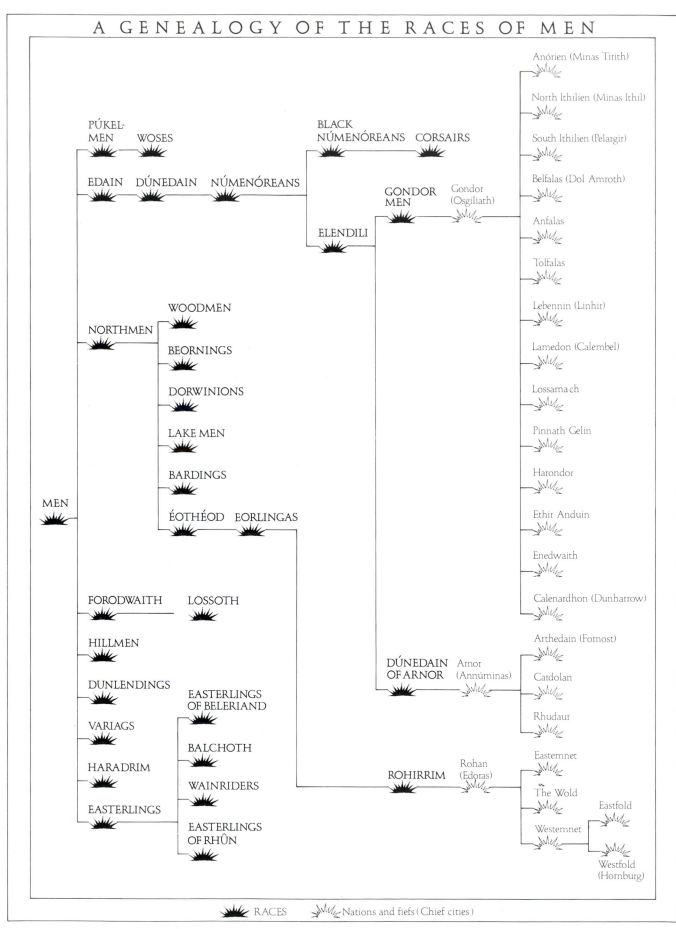

PÚKEL-MEN — WOSES

EDAIN — DÚNEDAIN — NÚMENÓREANS

BLACK NÚMENÓREANS — CORSAIRS

ELENDILI

GONDOR MEN — Gondor (Osgiliath)

Anórien (Minas Tirith)
North Ithilien (Minas Ithil)
South Ithilien (Pelargir)
Belfalas (Dol Amroth)
Anfalas
Tolfalas
Lebennin (Linhir)
Lamedon (Calembel)
Lossarnach
Pinnath Gelin
Harondor
Ethir Anduin
Enedwaith
Calenardhon (Dunharrow)

MEN

NORTHMEN
WOODMEN
BEORNINGS
DORWINIONS
LAKE MEN
BARDINGS
ÉOTHÉOD — EORLINGAS

FORODWAITH — LOSSOTH

HILLMEN

DUNLENDINGS

VARIAGS

HARADRIM

EASTERLINGS
EASTERLINGS OF BELERIAND
BALCHOTH
WAINRIDERS
EASTERLINGS OF RHÛN

DÚNEDAIN OF ARNOR — Arnor (Annúminas)
Arthedain (Fornost)
Cardolan
Rhudaur

ROHIRRIM — Rohan (Edoras)
Eastemnet
The Wold
Westemnet
Eastfold
Westfold (Hornburg)

RACES   Nations and fiefs (Chief cities)

278

INDEX OF PRINCIPAL SOURCES

This index refers the reader from the individual entries in "A Tolkien Bestiary" to the original texts of J.R.R. Tolkien in "The Silmarillion", "The Hobbit", "The Lord of the Rings" and "The Adventures of Tom Bombadil".

By referring back to Tolkien's works the reader can obtain fuller information than is given in the entries that make up this book: he or she can find out how various races played their parts in Tolkien's world and can re-read his tales with a new awareness of the backgrounds of the peoples, beasts and events.

The following abbreviations have been used:
S – "The Silmarillion"
    Ain. – Ainulindalë
    Val. – Valaquenta
    Quen. – Quenta
        Silmarillion
    Akal. – Akallabêth
    RofP – Of the Rings of
        Power and the
        Third Age
    Ind. – Index
    App. – Appendix
H – "The Hobbit"
    (numbers refer to
    chapters)
LR – "The Lord of the Rings"
    (roman numbers refer to
    books; arabic numbers to
    chapters)
    Prol. – Prologue
    App. – Appendixes

TB – "The Adventures of Tom Bombadil"
(numbers refer to the poems)

For example:
Balrogs S Val., Ind.; LR II 5, III 5, App. A
refers the reader to "The Silmarillion" Valaquenta and Index; and to "The Lord of the Rings" Book II chapter 5, also "The Lord of the Rings" Book III chapter 5 and Appendix A.

A

Ainur S Ain.
Alfirin LR V 9
Amanyar S Ind.
Apanónar see Men
Aratar S Val.
Asëa Aranion see Athelas
Atanatári see Edain
Atani see Edain
Athelas LR I 12, II 6, V 8
Avari S Quen.3, RofP

B

Balchoth LR App.A
Balrogs S Val., Ind.; LR II 5, III 5, App.A
Banakil see Hobbits
Bardings H 12,14; LR II 1, III 2, App.E,F
Barrow-wights LR I 7,8, II 2, App.A; TB 1
Bats S Quen.19; H 13,17
Belain see Valar
Beornings H 7,18; LR II 1
Big Folk see Men

Black Númenóreans S Akal.; LR V 10, App.A
Black Riders see Nazgûl
Boars LR App.A
Brambles of Mordor LR VI 2
Brethil S App.

C

Calaquendi see Light Elves
Cold-drakes LR App.A
Corsairs LR V 6,9, App.A
Crebain LR II 3
Crows LR III 2,10
Culumalda S Quen.1, App.

D

Dark Elves S Quen.3,4,17, Ind.
Dead Men of Dunharrow LR V 2,3,9, App.F
Deep Elves see Noldor
Dorwinions H 9
Dragons S Quen.21,24; H 1,12
Dúlin see Tinúviel
Dumbledors TB 3
Dúnedain S Akal., RofP; LR Prol., II 2, IV 4,5, App.F
Dunlendings LR III 7, App.A,F
Dwarves S Quen.2,10,13,22; RofP H 1; LR II 4, App.A,F
Dwimmerlaik LR V 6

E

Eagles S Quen.2,13,18,19,22,23, Akal.; H 6,7; LR II 2, V 10, VI 4
East Elves see Avari
Easterlings S Quen.18,20,21,22,23
Edain S Quen.17,18,20, Akal.; LR App.A,F
Edhil see Elves
Eglath S Quen.5, Ind.

Elanor LR II 6
Eldalië S Quen.3,5,19,20,24
Eldar S Quen.3,5,24, RofP; LR II 2, App.A,B,F
Elendili S Akal., RofP
Elven-smiths see Gwaith-i-Mirdain
Elves S Quen.1,3,5,7,10,15,18,22,23; H 9; LR II 6 8, App.F
Engwar see Men
Ents LR I 2, III 2,4,5,8,9, VI 6, App.F
Eorlingas see Rohirrim
Éothéod LR App.A
Eruhíni see Elves and Men
Erusën see Elves and Men
Evermind see Simbelmynë

F

Fair Elves see Vanyar
Fair Folk see Elves
Falathrim S Quen.5,10,14
Fallohides LR Prol., App.F
Falmari see Teleri
Fastitocalon TB 11
Fire-drakes S Quen.13,20,23; H 1,12; LR App.A
Firimar see Men
Firstborn see Elves
Flies of Mordor LR VI 2
Forgoil see Rohirrim
Forodwaith LR App.A

G

Galadhrim LR II 6, App.B,F
Galenas see Pipe-weed
Gallows-weed TB 9
Gaurhoth see Werewolves
Giants H 6
Glamhoth see Orcs
Goblins see Orcs
Golodhrim see Noldor